MAKING MULTICULTURALISM

Making Multiculturalism

BOUNDARIES AND MEANING

IN U.S. ENGLISH DEPARTMENTS

Bethany Bryson

Stanford University Press
Stanford, California
2005

Stanford University Press
Stanford, California

Printed in the United States of America on acid-free, archival-quality paper.

Library of Congress Cataloging-in-Publication Data

Bryson, Bethany Paige, 1967-
    Making multiculturalism : boundaries and meaning in U.S. English departments / Bethany Bryson.
        p.   cm.
    Includes bibliographical references and index.
    ISBN 0-8047-5163-3 (cloth : alk. paper)
    ISBN 0-8047-5164-1 (pbk. : alk. paper)
        1. Multicultural education—United States—Case studies.   2. English language—Study and teaching (Higher)—United States—Case studies.
    I. Title.

LC1099.3.B79 2005
370.117'0973—DC22

                                                        2004023932

Original Printing 2005

Last figure below indicates year of this printing:
14   13   12   11   10   09   08   07   06   05

To my parents, Jan and Jerry Bryson

Tables

Figures

ACKNOWLEDGMENTS

I owe my first and greatest debts to Michèle Lamont, Paul DiMaggio, Sharon Hays, Sarah Corse, and Patty Wonderley. When I decided I didn't have the guts to beg for interviews, my partner Patty flung me over that hurdle with the force of a single hilarious sentence: "Bethany, if you want to be a sociologist, you're gonna have to be more *social*." But that was just one of many trials that Patty saw me through. She paid the rent and put food on the table through graduate school. Her job as a UPS driver still provides most of our household income. She also tends our vegetable garden and fixes my car. She waited on me hand and "foot" after major surgery and then an automobile accident. When I face looming deadlines, Patty comes home from ten-to-twelve-hour days of hard labor and cooks dinner. When we couldn't get it all done, Patty's parents Eva Ann and Andrew Wonderley filled in the gaps. Patty gets it honest.

At the University of Virginia, I was lucky to be surrounded by a terrific group of smart and supportive friends. Most important, Sharon Hays has held my hand through the last years of this project, reading my work, providing support, and talking through problems. She would have pressed the keys for me if I'd let her. Sharon is the one person I can always count on for quick advice or a speedy read. Sarah Corse also made a big difference. I found her on the couch in my office when I joined the department in 1998, and she has since become a treasured source of friendship, guidance, and coffee. As my official mentor and associate chair of the department, she provided valuable resources and protected me from excessive obligations. The funding she secured for our collaborative project on dormitory décor paid for the laptop I am typing on today. Life just won't be the same now that she has her own office couch!

Countless other people have helped make this book possible. Without any one of them, I might not have made it. But I owe my greatest debt to Michèle Lamont, whose steadfast dedication to me and my research has remained every bit as strong as it was when I was her student at Princeton. From my early days in graduate school, Michèle pushed me to take the long road, to collect original data, to conduct in-depth interviews, and to incorporate a comparative methodology into my research. She prepared me for the pragmatic and analytical challenges I would face and helped me make the difficult transition to thinking of myself as a scholar. In the writing process, she offered lengthy and careful comments on more drafts than I want to admit. And, perhaps most important, she offered translations of my words into other sociological languages. I find much of my inspiration in her retelling of my contributions.

Michèle also co-chaired my dissertation committee with Paul DiMaggio, and the combination helped develop my passion for intellectual collaboration. They made room in their schedules for joint meetings and wrote lengthy comments on my work. Both managed to combine unconditional confidence in my abilities (far greater than my own), and both offered support in the form of funding, guidance, inspiration, collaboration, advocacy, and friendship. Each contributed more personal attention to my work than any graduate student could dare to expect from one mentor, much less two. Of course, their written work started it all. Bibliographic citations cannot do justice to the intellectual debt I owe these two scholars.

Paul has been at once an inspiration, an advocate, and a sparring partner. Some of my most rewarding moments in graduate study happened in the process of trying to change his mind. He also built institutions that were essential in my intellectual development. Two critical turning points in my research came in the form of presentations I made for the Princeton University Center for Arts and Cultural Policy Studies, a center he created with Stanley Katz during my study at Princeton. Through that center, I've had the opportunity to present this research to people whose comments made an important impact on the final product: Jennifer Hocschield, Amy Binder, Susan Herbst, Myra Marx-Feree, and Tali Mendelberg. Paul also sponsored my successful application for funding from the National Science Foundation and offered financial support in return for collaboration on two other research projects.

Two Princeton sociology workshops offered weekly occasions for even more intellectual exchange among graduate students and faculty. Princeton's notoriously collaborative atmosphere meant that numerous other professors and graduate students provided guidance and suggestions: Robert Wuthnow, Frank Dobbin, Miguel Centeno, Stanley Katz, Viviana Zelizer, Sara Curran, and Marvin Bressler.

But the most cherished gift I took away from Princeton is the best set of grad school buddies in the world. Julian Dierkes, Kieran Healy, Courtney Bender, John Evans, Brian Steensland, Steven Tepper, Jason Kaufman, Erin Kelly, Maureen Waller, John Schmaltzbauer, Jeff Hass, Becky Petit, Hugh Louch, Eszter Hargittai, and Marion Fourcade-Gourinchas have all provided crucial support and criticism over the years. Thanks, especially, to Espn Liszt. You are my lifeline.

This book also benefits from the careful attention of five anonymous reviewers and editorial suggestions from Kate Wahl and Doug Mitchell. Financial support for field research and interview transcription was provided by a National Science Foundation Dissertation Improvement Award and the Center for Domestic and Comparative Policy Studies. Support for analysis and writing came from the Princeton University Center for Arts and Cultural Policy Studies. Funding for travel to present portions of this project at workshops and conferences came from the Russell Sage Foundation and the Princeton University Department of Sociology. The James Madison University Department of Sociology and Anthropology (my alma mater) provided office space during an institutionally homeless summer. There, I owe special thanks to cherished colleagues Sue E. Spivey, Laurie Lewis, and Mary-Lou Wylie. Where office space is concerned, however, it should be noted that I wrote most of this draft at the Artful Dodger coffee shop in Harrisonburg, Virginia. Thanks, Deborah!

Finally, I owe much gratitude to the people and institutions that remain anonymous in this study. The project depended on the support of five institutional review boards (those of Princeton University and each of the four research sites), four English departments, seventy-six English professors, and several graduate student informants. "Ivory Towers" provided me with a visiting scholar position that furnished key resources, including access to computer labs and the library. I am saddened that my promise of anonymity prevents me from properly acknowledging all these vital gifts.

MAKING MULTICULTURALISM

Chapter 1

INTRODUCTION:
CULTURE TO THE RESCUE!

Hope for the future is routinely left at the doorstep of our schools and universities. To policy makers, cultural change seems easy and inexpensive: A brief memo should do it. Teach the children to stop being racist. Make textbooks more inclusive. Expand literary experience. Make well-rounded, deep-thinking, culturally sensitive citizens. According to this thinking, all social problems would dissolve in the face of a perfect culture.

The trend in the 1980s and 1990s toward multiculturalism in English literature was an attempt to orchestrate one of those cultural changes—to socialize children and young adults into a more diverse world by exposing them to a broader sampling of literary works. There was plenty of resistance, but multiculturalism, in one form or another, has been accepted into most corners of U.S. literary education. In fact, 92 percent of U.S. colleges have made curricular changes to address the diversity of American culture.[1] In 1991, 72 percent of college vice-presidents and deans surveyed reported that they talked about multiculturalism frequently or continually, and most were trying to increase faculty diversity. Moreover, curricular changes were more likely to happen in English departments than in any other discipline.

Many hoped that expanding the cultural horizons of new generations of college students would achieve something momentous. Students might become better prepared to operate in a global economy. They might develop more sophisticated cultural sensitivities, greater empathic capacities, fewer prejudices, and more elastic intellectual abilities. Some progressives even thought that multiculturalism could begin to erode the foundations of patriarchy and racism by reducing the extent to which students learn to associate greatness with certain categories of people (white men). After all, it is not only the physical attributes of the authors that matter. Linguistic styles, moral claims, religious influences, dark villains, and lily-white damsels lurk between the pages of those great books, just waiting to capture the imagination of our impressionable young students.

Defenders of traditional education, on the other hand, saw the situation differently and worried that de-emphasizing Western culture might be dangerous. The ideas contained in those classic works of literature are, they argued, "the glue that binds together our pluralistic nation." The quote is from William Bennett's infamous 1983 National Endowment for the Humanities (NEH) report titled *To Reclaim a Legacy*. The report, along with the media attention and opinion pieces it generated, is widely seen as the first volley in the national battle over English literature, and it set the stage for a full-scale attack on the Humanities. Soon, pundits such as Dinesh D'Souza and Roger Kimball jumped into the fray and escalated the rhetoric of cultural preservation to the point of frenzy, charging that multiculturalism would disintegrate U.S. national culture.[2]

Two decades of heated battle would ensue between members of what would become known as the Cultural Left and the Cultural Right—academics and public intellectuals who engaged the debate in the national media. Despite the appearance of an epic battle between opposing forces, however, the two "sides" shared an extraordinary premise: that every time an English teacher put together a reading list, the future of a nation hung in the balance.

But nothing so profound has come of multiculturalism since its national debut in the mid-1980s. Reading lists have changed some, but not at an unusual pace. (Reading lists always evolve over time.) College students and English professors alike are more conservative now than they were in the 1980s—never mind the 1960s! Shakespeare and Melville are still with us. They have been joined by Alice Walker and James Baldwin, but sexism, racism, and xenophobia persist. The Ivory Tower and U.S. national culture are both alive and well.[3]

Despite fiery claims to the contrary from both sides of the media frenzy, multiculturalism has neither dissolved the foundations of American life nor liberated the victims of cultural oppression. But this book is not devoted to merely claiming that our cultural critics are full of hot air. (They are full of hot air. But there's a reason for it, and that's an important part of the story.) Instead, I begin from the premise that multiculturalism really could have changed our world.

The following chapters will explain the reasons why multiculturalism has not proven to be an effective agent of change in American social life. Despite the powerful rhetoric coming from would-be cultural extremists, the bulk of multiculturalism's current existence was produced by *the center*—major institutions of public life in the United States, and especially the U.S. system of higher education. In other words, multiculturalism, the movement that some say threatens the core of American culture, is itself a product of that center.

In short, our cultural warriors were mistaken to think that their piece of culture could work alone.[4] In this story, our parcel of cultural treasure is a literary tradition. In other battles, the golden apple might be family values or patriotism. But in all these cases, the bits of culture we fight over get their meaning from something larger. If you take literary multiculturalism and put it in a box of crayons, the box will not explode. You'll just get a new assortment of crayons.

Crayola introduced their "multicultural crayons" in 1992, and they are still available today, but I don't mean to make light of that story. In fact, it illustrates what I mean when I say that culture is bigger than our "cultural critics" claim it to be. The fact that for a decade children sat down to draw with a crayon called "flesh" is a fairly profound cultural problem with a firm grounding in the material world. According to a 2000 press release, Crayola changed the name of their "flesh" crayon to "peach" in 1962. The only other name changes between 1900 and 2000 were those for "Prussian blue" and "Indian red." So it turns out that crayons can have cultural importance beyond their mechanical qualities. Crayola originally defined "flesh" as a peachy color, and now they define multiculturalism as "apricot, burnt sienna, mahogany, peach, sepia, tan, and," the marketing description explains, "black and white for blending."

That's essentially what happened in English literature, too. Pundits talked about both literature and multiculturalism in lofty terms, as though they were the only things that mattered in the world. It made for great reading, but it had almost nothing to do with the multiculturalism that now exists "inside the box" of everyday life in college classrooms and the outside world. Real multiculturalism—multiculturalism in action—is much different. It is more restricted, more resistant to cultural change, and more closely tied to stable social institutions.

There is no doubt that culture is real and important, but the myth of an omnipotent culture that can single-handedly change the world is more than harmless fantasy. It is the central problem that fuels the battles over culture, and it is the reason those battles never end. The myth keeps our intellectual wheels spinning, but it doesn't do much to inform concrete strategies for social action. The problem extends well beyond the battle over multiculturalism in English literature, of course. As we come to place more and more attention on the cultural aspects of social problems, we move our conversations farther and farther into the clouds.

In *Dogmatic Wisdom*, Russell Jacoby argued that battles over culture divert our political attention away from real national problems, material problems. In many ways, he is right. Important questions about material inequalities have lost the limelight, but that's no reason to argue that culture doesn't matter. The following chapters will suggest, conversely, that our difficulty lies not in the sheer fact that we've increased our focus on cultural problems but in the way our cultural warriors attempted to separate culture from its material existence—the material conditions that concern Jacoby. There is some value in making an analytic distinction between ideas and material structures (as I will explain later), but it makes very little sense to carry out a purely cultural "war" on the premise that ideas alone are responsible for justice, equity, and national survival.

In all of this, the story of multiculturalism in English literature is not merely a story of abstract theoretical relationships and naive cultural warriors. To get back on the ground, I decided to approach multiculturalism as a meaning-making problem. I asked professors in four college English departments to tell me how they make sense of the word "multiculturalism." I expected them to distance themselves from the overblown media reports that there was blood in the halls of academe. I knew that college professors make their living producing such arguments. That's what they do; it's no shock to them. But I was not prepared to find that multiculturalism was an entirely different creature inside English departments. The sweeping proclamations of those cultural warriors were virtually absent. There were some common elements: something about diversity and an occasional nod toward literary traditions. But those ideas were often overshadowed by more practical concerns: time constraints, teaching strategies, student abilities, and how well a given piece of literature performs in the classroom. In my research, I came to understand this effect, not as the difference between imaginary culture and real life, but as the difference between two kinds of culture, one abstract and the other grounded in material realities.

In addition to the constraints of the classroom, the meaning of multiculturalism in each university was also influenced by unrelated aspects of department administration. An efficient bureaucratic structure, for example, can turn a few ideas about multiculturalism into a sweeping curriculum change with shocking speed. An autonomous collection of scholars, on the other hand, may generate more radical ideas but never find a way to enact them, thereby keeping multiculturalism in the clouds. A lack of community can leave multiculturalism (and much else, for that matter) essentially meaningless and nonexistent.

In short, what happens to multiculturalism inside English departments bears very little resemblance to the picture we get from cultural critics. How can we expect that dramatic form of multiculturalism to have any effect when it does not even exist, perhaps cannot exist, inside English departments?

The answer lies in my claim that both versions are cultural. The grounded version of multiculturalism can be debated in a national forum. It can be printed in magazines and newspapers. It won't melt the page. It will only constrain the writer to address some less lofty ideas.

That disconnected view of culture is what made the canon wars irrelevant to real life both inside academe and in the political world beyond it. And it was also the isolation of this battle in the (imaginary) cultural realm that disabled its potential effects.

This book does not attempt to answer some of the more commonly posed questions about multiculturalism. I do not ask the "What's going on here?" question, and I do not address all the other very important places that multiculturalism happens on a college campus—within student movements, as a result of interest group pressures, or in recruitment and retention of faculty. Neither do I devote much attention to the problems that gave rise to the idea in the first place, such as racism, sexism, or global migration. I focus exclusively on the organizational conditions of meaning-making, and then only on the meanings associated with a grossly imperfect and problematic concept, multiculturalism. But I make all those concessions in order to study the problem in a new way. I ask what happened to the idea of multiculturalism in those places where its influence was most hotly debated—four college English departments where grand ideas collided with everyday life in four different ways.

With a focus, therefore, on questions of meaning-making and cultural change, this study offers a first glimpse into the way English professors have processed multiculturalism as a practical challenge. The short answer to the question of whether our social cohesion is in danger (or whether our appreciation for cultural difference will be greatly altered) is "No." Many English professors have indeed embraced the idea of multiculturalism, but they have done so primarily by shaping it into something that fits the pre-existing organizational routines and meanings that created the literary canon in the first place—the canon that traditionalists hope to preserve.[5] ("The canon" refers to those works most widely taught and respected as "great literature.")

English literature *is* different today from the way it was twenty years ago. Some portion of that change can even be attributed to multiculturalism, but multiculturalism within English literature departments does not challenge canons, Western culture, or the idea of greatness. When it came to deciding what multiculturalism would mean for any given class, professor, curriculum, or department, those choices hinged heavily on existing conceptions of literary education. Those versions of multiculturalism that allowed English professors to continue going about their business or, more important, those that allowed English professors to do their business *better,* were the ones that were finally etched into institutional structures through habit and policy.

The Myth of Omnipotent Culture

They Have a Theory, and You Should, Too

Exactly how powerful is culture? It is important to have a good answer to this question. Culture is everywhere, and our cultural choices are not always made as carefully as they could be. But which choices matter and why?

The plan for saving the world by changing culture has an implicit social theory. It assumes that culture steers human action by way of ideas or values, and that life is all about ideas and action. It views both culture and people as extremely powerful. And, as a consequence, it views everything else as mere byproducts. In theory, our culture determines our values and desires, then we do what we want, and the world becomes what we make of it. If we could improve the way they think, people would behave better and we would have a better, kinder, gentler society. Step 1: Change culture. Step 2: Relax—the rest will fall into place.

That's the popular version of the multicultural plan, and the people who were putting the idea to work prior to 1980 were pretty excited about it. They weren't sophisticated cultural theorists or literary critics; they were teachers (who sometimes actually used the word "multiculturalism") and parents who just wanted to teach their children about the world, to "socialize" them.

But when President Ronald Reagan appointed William Bennett to chair the National Endowment for the Humanities in December 1981, Bennett faced a serious problem. Students were fleeing from the humanities in droves to sign up for majors in business management and computer science. Bennett needed a way to reassert the value of the humanities, and he landed on the theory of omnipotent culture when he made that claim about cultural glue.

If this theory of omnipotent culture is correct, tinkering with culture could, indeed, be an easy way to change the world. But it could also be extremely dangerous—especially if it's *national* culture we want to alter. If we change that culture too much, life as we know it could disappear. In this view, culture is so powerful that everything else depends on it. So everything social is subject to the whims of human action, and is, therefore, terribly fragile. Economic systems, national sovereignty, family structures, baseball—all these things could evaporate if our nation's children aren't taught to value them. In short, the destruction of a value system can amount to the destruction of a nation. That was the central claim of the cultural Right.

Once the theory of omnipotent culture was established and the fear of a fragile society firmly planted in the popular imagination, the groundwork was laid for a free-for-all attack on the American system of education. Cultural diversity was everywhere. It was dangerous, and educators showed no interest in stopping it!

After William Bennett's NEH report, countless other academics and public intellectuals jumped on the bandwagon. The first splash came in 1987 from a pair of books that held top positions on the *New York Times* nonfiction best-seller list: Alan Bloom's *The Closing of the American Mind* and E. D. Hirsch's *Cultural Literacy*. Bloom's book remained on the list for more than a year in hardcover and then soared to the top again when the paperback edition was released the following year.

In 1990 and 1992, respectively, books by Dinesh D'Souza and Roger Kimball helped establish English literature as the main focus of attention, and major newspapers such as the *New York Times* and the *Washington Post* began publishing gossip-laden stories about a roiling war in English departments across the country.

The books continue to sell. Historian Arthur Schlesinger published *The Disuniting of America* in 1992, another *New York Times* best-seller that has been republished twice and is available on audiotape. Other memorable titles include: *The Twilight of Common Dreams*, a 1995 book from sociologist and card-carrying 1960s liberal Todd Gitlin; *The Unmaking of Americans*, from *National Review* author John Miller, in 1998; and in 2001, *The Death of the West: How Dying Populations and Immigrant Invasions Imperil Our Country and Civilization*, from conservative critic Pat Buchanan.

How should we proceed in the canon war (and other matters) if this theory of omnipotent culture is correct? The most obvious point is that we should pay a lot more attention to culture, especially national culture and national values. The theory of omnipotent culture tells us that it would be irresponsible to ignore a culture "war" simply on the grounds that no one is carrying a gun. This theory says that people decide to buy and use guns based on their beliefs and values. We should get a handle on it before there is bloodshed.

But there appear to be two possible directions in which to go with this information. One possibility is that we can use culture to our advantage. We can tinker with it and attempt improvements. The problem is that we don't really know what kinds of tinkering would work, and there is that looming cloud: if our collective existence is fragile, our cultural glue could lose its grip. In fact, because we are already headed down the multicultural path, our cultural as well as social cohesiveness could be in deep trouble. It is the issue of fragility that settles the question. The theory of omnipotent culture tells us that cultural change is too risky. We should turn around and head back to a culture with a proven track record.

Whenever questions about social change are countered by concerns about social stability, there is a theory at work that assumes social systems are fragile. The theory of omnipotent culture is only one such theory. Others claim that something else serves as the main support structure for social life. For advanced societies, it is usually an economic system that is posited to be the foundation on which everything else rests. In other contexts, an anthropologist might guess that an entire social system revolves around kinship. All these theories are elegant in that they are simple and clear, but they are too simplistic to predict the demise of complex and highly developed societies.

At some level, most of us can sense that these views of omnipotent culture and fragile societies are wrong. Perhaps many people who bought those bestselling books wished for a sturdier common culture. Or maybe some of them just wanted to have more in common with their children and grandchildren. It probably *is* disconcerting to have a college degree and still not be able to help your teenagers with their homework. But it doesn't appear that those readers were also stockpiling food and ammunition in the basement to prepare for the fall of civilization. (Well, maybe the Buchanan fans were doing that.)

What's missing from this theory is a credible explanation of social stability. There is no social autopilot, nothing to keep things chugging along in the event we get distracted from the task of maintaining our social existence. The theory also lacks an account of what sociologists call structure. And there is *lots* of structure out there. Some structures are pretty obvious. Like railroad tracks and walls, they shape human activity in a profound way, and we can see them at work. But even those visible structures can disappear from view just because we are so accustomed to them. We quickly learn to live inside walls and to stop thinking about what might be on the other side. Other structures are less visible but equally powerful. Anyone who has ever tried to kick a bad habit knows how powerful little routines can be.

Notice also that for our pundits culture is about values, and for multicultural educators it is about socialization. These two views of culture are similar, and they are far more narrow than the kind of culture I have in mind when I argue that culture *is* extraordinarily powerful. We can't really solve our nation's problems just by socializing our children to be better than we are. To do that, we also need to understand structured, grounded, and institutionalized culture.

Institutions Are Petrified Culture

The most common way to account for social stability is to think of culture as something that can be more permanently established in the form of institutions. Sociologists once thought of institutions as large, patterned collections of norms, values, roles, and expectations. They believed that the institution of marriage, for example, organized all the bits of culture relevant to marriage, and it explained why such a complicated thing could be so common across a society and how it managed to be such a permanent feature of social life.

But culture can also get its institutional permanence in the form of organizational structure, or even architectural structures. Our mealtime rituals, for example, are powerful forces shaping the structure of the workday. We erect our houses and other buildings according to social custom, placing walls to hide ritual behaviors that are coded as private rather than public. And much (though not all) of our legal system is a rigid institutional monument to national culture. Anthropologist Mary Douglas (1986) even argues that our beliefs about the function of the human brain shape our political organization, so that a single decision-making entity (a social "brain") normally controls and coordinates all the other parts of the social group (be they family, the corporation, or the nation).

Similar processes apply to English literature. Therefore, it is important not to overlook the details of organization in which questions about English literature and multiculturalism are situated. For example, that "canon" of important literary works is merely those works most often assigned in English classes. When viewed as a question of whether English classes are similar or different, the question changes to one of how English professors go about designing courses. So institutions can include norms and values, but they also shape culture and action in less obvious ways. In addition, "socializing" people won't automatically change institutions. There is more work to do than the theory of omnipotent culture claims.

The idea of a literary canon, for example, is firmly rooted in the institutionalized practices of education—of teaching, of reading, of taking classes, etc. If Professor Purple suddenly decides to assign a whole list of obscure authors in her course on the nineteenth-century novel, she will likely leave all the other elements of teaching literature in place. As a result, the experience for her students will not be especially unusual. But even that is an outlandish example. In practice, it's a rare literature class that does not include any of the works commonly considered to be classics of their period. There are all sorts of reasons why English professors stick to tried-and-true literary selections, and many of those reasons have little or nothing to do with preserving Western culture—at a conscious level, anyway. They include the practices of the publishing industry (especially with respect to the more established specialties, like Renaissance and medieval literature), the mysteries of making a classroom come alive, the problems of coordinating a larger curriculum, a professor's own love of particular works, and the desire to end the constant task of syllabus revision.

To fully understand cultural change, therefore, we need to look at institutions, not just battles over ideas. Institutions are cultural systems as well, but they are more stable forms of culture that are easy to overlook and thus, I would argue, more important to study.

Unlike the pundits and multiculturalists, most of the more academic players in the "canon wars" acknowledged the role of institutions by attending to the history of English literature or some other feature of institutional reality. The strategy helped them fend off the most inflated charges of politicians and pundits. Gerald Graff, for example, devoted his career to bringing the conflict out of the clouds, and he worked to that end in every relevant battlefield, first with his 1987 book, *Professing Literature: An Institutional History*, and then in a series of more popular pieces and unending interviews with the press about his suggestion that English professors should "teach the conflicts." Graff even organized a professional association for the cause called Teachers for a Democratic Culture.

But Graff was not alone. Michael Bérubé's 1995 book, *Public Access: Literary Theory and American Cultural Politics,* explained that we should be more worried about the institutional issues at stake in the canon wars than the kind of cultural fluff we hear about in the news. And Milton scholar and cultural warrior Stanley Fish attended to institutions in his analyses of the battle over English literature in books such as *There's No Such Thing as Free Speech . . . and It's a Good Thing, Too* (1994).

Institutional theories of cultural change are less threatening because they acknowledge some of the more tangible sources of social stability. This view also rings truer when applied to English classes, but it only muddies the question about the power of culture because it tells us that culture is tangled up with everything else. It doesn't give us any guiding principles for understanding the power of culture in a given situation. If we want to know how seriously to take those questions about literary canons (or family values, or television violence, etc.), we need to be more specific about the relationship between ideas and things.

The "Mutual Constitution" of Things and Ideas

To get out of the tangle between ideas and things, I operate from the premise that culture is not ultimately separable from the material structures and actions that give rise to it. Culture cannot be "merely" ideas. Books, clothing, CDs, videos, and paintings are obviously tangible. In fact, culture cannot exist if it only consists in the imperfectly communicated ideas hidden inside people's heads. Once those ideas are shared, they become tangible and contribute to the structure of human interaction. Therefore, scholars often refer to cultural patterns and material conditions as "mutually constituted structures."

In short, this view suggests that ideas and physical things cannot exist without each other. Ideas are communicated on paper and in sound waves. Moral convictions come alive as actions and stories. Moreover, physical objects can only be understood (inside our brains) as symbolic representations of objects. They don't exist for us until they become cultural. It's all culture, and it's all real.

It can't even be argued that the spoken word is always more ephemeral than the material world because both ideas and things can be characterized as more or less perishable. Ideas can be preserved in countless physical objects, and physical things can evaporate into thin air—even the word "evaporate" comes from the physical sciences. One minute it's a tornado, the next minute it's gone.

For navigating the canon wars, this view implies that we should take culture seriously, not because it determines our actions, but because it *is* our actions. There is no need to insert that extra step in which we try to determine how much culture controls other aspects of social life. That's just a sinkhole into which we pour way too much theoretical energy. Instead, the "mutual constitution" theory suggests that we should apply our energies to the previously ignored task of attending to the cultural aspects of physical things (oceans, highways, office chairs) and the physical aspects of cultural things (books, universities, concert halls). Moreover, changing culture and changing other structures should not be considered two separate processes at all. That is the reason cultural-change masters so rarely get to step two. Culture has far more staying power than we typically imagine, not only because it shapes the way we think, but also because it has a physical presence that we tend to ignore.

Abstract and Grounded Culture

If ideas and objects can't exist without each other, is there still a reason to distinguish between them? Yes! Although it is an inescapable fact that ideas can't be communicated without something physical and material objects can't exist without symbolic representation, the extent to which meanings are tied to material conditions can vary.[6] For those reasons (and others not discussed here), we *need* the analytic distinction.

When scholars and cultural critics debate the merits of multiculturalism, in the pages of a magazine, for example, there are countless ways that the battle is shaped, by such constraints as page limits and marketing strategies. But the debaters are generally free to make sweeping claims, about the connections between an English teacher's syllabus and the oppressive forces of a white-male value system or the fall of Western culture, for example. They will not be required to inspire a twenty-one–year-old mother of two who is attending night school to forgo sleep in favor of *Moby Dick*. Nor will they be expected to derive a plan for getting an eighteen-year-old white boy to read Zora Neale Hurston in his room—much less understand it—while the frat house rocks.

In the space of a few minutes, an English professor can move from abstract conversation about the fate of Western culture to grounded decisions about designing a course that can hold the attention of forty-eight young adults who have just been liberated from the control of their parents. Both kinds of activity are important. And both can be powerful factors in cultural stability or change. But they work in fundamentally different ways. So, the term "canon wars" refers to an abstract debate over the *idea* of national culture. In the process, that debate tackles persistent philosophical puzzles and, therefore, may never really be resolved. On the other hand, grounded cultural activities and discussion about grounded activities (aka grounded discussions) take place constantly. They are not waiting for the abstract debate to reach a conclusion that will guide activity from that point forward. Grounded cultural activity puts new ideas into practice, while the abstract debate rages on over our heads. Although many of these cultural practitioners also participate in abstract discussions, they cannot suspend their everyday lives during periods of cultural controversy.

Were my English professors schizophrenic? No. It's not that people are imperfect, it's that our theories are (often for good reason) too rigid to accommodate the complexities of real human activity. Much of culture is certainly material, but human beings are also capable of abstraction, and the capacity for (socially acceptable) abstraction varies by context.[7] For example, a person may be able to wax philosophical about the fine line between life and death, but not when her child is bleeding profusely from a small wound—afterward, perhaps. And though they don't have much theory to explain it, public opinion researchers consider it a well-established fact that abstract beliefs are different from concrete decisions. For example, survey respondents are far more likely to report supporting the racial integration of neighborhoods and schools in the abstract than when the survey question specifically refers to the respondents' own neighborhoods or schools.[8]

The extent to which activities oriented toward ideas are informed by physical circumstances can vary a great deal. Of course, actions devoted to the realm of ideas are profoundly structured by language, other ideas, etc., but that's another story. For now, I only want to suggest that we should give considerable attention to variations in the *groundedness* of cultural activities—the extent to which activities devoted to ideas are connected, at that moment, to ideas about material contexts.

A few examples are probably in order. When I talk with my students about income inequality, the conversation hinges, at some level, on the idea of justice—the just allocation of income in a corporation or across a society. I've done this many times over the years, and students generally enjoy the exercise. They like to uncover logical inconsistencies in the allocation of economic rewards. They like to point fingers at the guilty parties (including culture), and they are happy to construct new economic systems for the people represented in our statistical portrait. In most cases, students appreciate having abstract theoretical principles applied to the "real" world, but that application is not as real as it could be. When I suggest that my grading curve can be understood as a zero-sum economic system in which a limited number of points can be allocated to students according to some principle (merit?) and that the equitable thing would be to give everyone a "B," they freeze. Justice suddenly becomes something entirely different when they include themselves in the statistical puzzle. This exercise varies the groundedness of an abstract debate by moving from abstract theories of inequality, to hypothetical people, and, finally, to real people in the classroom. Our discussions do not really decide how resources are allocated, however. They remain hypothetical, but they vary in their abstractness. And the conversation changes dramatically (from equity to meritocracy, in some cases, becoming reactionary) as the conversation becomes more grounded.

Similarly, Sharon Hays's book, *The Cultural Contradictions of Motherhood*, finds that middle-class moms carry around two views of themselves—one for their working lives and one that better fits cultural expectations about mothering. Ann Swidler, in her book *Talk of Love*, also reports that her respondents talk about love in two distinct ways. One way fits in with an abstract belief system that is widely shared yet almost never practiced. The other way of talking about love is the one that literally "works" in her respondents' real lives. In short, people carry around at least two types of love, two types of justice, two types of motherhood, and two types of beliefs about cultural diversity.

Sociologist Paul DiMaggio also found a nearly identical pattern in his historical study of museum administrators from 1920 to 1940. He wrote that museum professionals "seem to have possessed a dual consciousness that enabled them to function as conservatives in organizational roles at the same time they used field-wide organizations to launch attacks on the system that employed them."[9] He further noted that the actions of these professionals inside their organizations were "grounded in routine," whereas field-wide discussions "permitted a decontextualization of discourse" that "offered sites for the development of critical alternatives to existing organizational arrangements."[10]

In the case of the canon wars, however, this book will demonstrate that no mechanism emerged to bring the two levels of reality together. In DiMaggio's terms, the field-wide debates over literary multiculturalism produced criticism and alternative goals but not alternative organizational arrangements. That is, the abstract debates never reached the grounded meanings of multiculturalism or discussions of the organizational routines that shape departments of English literature in the United States.

In short, the extent to which abstract debates produced at the field level can provide new courses of action for organizational change depends heavily on the extent to which grounded meanings can find their way back into those abstract discussions. So long as the two discourses remain separate, the ideas generated at the field level are unlikely to have any real consequences on the ground.

Moreover, Swidler's research on love and Hays's research on motherhood suggest that grounded meanings of multiculturalism may continue to thrive and guide everyday behaviors, even if the abstract and unrealistic form of multiculturalism generated in national debates becomes a powerful cultural ideal, like love or motherhood. The existence of an abstract ideal does not necessarily threaten the existence of a grounded one, though the contradictions may produce side effects, as is the case in all these examples.

Even the absence of specific talk about race and gender in my interviews can be understood through this lens. One of the most striking results of my study was the resounding silence of English professors on the details of these topics. To begin, there just aren't many African American English professors in the general population. Those that do exist are often seen as larger-than-life individuals, making the public think that English literature departments are diverse places, but the sad fact is that a sociologist asking for interviews among English professors will mostly encounter a bunch of white people and if one doesn't specifically ask white people to talk about race, they'll usually avoid the subject.[11] Multiculturalism offers an easy method for avoiding issues of race, gender, sexual identity, national identity, and any other human difference that makes people culturally uneasy.

In my interviews, I was interested to know how questions of race, gender, and cultural inequality influence emerging definitions of multiculturalism. Unfortunately, I found that these issues have almost no direct effect. Instead, it appears that the meaning-making process works in the opposite direction. At least when meaning emerges from a mire of complexity, the process of categorizing meaning is, in large part, a matter of *subtracting* possible meanings rather than adding them.[12] That is, multiculturalism can be understood as an *abstraction* of grounded cultural differences. Through the idea of diversity, multiculturalism selects only the common implications of cultural difference for literature, value, and pedagogy. It makes the *reality* of cultural difference disappear.[13]

As the following chapters will explain, all the nuances that make gender different from race, sexual identity, social class, nationality, ethnicity, or subculture—all the questions that bring richness to the experience of multiculturalism—must be subtracted to achieve a clear and manageable meaning for the word. As it turns out, the real bases of social inequality, then, disappear into the more nebulous but less threatening word, "multiculturalism." Most importantly, I found that clear meanings were largely imposed by organizational structures in the English departments I studied. That is, the professors I interviewed used the rules and routines of their daily lives as interpretive lenses for making sense of multiculturalism. Meaning relied on structure. Thus, subtracting complexity in the meaning-making process is one of the primary mechanisms through which colleges tamed multiculturalism and shaped it according to the imperatives of "the center"—the core institutions of American life.

The Research

In seeking to understand cultural change, I chose to study a battle that cut to the core of American culture, and I chose to focus my attention on the organizational units most clearly identified as those at the center of that debate—college English departments. It is no coincidence that national attention was focused on English professors. They have primary responsibility for creating and distributing a central piece of American culture—canonical literature. And, as a group, college professors reach more than half of our nation's eighteen-year-olds as they enter college-level education. Many of those students do not go on to earn bachelor's degrees, however, so the only thing we can say with any degree of certainty about this crucial collective experience for middle-class America is that those entering freshmen probably all took college English. *Monday Night Football* and *Oprah Winfrey* together do not reach as many young Americans on any given day.[14] And unlike literary training, television broadcasts don't hold the rank of "legitimate" culture—cultural resources that have a generalized (as opposed to specific) value in U.S. culture.

A mere fifty years ago, however, our system of higher education consisted of 1,851 colleges, the vast majority of which were private four-year institutions that provided culture and polish to our nation's budding young elites who were already destined for high-level occupations. In 1950, those institutions conferred bachelor's degrees on 432,058 students. Today, however, there are more than twice as many institutions and they serve *fifteen million* students. The public now understands higher education less as a source of culture than as a great equalizer—a large, presumably meritocratic, system intended to propel graduates into occupations commensurate with their educational achievements. In short, we hope that those fifteen million young adults will all go on to join the ranks of the elite group that once held a monopoly on higher education. As a result, colleges and students alike have refocused their energies on the acquisition of vocational skills rather than on cultural diffusion, canonical or otherwise. That was the reason for the precipitous drop in English majors that sparked the so-called "crisis" in the humanities. To date, no treatment of the battle over multiculturalism in college English departments has acknowledged the profound effect of these structural inequalities on the way multiculturalism took shape in institutions of higher learning across the country.

In order to study all these effects, however, I would have needed more detail than any quantitative survey could offer. Moreover, even the most detailed case-study approach would not have allowed me to examine the effects of differences among English departments and universities. Therefore, I chose to conduct four distinct case studies. The fieldwork took me a year and a half, but the comparative method offered many advantages over studying a single site. It avoided the flattening effect of both quantitative analyses and single-case studies, and it provided the opportunity to compare a multitude of structural conditions—not just the ones I considered when choosing research sites. Studying four different departments also allowed me to avoid thinking that the quirky aspects of one department might be representative of all English departments. I was also able to see similarities in the four departments. Those similarities might not extend to every U.S. English department, but at least I could say that they weren't unique to a single location and that they weren't caused by the prestige factor or by any of the other factors that varied across the four sites. In fact, I am still amazed at the similarities I did manage to find. These four departments are *vastly* different from each other.

I did try to hold some factors constant, however, when I selected the four English departments that I would study. I wanted to control for the demographic makeup of the undergraduate population, and I thought I should limit myself to relatively large institutions. I wanted the departments to be different, however, on the two factors that I considered most important to study: prestige and progressivism. Therefore, I chose two departments that could be described as fairly traditional, relative to multiculturalism, and two departments that could be described as more progressive. Both of the progressive departments I selected (Ivory Towers and Multicultural State) encouraged wide-ranging course work in non-traditional areas of English literature. Conversely, the traditional departments (State Star and Cathletic University) stressed more extensive study of literary classics, major literary figures, and historical survey courses.

The second important factor I wanted to study was prestige, and the pseudonyms help keep track of this variable. The elite universities are Ivory Towers and State Star; the non-elite sites are Multicultural State and Cathletic. Including both elite and non-elite departments in my research design ensured that I would be able to examine multiculturalism in famous universities like the ones covered by the press while also gaining an understanding of the way multiculturalism has been incorporated (or not) into the sort of non-elite English department that most college students encounter today.[15] The literature departments of both of my elite institutions have, in fact, been in the national news for their politics of multiculturalism, though perhaps not to the extent of some other elite institutions. The other two sites are inside non-elite universities that are reasonably well-known within their respective geographic regions (say, within a 100 to 300-mile radius) but are less well known across the nation. In terms of status in the discipline, these departments more closely resemble the departments that *most* college students experience today because most college students are not enrolled, for example, at Stanford and Duke (two universities that have made national headlines for battles over multiculturalism).

I tried to offer the same kind of memory aid for the multicultural–traditional dimension when I chose pseudonyms for the four universities, but I couldn't bring myself to grant a multicultural title to Ivory Towers because it would have mischaracterized the department so badly. There is no doubt that Ivory Towers' English department produces cutting-edge scholarship and that its curriculum and course offerings fit the multicultural bill. Right-wing cultural critics often included this department in their list of those multiculturalism-infested departments where Western culture is all but dead. Yet, on the ground, the department didn't feel at all multicultural. Ninety-five percent of the faculty described themselves as white or Caucasian. The place just felt elite, not at all multicultural. I'll say more about these pseudonyms in Chapter 3.

In this two-by-two design, then, one progressive university is elite (Ivory Towers) and one is non-elite (Multicultural State). The same is true for the traditional pair. One is elite (State Star) and one is non-elite (Cathletic University). All four sites are research or comprehensive universities (rather than liberal arts colleges) and have undergraduate student populations of at least four thousand, 25 percent of whom are non-white.

Deciding how to study college English wasn't easy, either. When I decided to break with current assumptions about the sources and processes of cultural conflict, I set myself up for a *big* project. To study meaning-making processes, I would need a qualitative method that offered data rich enough to reconstruct conceptual categories for building theory.[16] That meant long interviews, transcripts, coding categories, and cumbersome data-analysis software. (The one I used was called NUD★IST, Non-numerical Unstructured Data Indexing Searching and Theorizing.) To make matters more complicated, I would need to know about the context of the interviews: course offerings, curriculum structure, local culture, departmental governance, etc.[17]

To get both contextual information and enough depth to study meaning, I centered the research design on an analysis of multiculturalism in the four English departments and then sketched their broader milieu through secondary sources and data sets. At the national level, I studied media reports of battles over literary canons in the United States. I attended a meeting of the Modern Language Association (the primary professional organization for English professors). I talked to textbook sales representatives, and I studied other interpretations of the battle published by English professors in books and journals.

Inside departments, I collected orienting documents, including policy statements about the curriculum, faculty lists, course directories, and articles from local newspapers about multiculturalism or curriculum issues in the English department. And I spent from four to twelve weeks at each location (depending on the size of the department and the ease of scheduling interviews—something that was a lot more difficult in prestigious departments). During my time at each campus, I conducted interviews with faculty (76 in total), familiarized myself with their teaching and scholarship, and observed interactions whenever possible, which was not very often in most departments. The research wasn't what an anthropologist would describe as ethnographic. Unlike the dramatic public debates we read about in the paper, real academic politics is a closely guarded activity. Outsiders are not invited to faculty meetings, and English professors do most of their work in physical isolation from other humans. Therefore, the halls and other public spaces of English departments are mostly empty (though Multicultural State was an exception).

A Road Map for Cultural Change

In the next five chapters, I explore five distinct processes (one per chapter) that helped mold multiculturalism into its current shape. They are: meaning-making, local production, stance-taking, boundary management, and curriculum design.

In Chapter 2, I systematically map the meaning of multiculturalism for the professors I interviewed and show that there were important differences between the way English professors understood multiculturalism and the way it appeared in the national arena. This chapter lays the groundwork for the analyses that follow, and it helps demonstrate that the meaning of multiculturalism for English professors was largely a byproduct of the way their departments operate. But it also uncovers some useful insights into how the story of multiculturalism has played out. For example, the symbolic-boundaries method made it possible for me to identify key sites of contention, to expose some rhetorical tricks, to uncover the exact location of political pitfalls (especially what sorts of definitions were vulnerable to charges of racism), and to identify a crucial difference between abstract and "grounded" definitions of multiculturalism.

In Chapter 3, I describe my visit to each department and the main features of departmental organization in each. Then I connect those elements to the specific definitions of multiculturalism that professors in each department used. The chapter explores differences in each department's definitions and demonstrates that, despite the ominous power often attributed to multiculturalism, English professors found the concept to be vague and unworkable, so they changed it. They tamed it, and molded it to fit within their everyday routines—routines that are different in each of the four departments. Most important, this chapter demonstrates that many of the meanings emerging in each department could be predicted from conditions in the department that have nothing to do with multiculturalism per se. In short, I found that English professors used their organizational structure as an interpretive frame to make sense of multiculturalism and fit it into their existing work lives.

In Chapter 4, I turn to stance-taking—expressing support or opposition for multiculturalism. Here, I explain the surprising finding that local differences in the appearance of multiculturalism were not related to individual opinions on the issue or to the political atmosphere. Instead, other structural factors, such as prestige hierarchies, funding sources, and professional boundaries, had a much stronger influence on opinions toward multiculturalism. In addition, opinions about multiculturalism depended, in part, on the way the word was defined (or not defined), and the way the word was defined depended on departmental habit and structure.

Chapters 5 and 6 (which address boundary management and curriculum design, respectively) address processes that affected the relative ease or difficulty with which multiculturalism was incorporated into departmental activities. Together, these two chapters demonstrate how and why "structural" conditions played out on the cultural scene. I do not conclude, however, that organizations are more important than culture. Organizations *are* culture! And some of the most important conflict-management lessons emerging from these chapters involve cultural resources, such as the imaginary boundaries that protect literary questions from the influence of outsiders. The fate of the canon wars in these four departments depended more on the way the English departments did their work than on the ideological forces of traditionalism and multiculturalism.

I conclude in Chapter 7 by bringing the findings from the previous chapters to bear on the implicit theories of cultural change that are at work in the national rhetoric about multiculturalism. I give special attention to the role of abstraction in justifying social action (as opposed to informing social action), and I examine the paradoxical fact that cultural change appears to require engagement with social structure. I also provide an example of how these findings might be applied to specific cultural-policy decisions by discussing one of our nation's most difficult and ubiquitous cultural problems: institutional racism. Finally, I conclude that attending to the importance of structure in cultural change shifts the ground of personal responsibility from a "values and socialization" perspective to one that holds people responsible for social structure.

Chapter 2

PROFESSORS AND THE PRESS:
DEFINITIONS OF MULTICULTURALISM

I'm all in favor of multiculturalism. I wouldn't be teaching medieval literature if I thought we ought not engage with cultures
different from our own.

—*Senior professor at State Star University*

What? Medieval literature is multicultural? I was stunned and slightly amused
the first time I heard an English professor claim that literary classics could be
multicultural. In the interview, I maintained my composure, but I struggled
with this definition afterward. Sure, medieval culture would seem foreign to
most American college students, *but that's not what multiculturalism is! Right?*

Despite my plan to be agnostic about the definitions of multiculturalism I
might encounter, this one surprised me. It made me recognize that I *did* have
expectations. I thought multiculturalism would at least suggest some kind of
change for English literature. I had been unaware of my own preconceptions
until that moment when someone crossed the line and made a claim that
struck me as implausible.

It turns out that this wasn't an unusual way for English professors to think
of multiculturalism, and it wasn't just a reactionary way of defining the word,
either. It was one of many definitions that helped English professors make
sense of multiculturalism as a part of their working lives. This particular definition also helped its proponents separate multiculturalism from contentious
ideological battles by shifting the political landscape and bringing medieval
literature to the aid of multiculturalism. Most significantly, it exposed an
enormous gap between the definitions of multiculturalism available in the
national arena and those at work inside English departments.

Although my primary interest is in cultural change and the meaning-making *process*, the search for meanings associated with the term "multiculturalism" is a crucial mission in its own right. We need to know what the word means in order to make sense of the fact that nearly all colleges and universities in the United States now claim to offer it. Does medieval literature really count? There is a great deal of room for variation in the meaning of multiculturalism in practice and policy. And that variation could explain how it has managed to become entrenched without toppling the institutions it allegedly threatened.

For the most part, empirical research on the problem has focused on either the content of course syllabi or on ideological positioning in the debate.[1] These studies offer important insights into the conflict, but they miss what I found to be the most striking features of English professors' talk on multiculturalism, the gap between local and national struggles with the issue and a deep ambivalence about the word's meaning. Because sociological research on multiculturalism has (of necessity) imposed more stable meanings on its evidence, it has overlooked all the slippage that occurs between the moment when people make claims about the importance of culture and the moment when they (or others) take action on it. As a result, scholars have miscalculated the significance of this particular cultural change.

Rather than working with the assumption that political opinions and beliefs directly determine actions, I begin with meaning. Therefore, I do not use reading lists and public debates as indicators of political intention. Rather, I explore the way a political landscape is constructed from those actions (making reading lists, participating in debates, etc.).

The goal of this chapter is to uncover the variety of meanings multiculturalism has acquired in the four English departments—to the extent that it *has* acquired meaning—and to contrast those meanings with the ones put forward by a few of the most influential cultural warriors on the national scene. But doing that required a plan for assessing meaning, and I had to devise a new one. It started as a standard exercise in coding the themes that emerged in my interviews. I'll describe my method and how I developed it in more detail later in this chapter, but it operates on the principle of "symbolic boundaries."

The symbolic boundaries approach to meaning draws on the idea that meaning can have boundaries in the same way that nations, people, and cultures have boundaries.[2] Those familiar kinds of boundaries are marked by walls, fences, maps, secret passwords, and even symbolic indications of membership, such as clothing or mannerisms. All these boundaries are, in fact, the boundaries of ideas—of meaning—because even nations are ideas. That's why walking or driving across unguarded state or national boundaries can produce the eerie feeling that political entities are not as clear and obvious as they are in our imaginations.

Other meanings can be approached in the same way—by asking how we know what is and is not "green," for example, or "living," or "jazz," or "cold." Some meanings are more flexible than others, but people mark the boundaries of these meanings in much the same way we mark and protect other jurisdictions. In short, a focus on the boundaries of meaning is a focus on an exclusionary process—how we know something is green and not blue (and which kinds of things are ambiguous on that point).

The symbolic boundaries method offers several advantages over traditional cultural "coding." First, symbolic boundaries are more specific and less interpretive than the traditional understanding of themes, so I was able to develop a careful and systematic method that didn't require me to impose so many of my own meanings on the interview text. Second, it focuses attention on the *limits* of meaning. So, unlike interpretive approaches, I can account for the possibility that there might not be any meaning present. Third, boundaries allow me to make explicit connections between meanings and organizational conditions. Because boundaries can be both concrete fixtures and intangible ideas, they are the perfect mechanism for seeing how organizations and meanings influence each other. Finally, the fourth advantage of this method is an old-fashioned discovery: I found that it offered a careful and systematic measure of how *abstract* a meaning is.

When I contrasted national rhetoric with the definitions I uncovered inside English departments, the reason the national debate did not spur much real change became painfully obvious. In short, the meaning of multiculturalism in the national arena rested on two isolated realms of meaning (traditional literature and values). But their meanings literally did not reach into the classroom. Without being translated to the arenas that connected multiculturalism to students (specifically, diversity and teaching methods), the "war" was meaningless to English teachers.

Multiculturalism in the National Arena

Before the Canon War

Although the word "multiculturalism" is relatively new, the ideas generally associated with it are not. Multiculturalism emerged out of a tension between cultural diversity and social cohesion that has been a central theme in U.S. political culture since its inception. This was not the first time that a national concern about cultural difference had become entangled with normal scholarly debates about literary value, but it may have been one of the most dramatic convergences between the two.

Most treatments of multiculturalism do not include a definition of the word. There are good reasons for that omission. The exact meaning is not at all clear, and mere attempts at definition can produce conflict. At its most general level, multiculturalism implies the coexistence of multiple cultures. How complete those multiple cultures might be and how they might relate to each other varies from one definition to the next. Thus, the term can be applied narrowly, as in an elementary school classroom, a concert program, or a collection of sweaters, and it can be applied broadly to address cultural dynamics at a global level. Obviously, the social implications of multiculturalism would be vastly different in these instances.

In U.S. political culture, multiculturalism has its historical origins in racial and ethnic relations. During the 1960s and 1970s, the liberal position on racism argued that observed differences between "racial" groups, which served as the basis of racist beliefs in biological inferiority, could, in fact, be attributed to cultural rather than biological differences. Many racial inequalities could then be dissolved through cultural assimilation, popularly understood as "the Melting Pot." Once cultural differences disappeared, the theory suggested that racism and discrimination would also dissolve.[3]

History, however, has not proceeded in the way assimilationists expected. Eliminating legal segregation proved more difficult than originally expected, and removing social segregation was impossible to orchestrate from above. More important, assuming that cultural minorities would want to privilege U.S. culture over their own appears to have been a misstep. The apparent failure of assimilationism has lent strength to the alternative view, cultural pluralism, which has more recently been called multiculturalism. In the context of immigration, multiculturalism takes on a meaning closer to that of the Canadian multiculturalism program. It implies that there must be a way for groups within a social system to maintain unique cultures without jeopardizing social cohesion.[4]

The earliest references to multiculturalism in the news came from a Canadian political program aimed at negotiating French and Anglo cultural differences by drawing attention to other ethnicities (*New York Times*, October 10, 1971, 28), but practical uses of the term in the United States first appeared in books and articles about teaching methods in primary and secondary schools, where multicultural education is now a thriving field. The multiculturalism discussed in public schools is about cultural exclusion, personal expression, self-esteem, and the value of cultural differences. *Thus, the first references to multiculturalism (political and pedagogical) were not even remotely related to literary canons.*

Many emerging theoretical developments in literary criticism emphasize the power of culture and offer theoretical support for the idea of multiculturalism. But multiculturalism emerged independently in the national arena, without much more than a common-sense understanding of assimilation and non-assimilation.

The result was a simple coincidence of standpoints between well-established liberal political interests and the literary theory of the "New Left" in academe. Literary deconstructionists, neo-Marxists, feminists, and poststructuralists found themselves aligned with political multiculturalists on nearly all issues concerning socio-cultural inequality. Traditionalist literary scholars and assimilationists likewise shared a sense of threat as the other side attempted to "deconstruct" their canons, revealing the fragile state of their claims to cultural legitimacy. The two battles—one over theory, the other over cultural identity—came together in explosive fashion in the mid-1980s.

Such "battles" were not new to English professors, however. The struggle to institutionalize English literature—never mind *American* literature—in U.S. universities at the turn of the twentieth century was no less contentious, and participants were equally, if not more, concerned about the fate of their nation's culture.[5] In fact, the traditionalists in today's debate lament the loss of a canon that was invented by their immediate predecessors after World War I to emphasize cultural ties to Europe. This fact is documented by historian

Lawrence Levine in his 1996 book, *The Opening of the American Mind*, in which he explains that before World War I, college students read only Greek and Latin classics, and they read them in the original, "not as works of literature, but as examples of *grammar*" (16). The novels and plays that now dominate the American and British literary canons were not considered to be serious enough to deserve academic attention.

The battle of the late twentieth century, however, connected literary theory to cultural pluralism. As a result, the word "multiculturalism" became a pseudonym for canon expansion.[6] In fact, the two words, "canon" and "multiculturalism," have parallel histories in this debate because, although both words had obscure existences in the United States prior to that point, this battle made them famous. They emerged from the smoke as opposing forces in an epic battle over the fate of a nation, and they were catapulted into American homes on the front pages of the *New York Times*.

Fate-of-a-Nation Definitions

None of the complications I describe above were evident in the heated rhetoric that spewed forth from our cultural critics. In the press, multiculturalism was just a terrifying apparition. Dinesh D'Souza, Roger Kimball, and William Bennett, among others, argued that multiculturalism was a misconceived strategy of the cultural Left that threatened our national unity in the name of tolerance.[7] Members of the Left, however, argued that multiculturalism was an invention of the Right, caricatured for the purposes of waging war on the academy.[8]

Even the most notorious members of the Cultural Left steadfastly denied the existence of a specifically multicultural agenda in English literature. The main reason no one stepped up to defend multiculturalism in the way that the press expected, therefore, was that there was no such thing as a multicultural literary scholar of the sort the pundits described. Real, nihilistic cultural relativists would have no reason to promote any culture, much less multiple cultures, and advocates of non-dominant cultural integrity, such as Afro-centrists, were not interested in teaming up with other excluded cultures.[9]

Opponents of multiculturalism on the national scene were not especially interested in defining the word, either. They did talk about it, however. In fact, many cultural critics managed to go on at length about the dangers of multiculturalism, without bothering to specify what they meant by the word. The analysis that follows will reveal that denouncing multiculturalism as a threat to something valuable is a sort of rhetorical magic trick.

Roger Kimball, for example, introduced multiculturalism as an alternative to literary canons and added, "It is worth noting that the word *multiculture* and its variants have become code words for an approach to the humanities that is in effect *anti*cultural . . . instilling dissatisfaction and the desirability of undermining the traditional canon" (1990, 63). Notice that this statement makes no mention of cultural difference or what it might have to do with literary canons. In fact, culture is equated with "the traditional literary canon" (whatever that is). To support multiculturalism is to oppose the canon, and to oppose the canon is to oppose culture.

E. D. Hirsch's 1987 bestseller, *Cultural Literacy: What Every American Needs to Know*, for example, claimed that it is not so much the particulars of our common culture (the values it promotes) so much as its commonness that unites the nation. But that doesn't affect his conclusion because, he argues, canons *constitute* our common culture. It's the canon or bust, so multiculturalism is still the *anti-canon*.

Unlike Hirsch, most conservative literary scholars focused their attention on values (or literary value), but they mimicked Hirsch's strategy of separating that issue from the question of cultural diversity. Without the problem of U.S. national identity, books such as *The Western Canon* (1995), from literary scholar Harold Bloom, talk about canons in terms of their artistic value (aka aesthetics). These arguments often draw on issues of beauty, inspiration, deep impact, and the love of literature. Multiculturalists are simply people who want to destroy that beautiful and beloved canon of great literature by *politicizing* the idea of value (considering not only aesthetic value but also political and moral values). Multiculturalism is still the anti-canon. It's not about cultural difference, it is about the destruction of aesthetic value.

Let's try another influential pundit, Dinesh D'Souza. The closest thing to a definition offered in his *Illiberal Education* was this: "Diversity, tolerance, multiculturalism, pluralism—these phrases are . . . principles and slogans of the victim's revolution" (1992, 17). D'Souza also used catchy phrases like "tyranny of the minority," but he generally treated the state of higher education in the United States as a problem that has no name. In later writings, especially *The End of Racism,* he came to understand multiculturalism as a mandate for cultural relativism, by which he meant a doctrine of all cultures having equal value and deserving equal treatment. This is similar to the veiled reference that NEH Chair William Bennett made in his *Wall Street Journal* piece (the one that started it all). Without mentioning multiculturalism per se (yet), Bennett wrote, "In place of cultivation we advocate something called 'awareness,' which may be defined as a state of indiscriminate perception and uninformed judgment."

The "cultural relativism" definition of multiculturalism does begin to reference race and sometimes immigration, but it draws a direct line between race and values. By these definitions, any mention of adding "excluded groups" to the canon constituted an attack on core values because, critics argued, the original exclusions were based on values—good values. In this story, excluded groups were excluded on purpose, not because of racism or sexism, but because they didn't measure up to "our" lofty cultural expectations. If those judgments favor British literature over Chinese literature, it is because British literature better fits "our" superior understanding of literary value. Oh, and, um, our values are never wrong—unless, of course, they've changed recently. These cultural-relativism definitions hinge on diversity and value, and they are the sort of definition that attracts charges of racism.

Scholarly critics who worried about cultural fragmentation, such as historian Arthur Schlesinger, didn't normally claim that all things "American" (or English, or masculine, or white or Western or whatever) were better than the ideas that had been excluded. That is why Schlesinger could argue that racism was the underlying problem, while D'Souza argued that racism was bunk.

D'Souza's most recent (2003) book, *What's So Great about America*, takes that argument to its own extreme and explains why practicing academics don't use D'Souza's understanding of race and aesthetic value. One need not even buy the book to get his message about just how dangerous multiculturalism is. The jacket reads: "America is under attack as never before—not only from terrorists, but from people who provide a rationale for terrorism. Islamic intellectuals . . . Europeans . . . and left-wing multiculturalism—dominant in our own schools and universities—teaches students that Western and American culture is no better than, and probably worse than, Third World cultures."

It's the post-9/11 theory of cultural omnipotence: If we don't defend our traditional American culture, we'll be obliterated by terrorists.

My First Interview

When I walked into the office of Professor Ecks with my tape recorder and questionnaire, I suddenly realized that I didn't know what to expect. I had spent nearly a year preparing for this moment, devising research questions, selecting universities, honing my questions, getting institution approvals, sending letters of introduction, and begging for interviews. The review boards took forever, and all of them had an issue of some sort. For these Ivory Tower interviews, I would have to omit a question about tenure criteria. So much for the really juicy gossip.

Scheduling interviews was the hardest part, though. After spending half a day ringing unattended phones at Ivory Towers, I finally managed to catch Professor Ecks at her desk. I didn't know that I had landed an interview with one of the department's most famous authors, but I was plenty nervous, anyway.

Thankfully, I had a script to lean on. I began with my "consent" spiel, explaining that she could stop at any time and refuse to answer any questions she wanted (as though I were a white-coated scientist delivering electric shocks). I also reminded her that both she and her university would be anonymous. "Oh, so you won't use my name? You'll just write, 'Professor X said,' whatever?" "Right." "Then it won't be like that *Lingua Franca* reporter. To read his article you would have thought I was his Virgil, you know, leading him, like Dante, through the gates of hell . . . I never met the man!" (*Lingua Franca* was a popular but short-lived news magazine devoted to covering academic gossip.) We were off to a good start.

By the time we finished these introductions, I was perfectly at home. Being in her office was very much like meeting with my advisors at Princeton. In fact, it was *exactly* like that, once we established that I wasn't a reporter in disguise. Professor Ecks answered my questions. She even gave me some great sound bites and some bits of gossip. (Famous authors are clearly better at that than the average English professor.) But she also prodded me on key points, and she explained things.

Except for that uncomfortably legalistic "informed consent" conversation, my plan was to start my interviews slowly with warm-up questions. I began by asking how they had been drawn to the profession and how they would describe themselves to strangers—English teacher, college professor, literary critic, etc. (Nearly all answered that they would say, "I teach literature at such-and-such university.")

I didn't expect to get much from the answers to these questions, but telling their professional "life story" got them warmed up fast because it allowed them to talk about themselves in other contexts (their own college experience, graduate school, the profession, and other academic jobs, if there were any). Those stories provided important lubrication for the transition to talking about their departments and disciplinary politics. Their life stories would be incomplete if they withheld all the details in the last few chapters.

From there, I asked them how they conceived of good versus bad English professors, good books, and good students. I also asked whether they talked with their colleagues about teaching decisions and scholarly work (if applicable), and I asked whether their friendship circles tended to include colleagues in their departments. Finally, the last of the big questions was, *"How do you feel about multiculturalism?"*

As you might expect, it was a hard question for many of them to answer, and it was equally difficult for me to maintain my position that I didn't know what multiculturalism was—not because I was sure I had the right answer, but because so many of them wanted me to explain what *I* meant by the question. I tried very hard not to say "I want you to define it for me." Instead, I told them I just wanted their response to the word.

Although most of the professors I interviewed expressed frustration with the ambiguity surrounding multiculturalism (which interested me), all obliged me with their reactions, and I was able to glean a definition from most (88 percent). The 12 percent who did not employ multiculturalism as a meaningful word nevertheless contributed an interesting dimension to my analysis of the meaning-making process because they allowed me to examine not only which types of meanings emerge under what conditions, but also which conditions are conducive to meaning-making and which are hostile to it.

Most of my interviews at Ivory Towers followed the pattern established for me by Professor Ecks, in which I had to explain the differences between my research and that of the journalists they had encountered in the past. These professors had been in the news a lot, and journalists didn't always check their facts very carefully. The media version of life in the ivory tower sounded foreign to them, and most of them desperately wanted to correct it.

But despite their unusual exposure to public scrutiny, these Ivory Towers professors were like all the other English professors I interviewed in that they directed their concerns toward journalistic *misrepresentation* rather than toward the gap in expectations between lofty ideas and college classes. Misrepresentation is a valid complaint, but it also abandons the concerns that motivated those lofty ideas—cultural difference, value, and/or literacy. That is, the English professors I interviewed, and those who tried to defend their discipline in the press, wanted the world to know that even the most radical among them teaches canonical literature. Their message was, "We haven't strayed as far off course as you imagine." My analysis below, however, will suggest that such a response accepts the pundit's definition of the proper course—the one involving an omnipotent literary culture.

Making Sense of Multiculturalism

After each interview, I made notes on my observations, things that hadn't made their way onto the recorder. Once the interviews were transcribed, the next task was to start trying to categorize responses to the multiculturalism question.

I started with a pair of scissors and a magic marker, putting paragraphs into stacks according to their major themes, hoping to find what Zerubavel calls "islands of meaning"—big clear boundaries between multiculturalism and everything else.[10] But there is no island of meaning for multiculturalism—the term is far too nebulous to expect that I could simply describe its characteristics, all the factors that distinguish it from neighboring meanings. In trying to "force" responses into categories, I also found that I was drawing heavily on contextual information (such as what I knew of a professor's specialties or department) to make those determinations. Yet, multiculturalism *did* have *some* meaning. My task was to figure out how to describe it.

Eventually I succumbed to the mountain of paper and bought a qualitative analysis program that allowed me to assign a single answer to many different categories at once (like the paper and scissors method, but with a couple dozen copies of each interview and a better system for keeping track of where each sentence came from). The exact procedure I ultimately used was more elaborate than my original plan to describe a single boundary for the meaning of multiculturalism. But it was also a lot simpler, in that it required very little interpretive effort on my part.

To simplify the explanation, imagine trying to discover the difference between peaches and pears by comparing a dozen varieties of each. Rather than drawing a single line between the peaches and the pears and then describing that line as fully as possible, I chose to consider each criterion separately, as its own category of meaning. The category "sweet," for example, could be a rather large circle around all the fruit. The category "green" would apply to only a few pears—a smaller circle. Likewise, "round," "soft," "red," "grainy," etc., would apply to various portions of each set. If we used circles to enclose all the fruit that fit inside each boundary, the result would look far messier than the "fine line" dividing the two categories, but the sea of circles really represents a simpler, cleaner, and more specific approach to meaning because the process is more systematic and the defining criteria are more clearly identified. In short, I found that there is a lot more than water separating those islands of meaning.

The simplicity of the boundary metaphor (and method) requires an explanation of how people juggle all the boundaries in play at any given moment. And for meaning-making, the interplay turns out to have interesting effects. Consider interior lighting (because the human creative factor is stronger than it is for fruit). First, note that this method of identifying the overlapping properties of meaning is not (currently) typical of a symbolic boundaries approach. In fact, the idea of overlap may seem incongruent with symbolic boundaries on first examination because the concept of boundedness focuses attention on differentiation, exclusion, and separateness rather than overlap. So long as the analytic focus remains narrow, the way we distinguish lamps from other kinds of lights can seem clear. But if we examine lighting in the context of living rooms, the influence of other cultural categories comes into view. Floor lamps, table lamps, and ceiling fixtures exist because clear, bounded cultural categories influence each other. The overlap does not diminish our ability to distinguish between them, however. The existence of "floor lamps" doesn't blur the boundary between floors and lamps, it demonstrates that floors have physically influenced lights.

Similarly, when I allowed English professors to talk at liberty about multiculturalism, I got responses that ranged widely and defied narrow categorization. Making sense of the way this diverse group of professors talked about multiculturalism required a method that would allow a single thought to have several themes at once, the way a peach can be both round and sweet, yet a pear can be sweet without being round. In Zerubavel's terms, a sorting process combined with a matching process.

Adjusting my method to allow for both sorting and matching provided a breakthrough moment in my research when real patterns finally began to emerge. It made this analysis of meaning (and the organizational production of meaning) possible. But it also revealed a way to identify various definitions as more or less abstract according to the number of ideas attached to a single meaning. More connections reduce abstraction, as in the example where adding the idea of a floor to the idea of a light results in a specific type of lamp. Over the course of the next three chapters, abstraction will emerge as a key theme in the process of cultural change.

My method of categorizing meaning is a blind and inductive technique. I reduced whole sentences of transcribed text into two- or three-word phrases, allowing each respondent an unlimited number of these individual snippets. The quote at the beginning of this chapter, for example, was reduced to the phrase "medieval is multicultural." Other phrases included "can't define," "we try," "plugging in," "author's identity," "student demographics," "salad bowl," "global influences," "fresh air," etc. I didn't attempt to make sense of them at this stage, only to reduce them. The result was hundreds of phrases, all detached from the respondents who delivered them. I then sorted the various snippets into categories of meaning without feeling the influence of each respondent's other characteristics. Whereas complete interviews—even two consecutive paragraphs of interview text—would likely remind me of the respondent who delivered them, their demographic characteristics, and (most important) their departmental affiliation, this method allowed me to disable the tendency to think that certain responses might "go together" because they came from the same department. Once reduced to snippets and phrases, the responses became anonymous for me. Thus, I was able to sort responses into categories of meaning and discover whether other patterns, such as departmental affiliation, would reproduce themselves in the inductively coded data. (They did!)

I had to make several passes through that collection of snippets to discover a set of categories that made room for all the phrases without excluding too many of the mysterious ones (such as "fresh air"). And I had to allow each phrase to go in all the relevant categories. That was the key to discovering the four arenas of meaning at work in definitions of multiculturalism. The first sort, for example, turned hundreds of phrases into dozens of topics. In the next pass, I started combining topics into larger arenas. Then I returned to the individual snippets to make sure the new larger categories really applied to everything I'd placed inside them. Finally, when I arrived at the four key themes, I examined those responses in whole paragraphs to make sure that my method hadn't caused me to take some statements "out of context," in the negative sense of distorting the larger picture. At that stage, I did make some adjustments to account for the fact that my original selection of snippets was not specifically intended to categorize responses in relation to the four themes. So, in one case, for example, a respondent provided an example of how her definition of multiculturalism worked. At first, the original description and the example looked the same. But once the four key themes emerged, I paid more attention to those ideas and noticed that the example made a brief reference to literary value. In this second pass through the interview data, therefore, I made the necessary coding adjustments.[11]

Four Themes

The themes that emerged from English professors' talk about multiculturalism revealed four primary arenas of meaning: (1) cultural diversity, (2) literary preservation (i.e., canons and the anti-canon), (3) values, and (4) teaching methods (aka pedagogy). The four arenas do not describe mutually exclusive "types" of multiculturalism. Rather, they are the *elements* of multiculturalism, or at least, they are elements of literary multiculturalism. That is, when English professors talk about multiculturalism, they usually describe how cultural diversity affects canons, values, and teaching practices. But they do not necessarily invoke all of these themes at once.

All four elements of multiculturalism (diversity, canons, value, and pedagogy) may be used together to describe the overall scope of multiculturalism in English departments. They may be used independently, or they may be used in various combinations to produce a wide variety of specific definitions. Thus, one could draw on a single area, such as literary canon preservation, to say that multiculturalism is a threat to cultural tradition, as do most cultural critics. The *intersection* of two domains (literary canons and cultural diversity) produces one of the most popular definitions: multiculturalism, many professors said, is canon expansion—an attempt to make literary canons represent the cultural breadth that exists among their students or within the U.S. population.

Combining all four areas produces the narrowest and most specific definition. It can be considered a central or "core" definition, in the sense that it contains all the major characteristics that English professors attribute to multiculturalism. Thus, in its most specific form, "multiculturalism" suggests that *expanded canons help English professors teach the value of diversity*—the skills they believe their students need to navigate the cultural terrain of the twenty-first century.

Note that this core definition applies specifically to English professors. I did not restrict faculty to talking about their profession, but I did ask the question in the context of a larger conversation about their work. The word does have important applications outside English literature, but the scope of this particular definition is not wide enough to encompass its application to many other areas, including other movements in higher education such as affirmative action, retention strategies, cultural programming, and numerous other changes underway in other disciplines.[12]

To make sense of all the possible combinations and overlaps among the four arenas of meaning, I devised a Boolean-style diagram that depicts a space for each possible combination of overlaps. The result is Figure 2.1, a visual image of multiculturalism's turf, the emergent boundaries of meaning (symbolic boundaries) that define it, and their potential overlaps.

In Figure 2.1, the four white outer "petals" represent single arenas of meaning, and the various shades of gray indicate the number of arenas that overlap to form each specific definition. The darkest section, at the heart of the figure, represents the overlap of all four arenas at once—the core definition of multiculturalism. The size of the various overlapping regions is a function of geometry, however, and bears no relation to the importance of the definitions therein or to the number of professors who used such definitions. The labels in Figure 2.1 describe empirical findings in that category. Like the example of floors and lamps, putting two ideas together doesn't tell the whole story. People aren't making carpets from lightbulbs. Therefore, the area labels attempt to describe *how* the ideas are combined, to the extent possible, given

FIGURE 2.1

Conceptual Diagram: Four Arenas of Meaning and Their Intersections

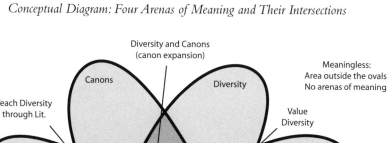

limited space. Together with the area outside the flower (representing the possibility that a respondent could claim no definition for the word), the four arenas of meaning generate sixteen possible definitions of multiculturalism.

Abstract definitions in Figure 2.1 have lighter shading, while more grounded definitions—those invoking more arenas of meaning—are darker. In contrast to Figure 2.1, Figure 2.2 uses shading to indicate the concentration of observed definitions among the professors I interviewed. In this figure, the color of the background area represents the proportion of professors who never used the word in a meaningful way. This same color-coding applies to all the figures in the following chapters, in which I separate these definitions according to department and stance-taking. Darker shading indicates more popular definitions.

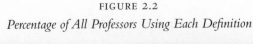

FIGURE 2.2

Percentage of All Professors Using Each Definition

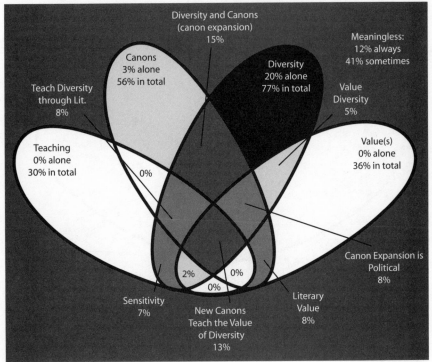

Meaninglessness

> I think it is really unfortunate that we allow ourselves to be
> ruled by a word that remains so amorphous and yet seems to be
> invested with such heavy moral authority. . . . It reminds me of
> that episode of *The Twilight Zone* where the children can send
> their parents to the corn field where they will vanish if the par-
> ents say the wrong thing, but the parents never know what the
> wrong thing will be.
>
> —*An Ivory Towers professor*

The first thing to notice about Figure 2.2 is that the background is fairly
dark. Forty-one percent of the English professors I interviewed began their

answer by explaining that they could not easily give their opinion on the matter because the word had no clear meaning, but most of them went on to describe the word, as they understood it. The 12 percent who maintained the position that multiculturalism was meaningless are represented in the background shading of Figure 2.2. Those who indicated a sense of ambiguity about the word but went on to offer some form of definition are also important—especially considering the sheer variety of definitions represented in Figure 2.2. Here's how a professor at State Star University described the experience of wanting to resist the word because of its unclear and politically tricky meaning while having a firm grasp on how the word operates in his world.

> I think the fact that you don't define the word is exactly the point. It's ceased to mean anything. It's a cliché, and part of my profession is that I'm a sworn enemy of cliché. But that doesn't mean that the kind of things that get discussed when people discuss multiculturalism don't mean anything to me. I'm in American literature and, because of multiculturalism, my field is expanding at a tremendous rate, a *tremendous* rate. What it means to me is: I need to work like hell and just read all the time everything available and try to be able to make judgments about what I'm going to use and teach and write about. Although I don't use the word and I feel a little squeamish when people do, I feel even more distant from people who always say it with a snide, deprecating pejorative tone.

The main reason for this kind of confusion is that the word "multiculturalism" comes from outside the discipline and is used to describe something far less sophisticated than either literary theory or non-traditional literary studies would advocate. In short, it just doesn't fit them very well, and it wouldn't have fit them very well even before the word became controversial and further complicated the situation. A tenured MC State professor who studies Native American oral traditions explained that situation when I asked whether multiculturalism had influenced her work. She said, "It has not." Then she paused and added, "But it has influenced the way others perceive me."

A professor from Ivory Towers highlighted the polarizing effects of the word "multiculturalism" in his explanation of its uselessness. "It gets implied very sloppily. Very, very few people mean 'multicultural' when they say 'mul-

ticultural.' They mean, 'things I like' or 'things I don't like.' The word 'multicultural' in the academy or the tabloid press is used the same way Newt Gin-
grich uses the word 'liberal.'"

These responses show that a word can cause controversy, not just in spite
of its vague meaning, but *because* of it, especially when the vagueness is centered on a touchy subject. All four of the ideas that multiculturalism invokes
(values, canons, diversity, and teaching) are important, morally salient arenas
of meaning for English professors or national culture. Because of the variety
of ways the four arenas are combined, however, combatants may talk past
each other by using different definitions of the word, or they may fight directly over its definition.

In addition, countless scholars have published definitions, but they offer
these new definitions as solutions to the debate or treaties in the battle.[13] That
is, they attempt to produce a definition that will make the word "acceptable."
Behind their strategy is a belief that a carefully constructed definition of multiculturalism can produce consensus if it acknowledges diversity and promotes equality without threatening any existing arrangements.

Of course, as the number and variety of these diplomatic definitions increase, the likelihood of achieving shared meaning decreases. My question,
"How do you feel about multiculturalism?" posed a problem for professors
who wanted to answer but could not do so in good conscience. As proponents of cultural enrichment, English professors are under tremendous pressure to offer meaningful responses to multiculturalism, so being uncertain
about its meaning made fulfilling that responsibility difficult. My question
only aggravated an already troublesome tension between having a responsibility to multiculturalism and not knowing what it was. An Ivory Towers
professor described the tension this way:

> I think that, like virtually every other department, our department is
> concerned with sending the right signals to the profession and to the up-
> per administration that it in fact endorses their definition of modern
> multiculturalism. . . . The upper administration is anxious, so we have in
> a certain sense, a kind of hierarchy of paranoia that is driven by a word
> for which nobody has a definition.

Where did that leave English professors? The word "multiculturalism"
landed in their laps, but, as one professor from MC State said, "We're pretty

damn close to absolutely clueless about what to do with it." And yet, there it was: a meaningless word that wouldn't go away. There was only one thing to do. Add meaning. In the next chapter, we will see that this professor's department has done more than any other in my study—more than most in the nation, in fact—to add meaning to the word "multiculturalism."

Diversity

Among the professors who *did* offer some meaning for the word, the dominant theme was diversity. Twenty percent (those represented in the outer portion of the diversity "petal" of Figure 2.2) even managed to use diversity *alone* to define multiculturalism, without addressing questions of value, canons, or pedagogy. Many definitions in this category understand multiculturalism as a social condition much broader and more serious than the concerns of English literature. Some professors, such as this one from Ivory Towers, argued that the attempts of literary and cultural critics to make sense of multiculturalism are pointless, saying, "It's a fact of life," and, "It's a demographic reality. It doesn't want a philosophy." Notice, however, that disciplinary *boundaries* still play an important role in these definitions. Professors who used this approach described the place of multiculturalism relative to the boundaries of English literature—to exclude it, to bring it inside, or to make connections.

More often, however, respondents who referred only to diversity did so in order to critique literary approaches to social justice, arguing that English professors have overstated their own importance in the battle over multiculturalism. For example, an Ivory Towers professor said, "I would be in favor of a multicultural requirement at this university, provided it was rigorous. If students were, say, required to learn a non-Western language, if they were required to know the history of a culture other than their own." Another invoked the shallowness of defining cultural difference as the identity politics of elite English professors when he said, "It's hard to be multicultural here. It's like a multicultural country club." In the next chapter, we'll get to see the Ivory Towers campus, where it will become clear that his characterization of the place as a country club is disarmingly accurate.

The quote that opened this chapter (the one that claims medieval literature is multicultural) is another example of the "diversity alone" definition of multiculturalism. Although the quoted professor is making a reference to literature, he isn't connecting the matter of literary diversity to contentious canon debates. Instead, he argues that diversity is the whole point and it always was the point.

I didn't come easily to this conclusion. During the interview phase, I thought this professor and two other white-male full professors who made similar statements were merely trying to justify their decisions to ignore emerging work in their field by claiming that they had multiculturalism covered. Then I heard the same view espoused by a female assistant professor, fresh out of graduate school, who put the male professors' view together with a more common understanding of diversity. She said, after a long pause:

> I really think that *most* of us are engaged to a greater or lesser degree
> with multiculturalism. When I teach the distant past, that is a species of
> multiculturalism. When an Americanist teaches the more recent past, that
> also is a species of multiculturalism, and I can't, for the life of me,
> understand why anyone would object to a definition of multiculturalism
> that says we ought to teach not only along the temporal spectrum but
> also across a number of cultures in our own country and outside.

In other words, the idea that literature can transport readers to foreign worlds has been part of the literary raison d'être for as long as anyone can remember. From this perspective, the reason to teach literature to students is not that it is their culture but that it isn't. Although these professors didn't include classroom experiences in their definitions of multiculturalism, other interviews would reveal that student discomfort with canonical literature is a central tension in the professors' working lives. Some imaginary ideal tells them that reading great Western literature should be a rich and rewarding exercise in reflexive cultural introspection—an indulgent form of self-study. But their students disprove that ideal every day in the classroom. This is just one example of how English professors absorbed multiculturalism into their long-standing sense of purpose.

Both of these groups, the professors who never defined multiculturalism and the ones who did not connect the idea to their working lives, left multiculturalism in the clouds. But these professors were the exception, in that they talked about multiculturalism in a different realm from that of their concrete scholarly and pedagogical practices.

Together, the two groups made up less than a third of my total interviewees. This might suggest that the professors who used these definitions had not thought much about multiculturalism at all. Examining the members of this group individually, however, revealed that no more than half of those professors' disconnected definitions could have resulted from a lack of interest in multiculturalism, especially as it related to teaching and scholarship. The others were *very* interested in multiculturalism. Many were active participants in local or national battles over the appropriateness of multicultural changes within the discipline. In short, these professors think of multiculturalism as an important topic for public debate that is largely irrelevant to their own work. It may be that active participation in public debate encourages participants to embrace more abstract understandings of the issues and decreases one's ability to apply those abstract concerns to concrete situations. More evidence supporting this possibility will emerge in the next chapter.

Non-Diversity (Literary Value and the Anti-Canon)

If the connection between multiculturalism and diversity seems obvious, it should be noted that 12 percent of my respondents (seven professors) managed to talk at length about multiculturalism without mentioning diversity or anything I could identify as *related* to diversity, such as gender, race, ethnicity, cultural difference, pluralism, otherness, or even historical or stylistic diversity. Such non-diversity definitions appeared in only two of eleven possible forms, however, addressing only literary canons or adding the idea of value(s) to concerns for the canon.

The most common way of talking about multiculturalism without referring to diversity involved "literary value" (at the intersection of canons and value). These five professors primarily avoided questions of diversity by defining multiculturalism as a politically motivated agent of disorder that threatens the idea of literary value or quality. A professor at Ivory Towers, for example, said, "What we are winding up with is a smorgasbord of texts but no way of accounting [for] why they ought to be there other than our sense of preemptive political righteousness." A Multicultural State professor went so far as to say, "I don't like the idea of breaking down the barriers and having, you know, *just literature*." In short, these professors argue that the reasons for changing definitions of literary worthiness are irrelevant. What matters, they claim, is that previously accepted standards of greatness appear to be weakening.

Here is that rhetorical magic trick. The unspoken implication of the definition of multiculturalism that says it is an assault on literary value is the D'-Souza problem: if "the canon" was carefully selected based on aesthetic value, then excluded groups must have been excluded because they have bad values or poor skills. The racist implication of that argument, however, makes it unpopular in universities, so academic opponents of multiculturalism just skip the whole idea of cultural difference when they complain about multiculturalism. This is an often-successful attempt to avoid charges of racism, but it leaves multiculturalism without any connection to diversity and, thus, without much useful meaning. It is one of the most serious ways that multiculturalism erases the specifics of race, gender, and cultural differences.

One professor at State Star stood out for his ability to articulate this view of multiculturalism in a way that exposes its allure and the political difficulties it poses. First, he explained his attraction to aesthetics and placed that attraction not only in his own appreciation for beauty, but also in his experiences of having attended college during the World War II era (he finished his Ph.D. in the mid-1950s).

> I've been thinking about this for a long time and maybe saying it this way makes sense. One of the courses I took as a freshman at Princeton was a marvelous course on Plato—the idea that the good, the true, and the beautiful were finally one thing. I sort of believe that, and I, uh, find that in the sort of criticism I've been talking about that I find so repelling—it's as if they lopped off the beautiful. And, indeed, the true isn't there anymore. It's some kind of subjective and relative thing, so that's gone. And what you get is—is the *good*, which is defined in terms of political correctness. . . . And I just find it rather unappealing, frankly.

Next, he tried to separate aesthetic value from what he calls politics, which appears to include both formal politics (voting behavior) and identity politics. He began with a stuttering attempt to characterize his politics as 1960s liberalism and connected that idea (via Kimball's "tenured radicals" thesis) to multiculturalism.

> I try to make an effort to place these authors in the context of their times, rather than trying to impose our expectations as post-1960 people.

—Uh, and they're my expectations—I—my . . . As I say, I'm sympathetic with them, politically. I vote Democratic, I've never voted for anybody who wasn't a Democrat. Sometimes the Democrats are women; sometimes they're black; sometimes, for all I know, they're homosexuals. That doesn't figure into my appreciation of literature.

Note that although this professor makes reference to demographic differences in the context of talking about multiculturalism, he does so in order to say that such concerns ought to be excluded. That is, he says that, even though he might interpret the actions of characters or authors as, for example, racist, if they happened today, he doesn't think it makes sense to apply modern understandings of racism to older texts. In short, he brackets his own "political" concerns when he studies literature in order to focus on aesthetics. For that reason, I didn't code these definitions under diversity, though I could have. (Has he excluded the problem of diversity or highlighted it?) One thing is certain, however. As we will see in the next two chapters, there is some heated action here at the border of diversity and value.

The second type of non-diversity definition drew exclusively on the arena of canons and was employed by only two professors, one of whom said, for example, "I think of it as more sort of a canon issue rather than a multicultural issue." Both of the professors who avoided the topic of diversity by directing attention to the canon alone did so by treating the canon as an externally generated body of knowledge that they were duty-bound to teach. They did not seem to think of themselves as qualified to question the canon or to alter it. As a result, their responses to multiculturalism inferred that such issues were the responsibility of more important scholars. They teach "the canon"; someone else defines it.

In short, multiculturalism was only a problem for those who would dare participate in defining the canon. This position makes obvious the importance of professional status in the way English professors process the idea of multiculturalism. Professors who don't think of themselves as leading scholars in their field may avoid the issue altogether by resolving to teach whatever appears in the latest anthology or textbook. This approach allows elite scholars and the publishing industry to determine the appropriate role of multiculturalism in English literary canons, and it deflects potential conflicts to those levels as well. These kinds of effects will become even more obvious in the next chapter when we visit the four departments.

Most important for the ultimate meaning of multiculturalism, all seven definitions that avoided diversity follow Harold Bloom and other cultural critics in defining multiculturalism as the anti-canon, or an assault on aesthetic value. But definitions mimicking those of popular cultural critics were rare. An equal number of professors (seven) avoided talk of diversity by claiming that the word had no meaning at all. Both groups—those using an anti-canon definition and those claiming no meaning—demonstrated uneasiness with the concept of cultural difference. Those who claimed no meaning merely refused to make use of the term "multiculturalism" as a concept relevant to their daily lives as English professors, while those who employed an anti-canon definition defined multiculturalism as a threat to canons and/or literary value.

Connections

> I guess I think of multiculturalism not as a matter of making sure I'm sensitive to Hispanics and never say awful things about black folks, but trying to help people become more sensitive to their environment and also to realize that any environment that is interesting is almost certain to be a multicultural environment. In fact, that's a line that I try to demonstrate in composition class: "It's our differences make us interesting."
>
> —*An MC State professor connecting diversity, value, and teaching methods*

Richer understandings of multiculturalism begin to appear when professors connect diversity to at least one other category of meaning—and the majority of professors tried to do so. In my search for meaning, this is where the action is, and it matters in two ways. First, there is the sheer importance of putting two ideas together. Unlike the abstract philosophical attention to one nebulous domain, putting two ideas together defines the situation in far more concrete terms. The second interesting thing about connected definitions is that they start to take on real shapes—meanings that aren't merely A + B. Unlike the ubiquitous, abstract realm of diversity, where almost anything goes, these combined definitions really mean something recognizable.

I made this discovery early in the process of coding categories and deciding how to represent their combinations. As I tinkered with the geometric puzzle of showing all the possible overlaps in a single diagram, I started labeling the categories: "canons + diversity," "teaching + value," etc. As the number of overlapping arenas increased, however, the space for labels shrank. I started trying to summarize the overlaps in fewer words, but I did that before analyzing my results. As a result, I put the ideas together in ways that made sense to *me*, rather than ways that would make sense to English professors.

For example, "canons + diversity" might be described as "representation." Already, the effect of meaning-making is clear. "Representation" is far more specific than "canons + diversity." My first guesses about how those ideas went together were mostly wrong. Representation, for example, does matter to English professors, but it only matters to those who care about teaching, so the idea of representation didn't make an appearance in the "canons + diversity" category. Instead, as I will explain below, definitions in this category assumed that diversity would be additive—an expanding cannon.

Canon Expansion

Among the professors who connected the idea of diversity to their everyday activities, discussion of literary canons and issues of text selection were more often important than were pedagogical concerns. That is, the question of what they taught took precedence over question of how they taught it. This is no surprise, given that the typical training of English professors focuses on literature to the exclusion of pedagogy.

As a result, cultural diversity, in the nation or in the classroom, makes English professors rethink their choices of reading assignments more often than it makes them rethink their teaching practices. In addition, professors who combined these two arenas (and no others) specifically defined multiculturalism as the *expansion* of literary canons, rather than text substitution, replacement, or obliteration, saying, for example, "I think of multiculturalism as a way of adding to the richness of the discipline, rather than replacing what already exists."

In all, more than half of my respondents invoked the idea of literary canons to talk about multiculturalism—alone or in combination with other fields, mostly diversity. Of course, we already knew this much. Despite adamant claims that the word has no meaning, any observer could have guessed that multiculturalism in English literature will have something to do with the effect of cultural diversity on literary canons. The more interesting action in defining multiculturalism happens when the idea of canon expansion is brought to bear on other realms of practical or moral relevance. Therefore, definitions at the intersection of canons and diversity (alone) tended to be dry and matter-of-fact. Professors spoke of "plugging in" works by people from "different cultural backgrounds." Apart from the implied effect of cultural diversity at a societal level, these professors omitted specific implications of canon expansion. We'll see in later chapters that a dry and matter-of-fact approach to multiculturalism can be handy for reducing conflict.

Literary Value and Canon Expansion

An infinitely expanding canon of great literary works is a nice idea, in theory. But in real life, it complicates the question of what should go on a syllabus:

> I have no problem with multiculturalism except that there's only so much time you can give to the study of literature in four years. If you're going to give time to the writers that, in my terms, are not very good writers—at least not compared to Milton and Shakespeare and other people in the canon—then we're losing some of the canon. You can't have it all.

The syllabus is one real-life constraint that causes English professors to think about literary value. What makes one syllabus work better or be more suited to a college course than another? Reading lists produced the zero-sum approach to multiculturalism and the canon. Like the State Star professor quoted above, this Ivory Towers professor is also concerned with how big the canon ought to be, but he adds a new twist to the issue. He begins in a familiar way:

> My sense is that it's a mistake, really, to think that the road to salvation lies with a gradual broadening of the curriculum. The affirmative action approach to the curriculum is not helpful because it essentially provides no rationale other than a perfectly amorphous and unspecified criteria that everybody has to be included.

Think this professor is a traditionalist who opposes change? Think again. Like the previous professor, he situates the crux of the expansion problem on literary value, but then he turns the aesthetic problem on its head:

> My sense is that as long as we work with the model of literature as a particular aesthetic form, the curriculum will be, in fact, always too narrow. The category itself, in a certain sense, becomes more an obstacle than anything else.

A professor from MC State even went so far as to suggest what other professors should do. It's important to note that the following comment stands out in that respect. It is not unusual for scholars and professors to claim that they are right and everyone else is wrong, but it is unusual to hear them say "Those people over there should change." It sounds like a subtle difference, but it's striking in context. The first few words out of this professor's mouth sound as though she's talking about a team of hourly workers she's supervising. As we'll see in the next chapter, her statement predictably reflects the conditions of academic life at MC State (and many other non-elite colleges).

> I think that it's about time! A lot more effort needs to be made among traditional English professors to recognize, and place value on, African American and other cultural creations, other ethnic cultural creations. Not necessarily to judge them from the same perspective as they would something by Hemingway or Faulkner.

Professors who included references to value(s) in their "canon expansion" definition of multiculturalism gave livelier definitions, in which clearer meanings began to emerge. In particular, the five professors who combined canons, diversity, and value in their definition of multiculturalism were remarkably similar in the way they made those connections. Although there are an infinite number of ways the three themes might be combined, these professors all advanced the argument that canon expansion is a value-laden, even political, process.

Teaching Diversity through Literature

Less than a third of respondents (30 percent) included pedagogical concerns in their definitions of multiculturalism. I want to emphasize, however, that this does not mean less than a third were concerned about teaching. It means that only 30 percent regarded multiculturalism as *relevant* to teaching methods. What sets this group of English professors apart is a belief that multiculturalism has (or should have) something to do with the relationship between teachers and students.

Because professors who combined diversity and canons with teaching concerns had given some thought to how they might put multiculturalism into practice, they were more confident in their ability to define the word and to respond to it in an appropriate way. Each of these professors argued, in one way or another, that teaching multicultural literature conveys something vital to students, specifically because of multicultural realities outside of the literature classroom that are beyond the professors' control.

For example, a professor at MC State observed that multicultural literature is an important part of improving cultural understanding, but he wanted to push the discipline (or at least textbook publishers) further on that point. When describing the importance of new literary works on the lives of his students, he said, "I just believe that all of us grow up monoculturalists. If I have cause with other multiculturalists, it's because their multiculturalism isn't multicultural enough."

A Cathletic professor (who, incidentally, was vehemently opposed to the theoretical changes underway in English literature) put together a strong argument for instilling a broader sense of cultural understanding through the study of ancient literatures.

> We've integrated Arabic materials [into the Great Books course] in the past five years, so that the students don't think of them as rag-heads, fundamentalists, and all that kind of thing. We [Europeans] were still practically swinging in trees when they were starting medical schools, beautiful architecture, elegant conversation, magnificent poetry, ice in the desert. They could make ice! It's amazing, you know? They just built a big wall that made a shadow, and at night they would flood it with layers of water, which freeze, and then they store it underground. For thousands of years, the Arabs have had sherbets and things out in the desert and just about all they wanted, and air conditioning just using the wind itself.

Another way to conceive of the importance of canon expansion in the lives of one's students is to consider the importance of getting students to identify with authors and to start to think of themselves as writers. A female professor at Cathletic University, for example, drew on that idea and her own experience to argue in favor of expanded canons to help her reach non-white and female students: "I do think it's important to teach works that aren't all by the same kind of person . . . because it was important to me as a kid to read works by women."

Finally, much of the debate over canon expansion is based on assumptions about literary value and the future of Western culture—far removed from concerns about how students might use their knowledge of literature in their future lives. As a case in point, take the (empty) intersection of teaching and canons. Even though canons were central to the anti-multiculturalist positions of E. D. Hirsch, William Bennett, and Allan Bloom, no professor responded to my question by saying that multiculturalism threatens the goal of conveying traditional cultural literacy to students. Again, this does not mean that my respondents were unconcerned about their responsibility to convey such skills. In fact, that connection emerged as a dominant theme in my questions about syllabus construction. That this intersection is empty only indicates that multiculturalism is irrelevant to the methods one would use to teach *traditional* canons. *Professors who thought about multiculturalism as a pedagogical issue never denied its connection to cultural diversity.*

Although none of the professors I spoke to defined multiculturalism as an issue related to traditional cultural literacy, two elite professors considered the importance of a student's familiarity with the *expanded* canon as an important part of their multicultural literacy.

> At least familiarity with the names. If, at a cocktail party, someone says *"Moby Dick"* and you say, "Well, I've never liked Melville, but I sure like Frederick Douglass," you know, you've at least been able to make connections back and forth. . . . I would be very—I would feel I'd failed as an English teacher, as an Americanist, if someone—one of my students—went to a cocktail party and someone said, "I love *Moby Dick*," and [my student] said, "What's that?" . . . or "I really love Morrison," and my student said, "When did Morrison write? Who is Morrison?" I think that that is important.

Sensitivity: Teaching Diverse Students

In turn, the definitions above have a very different character than definitions that attend to teaching and diversity alone—not canons or value. In practice, "diversity + pedagogy" equals "sensitivity."

Responses that combined the ideas of teaching and diversity share the spirit of those just discussed, except that they do not make claims about the importance of literary works in multicultural teaching practices, and more surprisingly, they show even less concern for the "out there" world students will face after leaving the university. That is, these responses defined multiculturalism as a push toward teaching methods that are sensitive to various sorts of diversity in the classroom and to positive classroom experiences, rather than cultural preparation. All four of these responses came out of Multicultural State, where the focus on pedagogy is evident. For example, one professor there noted that, when "multicultural issues come up in the classroom, we would encourage teachers not to back down from it." Another professor put more emphasis on his students' feelings, saying, "I really think it is very important for creating a classroom where everybody feels that they are a part of things."

The Heart of the Multicultural Lotus

When all four arenas of meaning are applied to multiculturalism, the idea becomes grounded in practical considerations that make it seem more real, more important for the topic at hand, and less radical:

> The kinds of debates I've experienced in the academic world are much more sensible than, I think, is reported by the media, so I think there should be more effort on the part of leading academics to show that there's not this mass brainwashing of America going on. It's very smart, balanced, sensitive people who are trying to teach values of critical thinking and critical tolerance and a kind of acceptance to other students—basically standard, moderate, traditional American values, in that sense. *And in that sense, multiculturalism is part of traditional American values.*

The crucial difference between these intensely grounded definitions and the more abstract definitions is a consideration of teaching practices. In short, applying those abstract ideas about values, canons, and cultural diversity inside the classroom changes everything. To explore that process, consider what happens to the idea of literary value when it is applied to teaching practices. One would think that canons and reading lists for traditional survey courses would be informed by similar understandings of literary value—especially since "the canon" invoked by cultural critics is only important insofar as it is conveyed to students. According to a graduate student at Ivory Towers, however, it doesn't work that way. Attention to teaching complicates all those big ideas that draw on abstract meanings. They work better in the newspapers than they do in the classroom:

> If you went and asked the senior Renaissance faculty here, "Why don't you teach Sydney's *Arcadia* to undergraduates?" You don't have to have heard of that text. [It was] probably the most widely read piece of prose fiction in the English language for a hundred years between when it came out in the 1590s and the 1690s. Everybody read it. Um. They will say, "Oh, you just can't teach it to undergraduates. They don't get it. They get frustrated with it." That's the polite version. . . . Many of them write about it and like it, but there's a gap. It's a great text, but you couldn't teach it to undergraduates.[14]

This quote echoes a sentiment expressed by several professors who guessed that there is something about the age and life stage of college students that makes them respond better to certain works. As a result, some of the touchstone pieces of the American literary canon are just bits of bait for the eighteen-year-old mind, not anything scholars consider to be particularly good examples of great literature.

> It's crazy! To choose all those things students won't like is crazy. Some [books], they won't like until we discuss it—*Middlemarch, Tender Buttons, Portrait of a Lady*—things that I enjoy teaching more. *The Great Gatsby* is the highlight of any course on the modern novel for an undergraduate, and usually sort of a ho-hum for me. *The Sun Also Rises* . . . I think it's, that it has, sort of, what I would consider an adolescent vision of the world which they are perfectly entitled to identify with, but that I don't.

The other interesting thing about the age gap between students and professors/scholars is that nearly all professors learn this lesson the hard way.

Just last week, I used a poem that I just realized I'm not going to use in this class anymore because the basic meaning of the poem, unless you are an older person, I've decided, you just can't get it. These people have worked with this poem and I have told them a lot of stuff about the poem and they don't . . . There's a key thing about human life that, apparently, it just takes being older to get. The older students get it right now and the younger students don't, not because they're dumb or not trying. You have to take that into account.

The important point to take away, here, is the widespread assumption that some books will not remain important to students as they age. Even operating inside the traditional canon, English professors know that literary value is contextual.[15] As this State Star professor demonstrates, even the literary value of Shakespeare's various works changes over time.

I never teach *The Tempest* anymore because I haven't had a thought on that in years and neither has anyone else. It's just boring . . . [In the classroom,] it doesn't *do* anything. I don't have any thoughts on it. Students don't have any thoughts on it. It doesn't generate any discussion.

Finally, I should point out that English professors do not let their students' tastes drive their syllabus decisions directly. Like everything else they do, it's a balancing act. Here, a Cathletic professor explains his decision to give up on two works while forcing a third on his unwilling audience, and the factors are multiple: the interpretive capacities of the adolescent mind, canonicity, historical importance, time constraints, reading abilities, and stylistic exposure. Even the weather plays a role in the way this professor constructs his syllabus.

I tried to do *Heart of Darkness,* and they really hated it. . . . It was just a bit too abstract for them, and I think they had a hard time with the whole narrative structure of it. They just found it really difficult to understand what was going on. It's also very depressing, and I don't think they wanted to think in those terms, especially considering it's a spring semester course. So you know, the birds are singing, the trees are blooming, and we're all in class going, "The horror! The horror!" . . . [But] in my American course, we just did [Melville's] *Billy Budd,* which they hated. They hated *Billy Budd,* and I don't care. I'll do *Billy Budd* again, only because it does a lot of the kind of stuff that *Moby Dick* does and since we can't read *Moby Dick* [because it's too long and difficult], it's sort of essential.

In total, eight professors (13 percent of those I interviewed) gave responses to multiculturalism that involved all four arenas of meaning (values, diversity, canons, and teaching)—making it the third most popular definition. Four of those eight professors, however, only managed to cover the four arenas by offering a long rambling discussion that eventually touched on each topic. Although these four respondents help support the idea that multiculturalism is relevant to all four arenas, and contribute to its meaning, they do not contribute to the development of a unified definition for multiculturalism, one that can be expressed in a clear sentence or two, in the context of English literature. Of course, many words manage to acquire meaning without having clear, unified definitions.

The first attempt at a unified definition I encountered came from a Multicultural State professor, who began by explaining that multiculturalism is a centerpiece of his department's course in Literary Theory: "It's a theory of power and a theory of art that reflects where we are on this planet, and we had better start learning something about it."

Another Multicultural State professor offered a less formal response to multiculturalism when he said, "*This* is the real world. This is where multiculturalism happens. The segregation is out there in the banks, in the workplace. So we are doing a real honest-to-God effort here." At State Star, one professor said, "I guess I feel like, whether we like it or not, we're living in it. . . . The institution has a responsibility to serve the needs of its students. I tend to be fairly open-minded about notions of literary value, for instance." It was another professor at State Star, however, who provided the closest estimation of the sentiment all these professors shared. For this professor, and many others, multiculturalism is

> . . . attention to different kinds of cultures and their influence, especially on Anglo-American trends in teaching literature—people who are trying to teach values of critical thinking and critical tolerance.[16]

Together, these responses indicate that the "central" definition of literary multiculturalism was not merely a theoretical possibility; it was in active use by the professors I interviewed, especially those who spent a lot of time thinking or talking about multiculturalism. None of these professors exactly produced the one-sentence definition that I derived from my inductive coding of their talk about multiculturalism. But I had not asked them to define the word. I asked them to talk about it. In their talk, they repeatedly covered a common territory—the territory defined by value, pedagogy, canons, and diversity, that is, the "turf" of multiculturalism as viewed by these English professors. Though not all of my respondents ventured into all four arenas of meaning, many did, and only a few managed to keep their use of the word in the smaller realm of meaning traversed by popular cultural critics.

Fighting Words

The core definition of multiculturalism—the one drawing on all four realms of meaning—suggests that expanded canons help English professors teach the value of diversity. There are certainly other ways to combine the four arenas, but any version of that central definition derived by combining all four arenas would be a far cry from E. D. Hirsch's use of the term as something that might "supplant or interfere with our school's responsibility to ensure our children's mastery of American literature" (1987, 18). Again, multiculturalism is the anti-canon for Hirsch, and although students do appear in Hirsch's story, pedagogy does not. Students, in his view, do not need good teachers or better methods; they need the canon. Note, however, that these are fighting words.

When cultural critics describe multiculturalism, they do so with a special purpose in mind. They want to elicit a response, or at least they want to attract attention. Their counterparts who appear to defend multiculturalism make even less use of the word, preferring to use words with more specific meanings. When they do use the word multiculturalism, it mostly serves to describe the opposition's complaint. Scholars who work on the specifics of what teachers should do about cultural diversity are not usually part of this battle.[17]

Thus, cultural critics use "thinner" definitions of multiculturalism (those drawing on fewer realms of meaning) than do practicing English professors, who spend more time in the classroom. Thinner definitions are more abstract in that they focus on one conceptual realm (or possibly two) in unrealistic isolation from the other realms of meaning that bring words like "multiculturalism" and "the canon" to life. Of course, abstraction is also an important conceptual tool. Just as philosophers sometimes allow themselves to contemplate ideas such as "truth," "beauty," and "democracy" without the inconvenience of human nature or other constraining realities, so do cultural critics debate the merits of multiculturalism without concern for the details of everyday life in English literature classrooms.

On paper, it is possible to make a direct connection between literary canons and the fate of Western culture. In the classroom, however, the fate of Western culture also hinges on how many students are asleep and why. In non-elite universities, the reason is as likely to be the effect of a student's full-time job or child-care responsibilities (or both) as it is the curriculum. At MC State, for example, multiculturalism is an important tool for reaching students with powerful literary ideas (i.e., for keeping them awake) in the face of the challenges posed by their less privileged outside lives. This reality has not been part of our national debates over multiculturalism, and it is only one of many unfortunate omissions.

If the goal of the canon wars was to affect the quality of literary education across the nation, the debates should have been informed by all four realms of meaning. The tendency for public intellectuals and cultural critics to define multiculturalism in only one realm of meaning allowed their ideas to spread over great distances. Introducing a second arena, as many did, reigned in the scope of their arguments a bit and made them sound better informed, but two realms of meaning were not enough to make real connections to classroom practices. To do that, our public intellectuals needed to consider students as real people, at very least, and not merely display cases for values and ideas.

I want to finish this chapter where I started it, with the famous author and Ivory Towers scholar, Professor Ecks, who was my first and most memorable interview. As we moved through the interview questions, she fed me bits of information about the circumstances of her recruitment to the department. She provided lively descriptions of her teaching methods. She told me about her friends in the department and how much she loved them. In short, she provided rich, personal, detailed, and intensely "grounded" answers to all my questions, but when I asked her how she felt about multiculturalism, she shifted into "public intellectual" mode. She began by referencing her written work, so I knew that we had been transported out of her office and onto the pages of a journal, but even her language also shifted into a more formal mode:

I've written so much about this I feel like a broken record. . . . Only for a relatively brief time in American literary studies was there ever a moment when multiculturalism was not the same thing as American literature.

Because of this answer (upon which she elaborated with a critical history of the American literary canon), I coded her definition of multiculturalism for its references to the canon of American literature and for her claim that it has always been diverse. This position fits Professor Ecks's teaching practices only to the extent that she counters the position of "traditionalists" by arguing that their sense of tradition is ill informed. In her classes, however, literary value depends, in part, on the experiences of her students. In her scholarly mode, students have disappeared. In the next chapter I show how other Ivory Towers professors often made this kind of shift from grounded to abstract thinking about multiculturalism, but Professor Ecks's transformation was especially striking because she had demonstrated, more clearly than any other elite professor in my sample, that she thinks very hard about all those issues when she is teaching.

For contrast, I'll leave you with Professor Ecks talking about *exactly* what an MC State professor would consider to be multiculturalism. This is Professor Ecks in her "grounded" mode, talking about choosing readings for her classes—before I asked her to define multiculturalism.

PROFESSOR ECKS: It's in an ability of the writer to speak to issues—whether they're political, social, or issues of the heart, mortality, other kinds of issues, love, whatever—that are crucial to the lives of my students. You know, issues that my students are concerned about—even the dullest fraternity student. If you get him sober enough to talk about it, the dullest fraternity student will admit it's an important issue. That's my baseline criteria. . . .

Several years ago, I started teaching an American Indian writer named—the Indian name that she took was Zitkala-Sa, her Christian name was Gertrude Simmons Bonnin. . . . I taught one story of hers to an undergraduate class, and male and female students were weeping as they were talking about the story, and I thought, "This is very interesting." I gradually taught more and more of her work in my classes, with equally amazing results. She's just an incredibly wonderful writer, and on course evaluations, though we were reading James and Twain and, you know, the major writers as well as lesser known authors, people will say she's the best writer.

AUTHOR: And you didn't expect that?

PROFESSOR ECKS: No, I found it very moving but . . . It's a story of childhood adolescence and adult recollecting of childhood adolescence. I think it has a special meaning for students who are away from home and contemplating those issues—contemplating changes in their own life.

I would say most of my undergraduates in that particular class, probably 75 percent, were students who would have called themselves conservative. And if I'd ever used the words "canonical," "non-canonical," or "culture wars," which I don't—I refuse to use any of those terms. If I'd used those terms, they would have decided they wanted major literature, but suddenly they were reading a story that no one had ever heard of. . . . Then I was able to step back and talk about what it means to rediscover why some things get forgotten and why others don't.

In other words, why do we very quickly dismiss certain things without really investigating why? Why did the culture wars get started by people who've never watched anything but *Melrose Place*? I mean, what is the hypocrisy of assuming high cultural values and making high cultural distinctions without really knowing a damn thing about high culture? I think it's about larger ideas, not only making emotional connections but giving people intellectual tools that are applicable in a variety of situations outside the literature classroom. You want to make them life-long readers. Anything I can do to help a student become a life-long reader is important.

TABLE 3.1
Four U.S. College English Departments

	Ivory Towers	State Star	MC State	Cathletic
Tuition	$20,000	$5,000/ $16,000	$2,000/ $9,000	$15,000
Founded	Early 1800s	Early 1800s	1950s	Mid-1800s
Affiliation	Private	Public	Public	Catholic
Campus	Majestic	Classical	Functional	Ornate
University Rank	Top 25	Top 25	Not Ranked	Not Ranked
Department Rank	Top 25	Top 25	No Ph.D.	No Ph.D.
Admissions Rate	30%	36%	75%	80%
Undergraduate Women	49%	52%	54%	56%
Non-Hispanic Whites	75%	75%	75%	75%
Graduation Rate	90%	90%	50%	65%
Student– Teacher Ratio	11:1	13:1	16:1	14:1
Average SAT score	1300–1480	1200–1410	900–1220	930–1140
Part-Time Students	Less than 1%	6%	32%	17%
Undergrad- uates	6,500	13,000	14,000	5,000
	(15% in-state)	(69% in-state)	(86% in-state)	(85% in-state)

Chapter 3

ABSTRACTION IN ACTION:
DEPARTMENTAL MULTICULTURALISM

There's a cartoon on the wall in another office. This sort of hag-
gard-looking guy, drooped over a desk, saying to somebody,
"Hey, if I leave here at 10 and drive 80 miles an hour to Center-
ville campus, I can teach the two classes there and still get out
in time to get to my other one at Wherever and make enough
money to pay the rent." . . . I came out with an MA from a
good program, but I didn't have any teaching experience so I
sort of stumbled. I came along at the right time in the fall, when
they needed somebody at [Local Tech] to pick up a literature
course. Did well with that and picked up three more there.
Then, here [at MC State], one of the full-time faculty members
had to take a medical leave all of the sudden, right after the semester began. So they had to reshuffle classes. I had sent letters
and CV's all around, so they pulled my name out and said, "Are
you still interested?" And I said, "Yeah," because at that point, I
had three classes at Local Tech and I was looking at the income
and outgo and thinking, I've got to get a 15–20-hour-a-week
job somewhere. So that was sort of a godsend for me.

—*Instructor at Multicultural State*

Life in non-elite English departments is nothing like the picture we get from
Alan Bloom's images of clever young men debating the finer points of Plato's
Republic with their venerable professors in the University of Chicago's hal-
lowed halls.[1] Non-elite college students don't have the luxury of spending
long afternoons pondering the meaning of life or the size of the universe, and
neither do their teachers.

Multicultural State University didn't even exist when Alan Bloom was a
young college student (see Table 3.1). I'm not sure whether our cultural critics even care about the study of English literature in non-elite universities.

Many of them write as though the whole nation lives in their privileged worlds where ideas provide the better part of their sustenance and whole worlds (or at least whole worldviews) could topple without them. I *do* know, however, that our cultural critics care about places like Ivory Towers. And they worry. This is where some of our nation's brightest young men and women are groomed to glorious cultural perfection and prepared to lead us into tomorrow . . . or something like that, anyway. Most of them will be paper-pushing lawyers, middle-managers, and stockbrokers. But some will eventually become quite powerful, even if they don't choose public service.

Each of the four departments I studied faced the same set of national problems: declining enrollments, attacks from politicians in the press, and impossible standards set by abstract versions of both Western culture and multiculturalism. The relevance of these challenges, however, was different in each department because of the different ways they organized themselves, defined their mission, and related to national culture and national politics. As a result, professors in the four departments understood multiculturalism in different and distinguishable ways.

Ivory Towers

What would our budding young leaders find in the English department at Ivory Towers? I headed off to find out, just before the start of classes in January 1995. Ivory Towers was the first department I visited, and I had a fairly high level of anxiety about potential rejection from my would-be hosts. Ivory Towers had a reputation as a site for real conflict, and the stories of upheaval and controversy emanating from this department were just too juicy to miss. My first attempt to contact the English department was a smashing success. The chair welcomed me warmly and arranged to secure a visiting scholar appointment for me so that I could have a department mailbox and use university resources such as the library and computer labs. To this middle-class girl from James Madison University, it was like a fairytale; I mentioned my Ivy League graduate school credentials and the gates swung open!

It wasn't until much later that I would come to question the smoothness of these first encounters. No one opposed the chair's decision to welcome a sociologist into their midst. (I doubt he bothered to tell them about our conversation.) And there were no disgruntled right-wingers complaining about the office being closed for MLK Day. This seemed normal to me. It matched my graduate school experiences at Princeton. The faculty at Ivory Towers took these things for granted, and so did I. The lack of opposition to my presence, and to the office closures, did not imply that the faculty agreed on these matters; they indicated that *no one cared*. I would later discover that professors in less elite departments care intensely about such details.

Ivory Towers is located in a bona fide city, with its share of cultural events (high culture and otherwise), restaurants, industrial areas, and urban decay, but none of that was visible from the inside—once I found my way in. Most of the sprawling campus is separated from the business district by expansive wooded buffer zones, though some borders blur into residential areas that are populated almost exclusively by faculty and students. The architecture of the main campus is strikingly beautiful, though somewhat overbearing. Most of the campus consists of large, grassy areas enveloped by towering trees. Yeah. It's a country club.

I ventured to the department for the first time on a Monday, only to find the office and mailroom closed for Martin Luther King Day, despite the fact that the university itself was open. Although my plans for the day had been foiled, I was happy to have collected my first piece of evidence that the department did indeed have race-conscious policies embedded into its formal operations.

The mere task of orienting myself, however, provided evidence that the department was in good favor with the university administration. Their offices had recently been moved into one of the original buildings on campus. Centrally located, their new location was described by the faculty as prime real estate. There were a few seminar rooms in the building, but most classes were conducted elsewhere, protecting faculty offices from the traffic of class changes and drop-in business from undergraduates. As for the writing program and its directors (both of whom had appointments in the English department), it was housed in less prestigious accommodations (a couple of trailers) at a distant location.

The next day, while stuffing mailboxes with my letter of introduction, I overheard an important conversation between a faculty member and a graduate instructor. The professor discouraged the graduate student from overfilling his literary seminar on baseball. He explained that other graduate instructors who were teaching seminars at the same level but with less-enticing titles would have trouble filling those classes if the baseball seminar took a disproportionate number of students. *Baseball?* I spent that evening reading the course catalog!

The following week, I had my first interview (with Professor Ecks) and scheduled four others. My project was off to a strong start, but the rhythm of academic life at Ivory Towers soon took a toll on my progress. Two weeks later, the halls were empty. There were no more conversations in the mailroom, and professors were even less likely to answer their telephones. Interviews trickled in at the rate of one or two per week for the rest of the semester.

Despite a general emptiness in the atmosphere, I was able to discern a departmental culture, evidence for which ran through my interviews. Professors spoke kindly of each other and of their department. In general, they portrayed all their colleagues as renowned experts in fields foreign to their own expertise—which produced a sort of distant, uncritical respect for all others without much intellectual engagement among colleagues in the department. There were a few exceptions to this comparative generalization of little intellectual engagement, of course: a women's writing group existed in the department and there were even a few close friendships among professors. One respondent emphasized the importance of understanding the department's professors as both cohesive and reclusive, saying, "This is a very individualized community, and that's not an oxymoron. This is a very diverse department. Everyone is different. It's a community of scholars." Most described themselves as people who work best alone, with the exception of specialized conferences, when professors would meet with the dozen or so other people in the country who shared their particular interests.

Media attention from the canon wars also played an important role in the departmental representation that came through in the interviews. Respondents often seemed to be having a conversation with their own collective media image. Graduate students continually forgot that their department would remain anonymous in my study and treated me as the person who would finally correct the record. It wasn't that they were trying to portray their department and their colleagues in an unnaturally favorable light, however. I got plenty of gossip about which professors seemed to be getting a disproportionate share of university resources, which professors could get away with little or no teaching, and how the department handled tenured deadbeats.

The following "country club" quote provides a nice example of the kind of rich, witty, and self-critical defense these professors offered:

> You know we're accused of being the hotbed of all these things, and yet we're not really multicultural in the sense that it's fairly hard to be multicultural at [Ivory Towers]. It's like a multicultural country club. I mean, everybody comes from the same kind of background, and everybody socializes well because we are of the same class, more or less, and we teach kids of the same class. I mean, also, the people of color on this campus are upper-middle-class people. So to think that [Ivory Towers] is a hotbed of extremism is very funny to me. When I hear, you know, Rush Limbaugh go on about—It's a hoot. I mean, [sarcastically] he's not classy enough to be here. And it's not because he's stupid; it's because he's *obnoxious*.

Although my interviews and observations at Ivory Towers uncovered no open conflict, it did appear that there *could* have been a battle there, of sorts. Many of the faculty were well-known intellectuals on the cutting edge of English literary scholarship, and some worked beyond that edge. There were also staunch traditionalists who cooperated with the National Association of Scholars (NAS) in a failed attempt to forestall the progressive takeover of their quiet department.

The NAS was adept at attracting media attention to such issues and bringing departments like Ivory Towers' under public scrutiny, but that appears to have been their only weapon. The NAS had no power inside the department, and those "staunch traditionalists" were not anything like the NAS or Dinesh D'Souza. For example, the most vocal and active member of the traditionalist block described himself as a fan of multiculturalism, and explained the quota system he used to make sure his syllabi were representative of African American, female, Jewish, and even gay/lesbian (one or the other, not both) authors. If there was any open conflict at Ivory Towers before my visit, it all happened inside the bounds of elite decorum and scholarly debate, which is not nearly as simplistic as the journalistic version.

In short, despite all those concerns about a left-wing takeover, the feel of the Ivory Towers English department was just elite (as the name so carefully implies). Professors there had a tremendous amount of autonomy in their

FIGURE 3.1

Percentage of Professors Using Each Definition, by Department

PROGRESSIVE

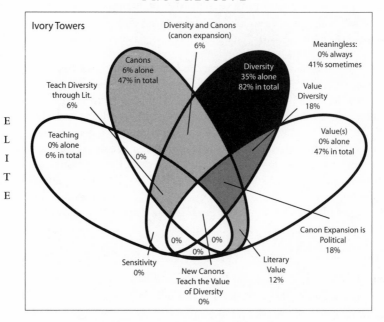

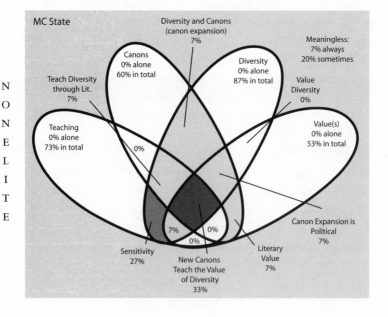

FIGURE 3.1 *(cont.)*

Percentage of Professors Using Each Definition, by Department

TRADITIONAL

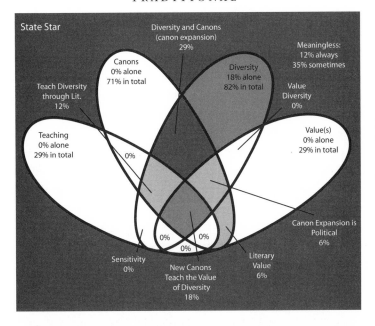

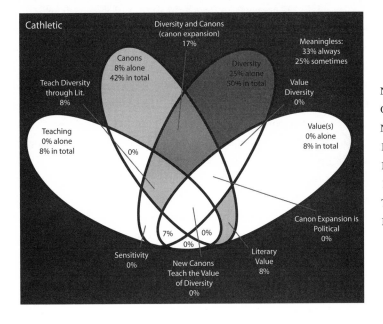

academic activities and relief from excessive bureaucratic regulation. Committee work and administrative tasks (central activities for professors in other departments) were minimal at Ivory Towers, and professors taught just two courses each semester. The most famous among them taught even less.

All this, of course, had a powerful shaping effect on the brand of multiculturalism that was generated in the Ivory Towers English department. As I return to those definitions, I will refer to Figure 3.1, where I have characterized each university I studied.

At Ivory Towers, the definition of multiculturalism hinged less on canons than on the breadth and diversity of American culture. By expressing a responsibility to culture, professors there indicated that they saw themselves as curators and producers of American culture—a role defined by the individual professors I interviewed, as well as by the university that had carefully lured this collection of intellectual superstars. English professors at Ivory Towers experienced multiculturalism as a (potentially positive) challenge to the traditional authority of the canon, on the one hand, and a (negative) threat to academic freedom, on the other.

Moreover, their approach to multiculturalism followed their pattern of work. Although they did select readings for their classes, they were less likely than professors in other departments to think of multiculturalism as a simple matter of "plugging in" works by authors from excluded cultural groups, as the "canon expansion" definition would imply. (The NAS activist was an exception, in that regard.) Instead, they considered their role as public intellectuals—not only as scholars of literature but also as interpreters of culture. Thus, the modal definition of multiculturalism at Ivory Towers was an unconnected reference to diversity.

Abstract definitions (those making the fewest connections to other arenas of meaning) provide the greatest flexibility for playing with ideas, for testing new connections, and for general philosophizing. Therefore, the abstract definition of multiculturalism at work in the Ivory Towers English department seems well suited to the professors' identity as public intellectuals. Note also that, to the extent that diversity *is* connected to another arena of meaning among Ivory Towers professors, it is equally associated with values and canons, and almost never associated with teaching. Although canons are the more obvious connection for English professors, it is through values that these cultural curators make the claim that literature matters for society, so the connection to values is equally important to the literary scholar *qua* public intellectual.

But the strongest evidence for the organizational structuring of meaning at Ivory Towers lies in the professors' tendency to ignore each other. As "sequestered scholars," a term several used to describe their social lives at the university, they recognized a responsibility to multiculturalism, but they did not discuss with each other its relevance to their work. Consequently, there was very little clear connection between the abstract idea of multiculturalism and the working lives of English professors at Ivory Towers.

Professors there were also aware of a significant shift in the department's value hierarchy, from a previous local culture that valued aesthetics to a newer model that placed more value on politics. Notably, this observation came from both staunch traditionalists and multicultural advocates. Given the centrality of this shift in scholarly and journalistic accounts of multiculturalism, it is not surprising that both "sides" at Ivory Towers agreed that literary studies had been politicized. The interesting pattern was that non-elite faculty failed to mention it.

Charges of politicization tended to come from professors in elite departments who drew on the traditional authority of literary canons to claim that social change is or should be irrelevant to (aesthetic) literary greatness. They experienced attempts to change the canon as the entrance of politics into an arena in which interest-based change is inappropriate—art, rather than merely work. Conversely, it would make little sense to say that work produced in highly bureaucratic, non-elite departments has become politicized, when participants in bureaucracies already see most of their occupational activities as political. Progressives in all four departments agreed that new work is self-consciously political, but they also argued that traditionalism is political in a much more insidious way, precisely because it denies its own political interest in maintaining the current status system.

State Star

The more traditional counterpart to Ivory Towers is State Star, a large, public, research university that was founded in the early 1800s and is now considered one of the nation's leading institutions of higher learning. It is one of those "crown jewel" public universities that competes with wealthier private universities in the national rankings. State Star's English department is consistently ranked among the top twenty-five Ph.D. programs in the country. (Anonymity prevents me from specifying the rank of the two elite departments beyond the selection criteria–top-25 in the *U.S. News and World Report* ranking of Ph.D. programs in English literature and overall undergraduate program.)

After finishing my fairy-tale semester "in residence" at Ivory Towers, I made a preliminary summer trip to State Star to secure my permissions, collect background information, and get my bearings. Although State Star did offer summer-session courses, I visited between terms and had the whole place to myself. The elite feel of State Star's deserted campus was significantly more understated than Ivory Towers' elaborate architecture. State Star's campus is thematically organized around the original architectural design, and although the design is rectangular, it offers cozy gardens as well as public areas with plenty of grass.

At the start of the fall semester, I returned to State Star to begin my interviews. As I walked across campus from the visitors' parking lot to the English department on the first day of classes, I passed a Confederate flag covering a first-floor dormitory window. I was shocked. "Must be a freshman," I thought, emphasizing the "man" in freshman. The flag was gone when I walked that route again the following week, making me think I must have been correct that its bearer was not yet accustomed to the politics of campus life. But there were others, especially on vehicles, but also one painted on the ceiling of a frat-house bedroom that was visible from the street.

The campus's classic architectural style was also reflected in the local culture, where understatement, honor, and sober responsibility were key themes that affected everything from parking policy to multiculturalism. Political culture throughout the university was often intensely democratic and notoriously slow. But the most curious element of political culture was the university's steadfast commitment to a tradition of progressivism. A significant number of campus leaders at State Star (students, faculty, and administrators alike) were preoccupied with the impossible task of reconciling the conflicting notions of tradition and tolerance. Those Confederate flags were a case in point, and, it turns out, a favorite topic of political conflict.

As elite English departments go, State Star's program was considered conservative, but the following pages will reveal that the culture of traditionalism and the organizational dynamics governing such issues are very different from the brand of conservatism practiced at Cathletic University. Rather than avoiding multiculturalism through outright rejection, the English faculty at State Star engaged the issue constantly, and they had made some concessions to it over time. Thus, the organizational culture at State Star can best be described as "deliberate democracy." Their traditionalism, relative to other top English departments in the United States, was primarily a result of slow deliberation, not, generally speaking, reactionary politics or rigid conservatism. (Nothing is that simple, of course, especially in large departments. State Star had its share of angry reactionaries, and many of the left-leaning scholars would argue that slow deliberation in the spirit of Enlightenment rationality constituted an aggressive ideological position that could be described as rigid, at the very least!)

Though I selected this research site, in part, because of its reputation for conservatism, State Star's English department was not one of the two or three that scholars point to as bastions of literary traditionalism. The department did not tout a "Great Books" curriculum, and none of the faculty sported Confederate flags on their cars or clothing. Its reputation was one of a strong, traditional department that hadn't devoted extensive resources to developing emergent fields in the discipline. As a result, the department's ranking had slipped a bit through the 1980s and 1990s, but it still remained in the top 25. The previous few academic hiring seasons had been notoriously dismal for Ph.D. graduates of State Star—as was the case for graduates from other universities across the nation.

Like Ivory Towers (and most top-ranked departments in almost any university), State Star's English department was in good favor with the university. English professors at State Star had (in general) the same teaching load as faculty at Ivory Towers: two courses each semester. That's half the teaching load of professors at Cathletic University. They also performed less committee work than their counterparts at non-elite universities did, but being public and democratic increased their commitment to deliberation and record keeping, relative to Ivory Towers. As a result, they spent more time on committee work than professors at many other elite universities, and they complained about it less often.

English was also the second most popular major at State Star, and the university had recently erected an impressive new building exclusively for the English department. A writing program that offered a Master of Fine Arts was also housed there. (Compare this to the way Ivory Towers banished their writing program to a pair of trailers three miles away.) Faculty offices and classrooms were housed on separate floors of the new building, maximizing both convenience and privacy for faculty. Inside the recently occupied English building, however, I felt uncomfortable.

Although most of the offices had big beautiful windows, public spaces in this building were the stuff of television nightmares—long, narrow, empty corridors of endless, evenly spaced doors—all closed and lacking both windows and personal embellishments. There was literally no place for me there in that long narrow hallway. I certainly wouldn't blend into the woodwork, and there were no graduate students around to provide cover for my intrusion. Neither Ivory Towers nor State Star provided office space for graduate students, but I did *see* them at Ivory Towers. At State Star, I had to contact them via e-mail and make appointments.

Between paper letters and e-mail follow-ups, I collected positive responses from thirty English professors, but appointments that were scheduled for later in the semester were more difficult to achieve. Many were rescheduled, and two professors eventually declined the interview due to time constraints. The rhythm of the semester was almost identical to that of the Ivory Towers department.

However, the public–private difference between Ivory Towers and State Star was more evident than I expected. The Ivory Towers campus wasn't exactly locked, but it was closed to outsiders in several ways. The library was not open to the public, visitor parking was extremely limited and available only for short-term, metered stays. (Invited guests were told to arrange for parking with their hosts.)

In contrast, the State Star campus was less guarded—literally. There was a large public parking deck. No one expected visitors to check in, and some of the most public buildings on campus were never locked. On the inside, however, things were more guarded at State Star than they were at Ivory Towers. A single key didn't do the trick. Computing labs and libraries were open, for example, but higher-level privileges such as borrowing books required state citizenship. Just being there didn't imply that you were a deserving member of the community the way it did at Ivory Towers.

I first noticed this pattern because my status there was tenuous, but the same theme was evident in the interviews. State Star is a big public place. It's easy to get in the gates. As a result, even real members must frequently prove themselves in various ways. The English department faculty, for example, judged each other's merits in ways that Ivory Towers professors never did. Status distinctions inside the university were far more obvious, and junior professors worried more openly about tenure (especially because I had a tape recorder). In short, there was a principle of social interaction at State Star that assumed open access to the right to be judged. At Ivory Towers, the principle of social interaction was more like a private club. There was a hierarchy, but it was deemphasized, even hidden, with the general principle being one of inclusion. Daily life at Ivory Towers was much easier for low-status and peripheral characters: junior faculty, graduate students, secretaries, and me! Here is but one example, related by a female associate professor at State Star:

> A couple—two or three—people here are pretty close intellectual colleagues, but I would say my closest [colleagues] are on the conference network. And it's not quite clear to me why. 'Cause you'd think it would be potentially more frightening. But you get more respect outside of your own. It's a very odd thing. For whatever reason, we don't respect each other's research in the same way—as the kind of acknowledgment you get from people outside.

Although departmental culture was not at all evident in the public spaces of the English building, my interviews revealed a high degree of thematic repetition. Overall, the faculty demonstrated a strong sense of their collective existence, with an undercurrent of uneasiness. State Star's collective democratic spirit was intentionally constructed with some effort, and that effort was often evident. This type of deliberate democracy will provide stark contrast to that of the Multicultural State English department, where the communal atmosphere felt easy and natural.

English professors at State Star did not consider themselves like-minded; they were aware of the scope of faculty opinion on various issues. They also claimed to value those differences, though very few offered evidence that they *enjoyed* their ideological diversity, via stories or examples of its positive effect on their individual work or lives. Professors were, however, able to identify vast areas of common ground (again, carefully and deliberately).

This department is among the least riven of the top departments that I'm
aware of. I mean, the fact is, we house a wide variety of people here.
Uh. Most of us are glad we do house that large variety of people. Uh,
but we're not on Mars, right? I mean, there are debates about what one's
mission is. I have a colleague here, whom I respect very much, who says
my job is basically to make my students understand how Shakespeare
connects with their life. We have another person also teaching Shakespeare, whom I like very much, who says my job is to make my students
aware of historical and cultural context. You know, and so on, and so on,
and so on. To me, that's no problem. . . . I don't think homogeneity is
desirable.

Many of my interviewees cited the department's size in their accounts of
difference and commonality. They described the department as a place large
enough to accommodate a wide range of differences while allowing them to
carve out almost any sort of niche they wanted. It might be possible to feel
outnumbered on one issue or another, but it would be rare to feel alone. This
characteristic *did* present itself in the interviews as a salient feature of departmental life, one rich with examples and stories of its importance. As was the
case for the earlier quote about getting greater respect outside the department, being able to collect one or two close colleagues was crucial to surviv-
ing the disconnect.

Despite the university-wide tradition of self-governance, this department
had not had a long history of collective governance and introspection. In fact,
the wave of faculty hires that had brought acclaim to the department in the
1960s occurred under the relatively authoritarian leadership of a powerful
department chair. State Star's experiment with collective governance was
new.

It was also clear that the high level of consensus in effect at the time of my
visit was something of an anomaly for State Star's English department. Many
expressed surprise at discovering that they were in agreement on central issues of teaching and research, even despite differences in specialties, political
orientation, and professional age. The chair explained that questions of funding and control of higher education in the state legislature required each
public university in the state to justify its budget. To prepare for producing a
formal departmental report, he had begun a process of introspective justifica-
tion.

Because I found this department to be in the midst of a massive self-examination, my interviews there were full of references to the project. Many respondents found their answers to my questions in the front of their minds because of their committee assignments in the self-examination, and all spoke favorably of the process—even those who were willing to complain to me about other aspects of their professional life. The English department at State Star was collectively engaging the problem of multiculturalism in the curriculum head-on.

When I asked what divided the department or was a source of potential conflict (carefully avoiding the assumption that professors fight with one another), the most common response involved not multiculturalism or political orientation, but the balance of teaching and research. Concern about the equitable distribution of course relief (reduced teaching loads that allow professors to devote a larger portion of their time to scholarship) also dominated answers to another question I asked about the definition of a "good English professor." It appeared, then, that the most controversial issue in the department at the time of my interviews overshadowed the issues that the press considered to be the most divisive.

The evidence of antagonism over the distribution of teaching loads at State Star was almost certainly exacerbated by the departmental review.

> If you're going to have a sense that it's worth sustaining a writing academic to write, then that's the way the job description should read, and you should probably put it up front so you can't have, uh, some would-be whistle-blower from "State Central" coming in and saying, "Ah-hah! What you purport to be doing professionally is mainly teaching, and what you are really doing is mainly writing, so what's wrong with you?" . . . That's much on our mind because there's a great deal of talk in this state right now . . . about accountability. And what they mean by accountability is, um, "We want you to give an account of why, if it's legally within our power to make you teach three times as much, we shouldn't do it." That's what they mean.

I assume this particular antagonism subsided somewhat when the issue was removed from center stage. Moreover, I found no evidence of any outright conflict in which professors had taken sides against one another in face-to-face interactions. Instead, the department consciously used a decision-making model in which all members of a committee (or whatever unit might be relevant) approached problems as scholars rather than as combatants. Faculty tried to increase their understanding of the complexity underlying any given issue until they could agree to make some imperfect attempt to address the problem.

Finally, although the democratic culture significantly restricted the department's flexibility in dealing with individual differences, State Star professors still made ample use of professional autonomy to manage their disagreements.

> Last year, we had a lot of valuable exchange on questions precisely about that [multiculturalism]. I was on a committee that had to do with writing in various courses in the department. . . . We realized fairly early that everybody wanted something somewhat different and that we couldn't get everybody in step without running over the pluralism of the place because we are a very pluralistic department. And we're a department that tends to. . . . We have people occupying every conceivable place on the ideological spectrum, and, um, we have a tradition of respecting each other's preferences here. So, we're not gonna say, "Everybody has to have their students write theoretical papers," or "research papers," or "new critical analyses," or anything like that. It quickly became apparent that, although we all felt that we wanted more writing instruction in undergraduate classes, that different people were going to do it in different ways.

Definitions of multiculturalism at State Star demonstrate an important difference between the two elite departments. An abstract definition of multiculturalism as a nebulous matter of diversity operates in Ivory Towers' superstar department, where many professors view themselves as public intellectuals. Although diversity was a popular arena for the meaning of multiculturalism at State Star (overall, 82 percent), the importance of canons was nearly as strong, at 71 percent. Professors at State Star drew their disciplinary boundaries closer to literary studies (as we'll see more clearly in the following chapters) and thus made stronger connections between multiculturalism and canons (91 percent, compared to Ivory Towers' 47 percent). In fact, canon expansion (at the intersection of diversity and canons) was the modal definition of multiculturalism at State Star.

In addition, because canons join the mix, a tendency toward groundedness appears at State Star, compared to Ivory Towers. These grounded definitions are less flexible in philosophical discussions, but more useful for making collective decisions about concrete curricular changes. That's handy because State Star spends a lot of energy making collective decisions.

State Star's definition of multiculturalism stands out as the "cleanest" among the four departments. The strong tendency toward a widely recognizable definition (canon expansion) helped provide a center for discussion about the matter and reduced the ambiguity and complexity that could be associated with abstract and complex definitions, respectively. It is exactly the definition one might expect to emerge from a "common ground" approach to multiculturalism—one that promises to leave lots of room for individual variation in the application of specific ideas or policies. The "canon expansion" definition avoids the idea of values, as though they are a matter of private conviction, not to be discussed in public, per Nina Eliasoph's study, *Avoiding Politics*. And it avoids teaching practices because the plan is to leave those matters up to individual professors.

It is interesting to note, therefore, that these professors did not often add the missing pieces when I asked them how they felt about multiculturalism. I took a little bit of grief from professors, who winced at my touchy-feely choice of words when I asked them how they *felt*, but this issue highlights the importance of my attempt to elicit personal understandings. Despite my unrelenting focus on individual histories, decisions, and teaching practices, the multiculturalism question was the most likely to evoke distancing maneuvers. When I got a general analysis of public or scholarly debate, I even prodded, "Has the issue influenced your work at all?" That question occasionally extracted interesting information, but it rarely increased the personal or grounded nature of a definition.

In sum, the department's modal definition of multiculturalism was consistent with its policy response and its general tendency to search diligently for common ground. State Star was not progressive; some of its members worked on the cutting edge, but most worked just inside that boundary. Neither was it standing still, however, or taking drastic measures to resist multiculturalism. Its definition matches. It was there (not ambiguous or resisted), and it addressed the impact of cultural diversity on literary canons, but it left as much room as possible for individual variation.

Multicultural State

Most of the highly publicized battles over multiculturalism in English literature took place at elite universities like Ivory Towers, where English departments were making conspicuous moves toward avant-garde literary criticism. But cultural critics preferred to look for fault in the English curricula of elite universities (even if not much was going on there) than to turn their attention to a college or university that most of their readership would not be able to recognize. That's why nobody noticed the radical changes that were under way at Multicultural State.

I found MC State by chance. By the time I got to the point in the selection process where I started digging out college catalogs to examine the English curricula, I had narrowed my choices down to about twenty universities. And even then, the full extent to which MC State had embraced the principle of multiculturalism was not evident in the catalog. For that reason, I imagine that similarly drastic changes took place in many of our nation's lesser-known colleges and universities. But we still don't know for sure. While elite academic politics became such a national obsession that the slightest sneeze at Stanford, Chicago, or Duke would attract reporters to the scene, no one was watching the rest of the nation's colleges.

Multicultural State's brand of progressivism turned out to be quite different from that of its elite counterpart. Whereas Ivory Towers focused on the most innovative literary criticism and appeared to be fairly radical with respect to the political implications of the theory produced there, the greater potential for extreme progressivism in non-elite departments was immediately evident at Multicultural State. When I asked professors at MC State how they felt about multiculturalism, more than half mentioned the university's "multiculturalism policy." What was so special about MC State's approach to multiculturalism? It is mandated.

> We, the faculty of the [Multicultural State University] English Department, in accord with our belief that literature and language both reflect and shape culture, affirm the importance of representing in our courses the complementary contributions of both sexes and also of diverse cultural representations. We, therefore, adopt the policy that:
>
> a) we will make a genuine effort to appropriately include both men and women, as creators and critics, in our course curricula;

b) we will make a genuine effort to include works representing the various cultural perspectives appropriate to each course;

c) we will make a genuine effort to heighten, in any works we teach, our students' awareness of tendencies to stereotype differences in culture, religious beliefs, gender, class, age, race and sexual orientation, and will at the same time encourage understanding of the above difference.

I didn't learn about this policy until I started interviewing faculty, but, by then, I wasn't surprised by it. There were lots of rules at Multicultural State, and people didn't seem to mind. In fact, the English department faculty apparently enjoyed the intellectual process of devising good policy. Rules and structure were important and respected parts of daily life at Multicultural State, not the imposition on individual autonomy that Ivory Towers professors considered them to be.

MC State was the only campus where I had trouble figuring out what the rules might be and worried about breaking them by accident. Computing labs were guarded both by human and technological gatekeepers (login required), and there was no special "visitors" parking here. No one even dreamed of offering me a library card or a computer account. On the other hand, the constant flow of people through every sidewalk and hallway finally relieved me of the feeling that I might be an intruder.

The suburban campus of MC State was smaller and more compact than the campus of Ivory Towers or State Star, and the grounds were largely concrete. The most striking feature of the campus, however, was that sea of people who crowded the spaces between buildings. Multicultural State students had lives in the surrounding region quite separate from their college careers. Only 20 percent of students lived on campus, and many held full-time jobs and/or had families to care for. MC State was *not* a place where young adults could spend four years marinating in high culture, protected from the responsibilities of real life outside the university. These students juggled college into their lives like soccer moms. It's possible that some of them *were* soccer moms, but most were not that lucky.

I spent my undergraduate years at a large public university (James Madison University), and the obvious differences between that experience and media reports of multiculturalism at elite colleges had informed my original plan to compare elite and non-elite universities. But I was not prepared for the extent to which Multicultural State looked and felt like a high-school campus. In fact, I had considered the possibility and rejected it early in my planning. In my preparations, I had visited some local, two–year community colleges, where the high-school theme was unapologetically obvious (mostly crowded spaces, utilitarian architecture, and the lack of dormitories). Those visits had convinced me to make four-year colleges my point of comparison because community colleges were too different from elite universities. I hadn't expected to find a similar environment in an accredited four-year institution with a selective admissions process.

I spent my first day at MC State in culture shock, and the rest of my stay in (relative) ethnographic paradise. Gaining access on a social level was surprisingly easy. Not only were the hallways full of students, the offices were full of faculty. I met two professors in the mailroom, where I introduced myself and my purpose. They *talked* to me and introduced me to other professors and instructors as we passed in the hall. I secured most of my interviews by knocking on office doors—and even that knocking was just a formality because the doors were open.

The dramatic difference in collegiality between Multicultural State and the other three departments was shocking. Everyone was eager to talk with me, both formally and informally, and the hallway was a fine place to hang out, watch, listen, and chat. I was even fortunate enough to witness the text-book fair—a day when all the representatives of textbook publishing houses bring the books that match course descriptions for review by the faculty. On those days, the atmosphere was downright festive, and I learned a great deal about the relationship between the publishing industry and the teaching industry.

One or two professors came in less often and kept their office doors closed, but not everyone can be an extrovert. They were equally willing to schedule an interview with me. In a mere six weeks, I was finished, and in that brief time I had learned more about the inner workings of Multicultural State, while operating out of a hotel room, than I had learned about Ivory Towers, after an entire semester in residence.

Other things were different, too. There was no Ph.D. program in either of the two non-elite departments I studied, but both offered master's degrees and, in both cases, the M.A. program primarily served the local primary and secondary education system, which offered salary increases for public school teachers who earned advanced degrees. Although only 8 percent of undergraduates choose majors in the arts and humanities at MC State, English is, by far, the most popular major in that category. Professors pointed to two reasons for their success in attracting majors. The first was a strong program in technical writing that students could use as a vocational skill, and the second was a reputation for good advising.

Multicultural State professors teach three courses each semester and spend a great deal of time meeting with students and performing departmental service. In fact, many have been successful in securing external grants for teaching and curriculum development. But many have also published academic works of one kind or another (these included literary criticism, historical research, scholarship on pedagogical methods, original fiction, ethnography, and playwriting), but none felt exceptional pressure to do so.

In addition to tenured and tenure-track positions, MC State's English department employed an array of instructors of varying status, ranging from semi-permanent, renewable positions to part-time graduate instructors. All permanent full-time faculty had private offices (this included the top echelon of instructors, plus tenured and tenure-track faculty), while most other instructors shared office space with one other person. Part-time faculty and graduate instructors shared a single office that contained a few desks and was otherwise devoid of human presence (no books, photos, plants, etc.).

I arrived at MC State's English department at the beginning of a transition in governance that confused me at first. In the previous year, the university had hired a non-academic supervisor for the department's writing program and a new chair, who presented a warm, gracious demeanor but who spoke in a linguistic style that made him an unrealistically powerful actor in his own stories. He answered my questions as if he were an individual leader with a vision who could give consent for new ideas and make unilateral decisions. (A poignant example of his style is coming up.)

Professors in the department, conversely, had an unusually collective discursive style. Despite my questions about their personal decisions, their answers made heavy use of the word "we." Almost every individual action seemed to have a consciously collective element or history. Interview respondents at MC State gave me the impression that *everything* went through a communal decision-making process, but the cohesive feel was far more natural than that at State Star. Whatever was left to individual discretion was still likely to be the topic of a series of workshops and other (voluntary) community activities. A full-time instructor put it this way (In what follows, she refers to the department's faculty as "they" because we were discussing the possibility of her departure for a tenure-track position elsewhere. As the interview continued, she switched to using the word "we" when referring to the department and even, sometimes, when referring to her own teaching practices, saying, for example, "We can get better writing out of them"):

> I can go sit in anybody's class and learn. . . . Their faculty meetings—
> rather than one or two people saying this is our position and send it to
> the college, what they typically do is divide us all into small groups and
> we talk. Two or three or four of us just get together and talk out our is-
> sues, and then the group leader will go back to the faculty and say "This
> is what we thought," and everyone else does the same. They really care
> what we think [pause] *and do*.

So it turns out that hiring an authoritative department chair and a non-academic program administrator is not at all contradictory for this self-governing department because the chair works for them. Here is the chair talking about the backward flow of authority between himself and the writing-program director ("Carol" is a pseudonym):

> If Carol would let me, I wouldn't use [a textbook]. . . . Last time around,
> she wouldn't agree to it. She said, "No, you've got to use one of the
> texts," so I said, "Okay, I'll use one." . . . I think that this department is a
> very egalitarian department in a way which speaks to the fact that I, as
> chair, even though I can tell Carol, "No, I'm going to do this," I would-
> n't do that because it's her program. If I think her program is wrong,
> then I'll fire her and get somebody else in there. While she is director of
> the program, I should do what she says. I should not, as chair, ignore it.
> Neither should a full professor who is tenured ignore what the program
> says is the way they're trying to do these courses. I think, though, that
> that's the philosophy that I have brought to this department.

Despite the chair's paradoxical claim that he is in charge of the group's egalitarian philosophy, full-time members of the faculty do give off a strong sense of egalitarianism and collective governance. Instructors can barely be distinguished from tenured and tenure-track professors. They attend faculty meetings and actively participate in committees and workshops. One or two were even vying for tenure-track positions in the department (a rare com-modity, and in the tight job market, mostly going to new graduates of top-ranked programs). But many instructors had been hired for a vocational specialty (often without a Ph.D.) and were happy in their current positions. I talked to those with Ph.D.'s about their sense of attachment to the department, because when they get a job offer for an instructorship elsewhere, the calculation involves guessing which job is most likely to lead to a more permanent line. But for instructors at MC State, it is more difficult to leave. One said:

> I did send out my vitae [résumé] to about four or five local colleges, and I was offered part-time at two of those and a new one at full-time, but . . . I stayed here because I knew I would have more flexibility and they will let me teach more than freshman composition. And that—I mean, I'm lucky. I get to teach a lot of things.

Even the part-timers felt included, which is practically unheard of in English departments. At my other three research sites, I saw little or no mutual acknowledgment across that status divide—never mind friendships or participation in departmental affairs. One part-timer at MC State noted:

> There seems to be a much greater sense of, I don't know, collegiality, I guess, would be the best term, here. I teach three classes [at Local Tech] and one here, but I feel more a part of things and more comfortable here than I do there.

The most obvious distinguishing characteristic of multicultural meanings at MC State is its focus on teaching and pedagogy—already evident in the local culture. The faculty's self-definition as teachers and the importance they place on doing that well was apparent from my first day at Multicultural State, so I was not surprised to hear a large portion of them (27 percent) define multiculturalism as the influence of diversity on teaching methods.

> FACULTY MEMBER: I believe in diversity, and that takes into account a lot more than the bicultural that we have here in America, which is black and white. We also have a tendency to think, "I have multicultural literature—black literature and white literature. Oh, yeah, now I believe I'll throw in a Native American, and let's pull in a Chinese American now that they are coming in." *I* think diversity is slow learners, fast learners, medium learners. Diversity is Jewish and Protestant and Catholic, and it's Mexican, and Chinese, and it's people who are quiet

and people who are talkative, and people who can write and people who can speak. It's all of those things. Are you a person who is quiet, a person who writes well? Oh, yeah, you happen to have some Mexican American heritage? That's good. You know? Maybe that's where you will be coming from and maybe it won't be. You can't speak for all of a certain group just because you are that.

AUTHOR: Does that affect the way you choose your readings?

FACULTY MEMBER: Yeah, it does. I labored over the selections for my literature classes all summer. . . . While some of those are classics and I definitely included them, I did go through and try and get things that I thought dealt with maybe divorced parents, street people, homeless people, *issues* as well as, you know, types of people. You need to address issues as well—AIDS, etc.

The more interesting organizational effect, however, is that the most popular definition of multiculturalism at MC State was also the most grounded. A full one-third of the professors there touched on all four arenas of meaning in their talk about multiculturalism. MC State definitions dominated my discussion of this core meaning of multiculturalism in the previous chapter, but here, I can show how intricately this grounded understanding of values, canons, and diversity is woven into the foundational arena of teaching.

With this population that we've got in [the state], a lot of our students are first-generation college-goers, low income. A lot of them are commuter students, so they have not been exposed to things. I mean, I've had students that have told me more than once, you know, last week, when I was going to a conference, told me that they've never been out of the state! So we wanted them to realize that they have a sort of mindset that they have inherited. . . . We actually talk about different ways of reading . . . so that was part of it. The other part, I think, was that *we really did want to have people see that the discipline is not dead*—that it does live and it does live partly on debate, and that the academy is a safe place to learn how to argue and develop points of view and see that there are different ways of looking at the world.

To me, however, the most interesting example came from a white male senior professor who, in any other context, could have been the leader of the local resistance movement. The echoes of his generation's prejudices (his term) are still clear, but he has absorbed multiculturalism into those ideals, entirely, and he does that primarily by focusing on what he calls the "new canon," in contrast to the "former canon." Be sure to notice the punch line at the end.

> Most of my courses, depending on what the course is, represent what I consider to be interesting work for both me and the students from the former canon, and I also try to include works that I consider to be good and interesting that have come into the canon and into print in say the last fifteen to twenty years. By that, I mean works by women, people of color, and that kind of thing. I try and not choose works just because they are a multicultural collection. I try to ask myself, can I be comfortable feeling that these are superb uses of the language, you know. And I understand all the prejudices in a statement like that, but nevertheless, I was educated in the New Critical era, and I do have preference for dense, modernist texts, and so, therefore, I'm attracted to a writer, say, like Toni Morrison.

Toni Morrison is an active African American scholar, literary critic, and author of many influential and popular novels, such as *Beloved* and *Jazz,* whose theoretical perspective can loosely be described as deconstructionist. Although this professor is not alone in attributing some traditional characteristics to Morrison's work, what's surprising about his argument is that it began defensively. Anyone who says that they favor "New Criticism" (a term coined in the 1950s) is normally working up to explaining what's wrong with everything written after 1965. This professor's integrated position on multiculturalism resonates with MC State professors' tendency to talk with each other regularly about their work, through both informal hallway chats and formal mechanisms such as workshops. The result is not only a more consistent understanding of multiculturalism but also a more grounded one. Definitions of multiculturalism at Multicultural State are most likely to take an applied form, outlining the effect of diversity on some realm of intellectual or pedagogical activity.

It is also important to note that MC State professors were least likely to say that multiculturalism might be meaningless. In fact, only one professor there maintained that multiculturalism was meaningless, and he held an administrative position, with an office outside the department.

Like all English departments at the time of my interviews, Multicultural State faced institutional challenges related to both multiculturalism and the trend toward vocational education that had been robbing English depart-

ments of their students (English majors). Unlike most other English departments, however, MC State employed two successful but unusual strategies to
deal with those changes.

The first is the department's specialization in composition and related
fields, such as rhetoric, communications, pedagogy, and linguistics. We might
think of these as applied fields in English language and literature—a good
strategy for an English department in a vocationally oriented middle- to
lower-middle-class university. As indicated above, the faculty also related
pedagogical issues directly to multiculturalism, so that 73 percent understood
multiculturalism as at least partly a pedagogical issue.

The second strategy the MC State department employed in the face of
environmental changes, and the one more important to this study, was to find
a bureaucratic resolution to the problem of multiculturalism. Professors there
were the least likely to mention ambiguity surrounding the meaning of multiculturalism. There is no mystery to this cultural phenomenon, though. The
faculty there resolved the problem in 1983 when they devised their multiculturalism policy and voted that it be included on every syllabus. A (male) full
professor described the process for me:

> There was just a group of us. We were trying to institute a Women in
> Literature course, and yet we didn't want women's literature ghettoized.
> One of the since retired gentlemen in the department said, "Well, then,
> the next thing you know, someone's going to want to put in a Men in
> Literature course," and I said, "We've already got forty-eight of them.
> What are you talking about?" There was a little resistance, but by the
> time it came to a vote, the only reservation to the first document was
> they said it didn't go far enough, and it *didn't* go far enough. That's why
> we revised it—broadened out to include sexual orientation, ethnic
> groups, and ages—all kinds of things are now considered a part of it.
> That seemed too daring on the first go-round. It was voted on unani-
> mously, and then it was amended unanimously.

The policy statement, which was revised in 1989 to expand the list of
groups included and to add the term "multicultural" to its title, served to
clarify and define the academic responsibilities of faculty members with respect to multiculturalism. In fact, 64 percent of the faculty mentioned the
policy when I asked how they felt about multiculturalism. Thus, the policy
defined expectations for all members of the department, and it even defined

the word for many. The department also made heavy use of faculty workshops to help with various aspects of teaching, including multiculturalism, to help clarify elements of departmental policy and mission. These also helped to keep collective goals and ideas in the forefront of local culture. One such workshop was intended to give the faculty resources to broaden their syllabi in compliance with the policy. It was aptly titled "Institutionalizing Multiculturalism."

Finally, the last and most crucial feature of MC State's structural situation that made its innovative approach to multiculturalism possible was its apparent isolation from broader discussions of the topic in the discipline. This made it possible for MC State's faculty to ignore the implications their policy has for academic freedom—a central problem for any policy discussion of what should or shouldn't be included in a canon or a syllabus. Cultural critics in the national arena, of course, make no mention of such issues because their intent is merely to convince their audience that their position is the correct one.

Therefore, while most members of the department were familiar with the national debate, they did not have much exposure to the elite or semi-elite version of the academic debate. One professor, for example, expressed surprise at the difference between his department's view on the issue and that of (almost) everyone else in the discipline:

> I was at conference last year and we were talking about the problems surrounding multiculturalism. I was talking about the multicultural policy that we have, and a question came around: How does it get enforced? How do you enforce it? Immediately, people were jumping up at the table and talking about, about academic freedoms, etc., and I was—I didn't respond. *I'm not as fully aware of the other side of this argument or how passionately people feel about the other side of this argument.* On the other hand, when you look at somebody who's teaching a graduate-level course on twentieth-century American literature and doesn't include any people of color and who doesn't include any women, I don't know how you can ignore that—how a department head or anybody else can ignore that.

Cathletic

If journalists were not interested in Multicultural State, they were even less interested in places like Cathletic University, where the English department's rigorous traditional curriculum had remained unchanged for decades. In many ways, the situation at Cathletic University was unremarkable. There are hundreds of places just like it all across the nation. But something really shocking was happening at Cathletic University. The study of English literature was withering away from starvation, and the cause was essentially a market mechanism.

More than any other university in my study, Cathletic had suffered from the market-like competition for students. The 1995–96 annual report from the academic administration described a shortfall in student enrollments (and thus tuition revenues) that drastically reduced the academic budget for that year. As a result, the university hired a consulting firm to help them improve overall operations, including recruitment and the bureaucratic organization of academic work. The report further warned of continued decreasing capabilities in the student population, especially in English, where more than half of the 1995 incoming class required remedial course work.

Cathletic University was essentially playing an unwitting game of "catch-up" with national culture and losing. Nearly three-quarters of the classes offered by the department were either remedial (32 percent) or required for the bachelor's degree (41 percent), and even with the help of part-time instructors, professors spent two-thirds of their teaching efforts on remedial and service courses. Substantive courses for majors and graduate students were almost exclusively the domain of the department's three full professors, all of whom resisted the multicultural trends that had influenced their textbooks. Without students, there would be no department, but without multiculturalism, there were not many students.

For colleges like Cathletic, that were already accepting 80 percent of applicants and depended heavily on tuition dollars, declining average scores posed a frightening dilemma: accept lower scores or start downsizing. Many turned to advertising campaigns, and Cathletic did a little of that, though not in the blatant way that for-profit universities did.

I approached the chair of the Cathletic University English department just before their spring break with confidence, having three departments under my belt and having received a particularly warm reception at Multicultural State. I was, therefore, surprised by her hesitation. I always waited for permission before I began observing departments or soliciting interviews, but the Cathletic University chair was the first who forbade me to begin. She promised to ask the faculty's opinion on the matter at the next department meeting, but warned me that the outcome would probably be negative. Though I did finally gain approval, getting individual interviews also proved difficult in the beginning. The first three professors I contacted (all men) declined the interview. Then, all five women in the department agreed.

Although the gender breakdown seemed to indicate a rift in comfort with questions surrounding literary value (an important piece of evidence), I knew I could not get the whole story without being able to interview the men. My breakthrough finally came from the most senior member of the department, who sounded perfectly delighted to get my phone call. He expressed interest in my graduate work at Princeton and told me he had studied at Columbia. (That Princeton pedigree sure came in handy!) He then suggested that we do the interview over lunch. Conducting a formal, recorded interview around the jangley sounds of silverware and the interruptions of a meal is impractical, but I gladly accepted his invitation in order to gain inroads with the male faculty there. Eventually, I was able to get interviews with most of the other men by scheduling their interviews for the week of exams and the following week, when time pressures had subsided.

As I headed off to that lunch meeting (my first visit to Cathletic), I realized that this place would be like nothing I had experienced before, and I made my first mistake before I even got there. I chose to ignore the convoluted driving directions published by the university in favor of a more direct route. Cathletic sits in a small city on the outskirts of a major metropolitan area, so there was no reason to wander through town on my first trip. The map told me that the university was less than a mile from a different interstate exit. I got off the highway and turned onto the road that would lead me directly to the university. One turn. It would be much easier!

The interstate ramp led into damp concrete below the underpass and dumped me onto a deserted street with vegetation growing up not just along the edge of the road but also up through the road's cracks. Old, rundown townhouses peeked through vacant lots a block away, and I could make out some rusted playground equipment through a chain-link fence on the right.

I continued because it was not at all clear whether I could find a reentry route to the interstate. The street eventually came alive with shops—shops with bars on the windows—just as I approached the campus. I could see the chapel in the distance, but the last few blocks went slowly because African American men congregated on the sidewalks and dominated the street, making 25 miles per hour a hazardous driving speed through the poverty-stricken neighborhood that adjoined the north side of the university.

At the university entrance, the tiny Cathletic campus was separated from that neighborhood by a series of stone walls and iron gates. A security post guarded the main entrance, and I worried a little about gaining access, unannounced, in my 1975 Ford Grenada—a big, brown, rusted dinosaur so old it had a three-speed manual transmission lever on the steering column. The car looked more at home outside the gate than inside, but I was a blonde, blue-eyed, white girl who claimed to be from Princeton (no need to show that student ID). I was allowed to enter, and that meant I could also park in the faculty lot. Amazing!

The university's directions would not have had me dodging pedestrians in a rundown neighborhood, however. They dictated a meandering approach from the opposite direction, where a village of quaint little specialty shops and professional offices borders the campus. That area is populated primarily by upper-middle-class white locals and students, and there is no wall on that side. Other sides of the campus adjoin posh residential areas and feature keyed gates in the stone wall that surrounds part of the campus. The buildings inside the wall draw on widely varied architectural styles, and many of them are really beautiful.

A lecture series that invited famous authors to give live readings on campus was featured prominently on all the university's brochures, and many of the buildings gave the impression that Cathletic University was the sort of place that could inspire great writers. The feel of the English department, however, was unfriendly, and many, though not all, of the professors there seemed unhappy. All were wary about my research (except my new friend from Columbia), and many asked how my findings might affect them, as though I would report directly to their dean.

The nondescript building that housed the English department was also unfriendly to inhabitants and visitors alike. It wasn't one of those fabulous inspirational buildings. Although faculty offices in the English department all had magnificent views of a distant mountain range—compensation for climbing five flights of stairs each day—the offices were awkwardly long and narrow. In addition, there were two professors assigned to each of these narrow rooms, and that condition was exacerbated by the cramped quarters, which made concentration difficult for reading, writing, and even grading.

Although there was quite a bit of traffic in the hallways, there was very little collegial interaction. Part-time faculty and graduate instructors shared a single, windowless room on the other side of the hall. Loud chattering escaped from it whenever the door opened, punctuating an uncomfortable silence that normally loomed in the English department hallway.

The entire department was contained in fewer than ten adjacent rooms on a single hallway, so people appeared to be trying to go about their business without the inconvenience of engaging passersby. This was understandable; English department faculty taught four classes each semester, and some taught five or six, an extraordinarily heavy teaching load for professors in a university of this type.

Ironically, it was at Cathletic University that I saw my first "faculty activity report." To this point, I had no idea that most college professors have to file an annual report justifying the way they've spent their past year on the university's dime. It was only the bureaucratic paperwork that made the reports visible to me at that particular moment, but the thought of it was especially painful at Cathletic. These professors taught four to six classes each semester. Their teaching load alone was every bit as heavy as that of a high-school teacher, and then there was the additional pressure to publish (a serious pressure, unlike Multicultural State's approach). Add the tasks of student advising, faculty meetings, university level committee obligations, and administrative work, and you have a recipe for disaster.

The very idea of filling out an activity report—as though it was unclear how they spent their time—seemed inconceivable to me. But the recurring theme of lazy college professors wasting someone else's money loomed more ominously in my mind. That image, so firmly ingrained in our popular culture and the psyches of middle-class parents forking out college tuitions, does more harm to the enterprise than I was able to measure in this study. I was only able to see glimpses of its effect in the paranoid aspects of State Star's self-study and in the ludicrous implication that Cathletic professors might be free-riders.

There were also many ways in which Catholic traditions influenced university affairs, but there were not any direct mandates on the activities inside academic departments. And the Church's effect on thinking about multiculturalism at Cathletic University was less dramatic than was the influence of civic responsibility in the public universities I studied. Nevertheless, the organizational dynamic in the English department is best described as a "brittle hierarchy," and that characteristic goes a long way toward explaining the department's position on multiculturalism. It did not have a coherent philosophy motivating its preference for a traditional program in literature, nor did it have clear reasons for rejecting multiculturalism. Rather, it appeared that the department's professors were merely unable to respond at all. Moreover, multiculturalism was only one of several social and cultural changes in the university that threatened the viability of departmental life as the professors knew it.

I want to dissuade readers from the temptation to assign blame on this point to the hierarchical organization of the Catholic Church. In fact, the formal power structure at Cathletic is essentially identical to that of all the English departments in my study. At most, there might be an increased tendency to invoke those structures at Cathletic, but it would be a mistake to assume that the church is the source of all power plays among English professors there. The more serious problem for Cathletic was its lack of flexibility and responsiveness. Further exploration will show that much of that brittleness stems from the way the department responded to a painfully inadequate supply of resources and to other factors related to its decline *relative to the rest of the (Catholic) university.*

The hierarchically organized structure of authority at Cathletic University may have been part of the reason that students did not challenge the content of English courses there, however. (Remember that racial and ethnic diversity in the student population is a constant across all four research sites.) Students did not directly express dissatisfaction, but neither did they choose to major in English. At the time of my visit, there were dangerously few English majors there. The department had been able to fill some courses with non-majors, but the full-time faculty devoted most of its teaching time to composition courses for first-year college students. *The question of shaping our nation's literary canon makes no sense in this context.*

In stark contrast to Multicultural State's highly collaborative approach to "institutionalizing multiculturalism," Cathletic University tended to avoid multiculturalism—and nearly everything else, as well.

The differences in meanings associated with multiculturalism at the two non-elite universities were just as striking as the differences in their local culture. Most noticeable was the strong inclination for professors at Cathletic to avoid multiculturalism altogether by deeming the word meaningless and irrelevant to their work as English professors. A full 75 percent mentioned at least once that the word might be meaningless, and a third never offered any indication that it had acquired an operational definition for them. A tendency toward abstraction was also evident, with no professors covering all four arenas of meaning and many defining multiculturalism simply as diversity. Unlike Ivory Towers professors, however, those at Cathletic University did not make use of the more abstract definition to generate analytic flexibility.

The faculty at Cathletic University lacked clear meaning for the word because they rarely *used* it with each other. They rejected the word in a literal sense. However, it is important to remember that the newer members of the faculty cared a great deal about literary diversity (17 percent) and felt stifled by the predominant view at work in the department. These results support those from Multicultural State. Even the strong advocates of multiculturalism at Cathletic University used less-grounded definitions than their counterparts at Multicultural State who had the benefit of collective discussions.

In short, where engagement and collective governance were high, definitions of multiculturalism were clearer and more connected to applied arenas. Where engagement was low, there was more ambiguity surrounding the word and less ability to make sense of it in the context of work routines. The failure to address multiculturalism at the department level decreased the chances that the word would earn any meaning at all—never mind *shared* meaning or meaning that might inform social change.

To the extent that there was a definition at Cathletic, though, it centered on text selection. Choosing the books their students would read was a problem for the department because multiculturalism in the external environment had influenced anthologies and textbooks. Senior professors believed that the few traditional anthologies available on the market were too difficult for their students. In their own classes, which tended to be more advanced literature classes, these professors normally chose shorter works and progressed more slowly than they would have liked because of student abilities. Here's a concrete example.

> In Freshman English, I had a reader called *The World of Ideas*, but I've decided not to use it any more. It's too hard for them. The idea behind that book is: They're going to respond to readings anyway, why not have them read great stuff? But I decided there was too much framing and background one had to give for every single piece. It ended up taking too much time and students weren't getting it, so I'm going to dumb it down again.

Professors at MC State faced similar problems with student abilities, although we'll see that it affected them differently. In fact, when I visited, MC State had just decided to remove the study of literature from its year-long sequence in freshman English. The first semester would thereafter be devoted to a specific type of writing that the textbook publishers call "argumentation." While interviewing a professor who expressed a strong belief in the importance of literature for the lives of her students, I spied a rare source of potential conflict in MC State's happy department and asked, "Do you object to the recent decision to remove literature from [the college English sequence]?" To my surprise, she did *not* object. Instead, she confirmed the strength of the department's commitment to composition.

> It was a baby introduction to literature. . . . Argumentation is far more rigorous and it can model for all the other kinds of college writing we'll be doing, so I was one of the "movers and shakers." I know it sounds weird to say, "Throw the literature out," but it was just a gesture. The kids just forgot all about it, and then we had to start all over again in "Approaches to Literature."

In more advanced classes that were devoted to literature, professors in both non-elite departments again faced similar challenges. They found that anthologies induced a sense of inadequacy in both students and teachers because these courses can broach only a small portion of the anthology in a semester's time. The Cathletic professor quoted above described his dilemma in teaching the more advanced classes this way.

> In the American Literature survey course, I've used an anthology like the one we've got here. I'm now thinking of changing that. I probably won't do it [change books] this year, though, because I've got too much other

work to do. I like this anthology, it's just that I'm starting to think that since you can't cover everything anyway, and you always end up stretching and trying to fit people in, students aren't going to maintain all that anyway, so I'm starting to think that I should just select a handful of works.

Professors who were interested in maintaining traditional canons were not the only ones who felt the pinch of student abilities, however. Junior professors, who would prefer to expand students' reading lists rather than reduce them, expressed a similar sentiment. In this case, adjusting the reading list to student abilities meant reducing its canonical content.

> In the prose section and the short-fiction section, we did primarily women and minorities. Faulkner and Joyce were the only white men. Then, in the poetry section, there was a good mix, but not as good as I'd like, because we did less contemporary poetry. I had less time for it. The course at [my previous job] just met more often, for more hours, and the students were a little more able in reading, so we could do a little more. Then I hit a lot more of the classics, and I did *Midsummer Night's Dream.* But now, it's probably about fifty-fifty.

Compare those quotes to this complaint from an avid supporter of multiculturalism at MC State:

> In an upper-level course, you sincerely hope that they already know how to read, and you also would like to think that they already know how to write. Neither one of these hopes is particularly fruitful. They could not read *Melville.* They could not *decipher* the sentence structure. It wasn't the language [vocabulary]; it was the sentence structure. So we had to take it in terms of phrases and clauses. "See this punctuation mark? Let us read to there. Now what does that say?" You know? We had to decode a nineteenth-century American writer writing in basic English!

Although MC State professors faced similar challenges relative to student abilities, however, they did not agonize about the way such changes affected their ability to teach canonical versus non-canonical literature. Expectations about multiculturalism and the canon were defined elsewhere, so the challenge of student ability merely involved getting them through the task at hand, whatever it was. (The quote above about Melville comes from a specialist in African American literature, but she had no plans to remove

Moby Dick from her syllabus. She just developed a new strategy for teaching it.)

Cathletic professors, on the other hand, allowed such things as textbook offerings and student abilities to shape their decisions about the canon and multiculturalism. In committee meetings where professors decided what textbooks juniors, adjuncts, and part-timers would use in their freshman English courses, therefore, senior faculty often agreed (with reluctance) to allow multicultural texts because, they said, textbook publishers offer no realistic alternative at the level of ability they believe their students need. Such problems do not concern faculty at elite schools.

Cathletic and MC State had both abandoned the canon in their freshman English courses—the ones that matter for widespread cultural education. But the issue of canon expansion was not at the heart of either decision. In both cases, professors were faced with the daunting challenge of preparing their students to do college-level writing, and they found it impossible to do that while simultaneously teaching them to read difficult works. In these two non-elite universities, the goal of introducing students to a wide range of literature—canonical or otherwise—disappeared from sight long ago.

Organized Culture

These English professors chose to make sense of multiculturalism in a way that fit into the preexisting organizational routines and meanings that created literary canons in the first place. In short, the multiculturalism that emerged from the smoke of the canon war is a familiar creature. It is the product of one of our nation's most stable and important cultural institutions—higher education.

At Ivory Towers and State Star, multiculturalism took the shape of scholarly cultural production as well as the preservation, interpretation, and distribution of literary high culture. In so doing, however, the faculty in the state-funded university, State Star, used a "common ground" definition of multiculturalism that drew on two realms of meaning. Professors in Ivory Towers' superstar department, on the other hand, produced definitions that were more abstract—the sort that a public intellectual might find useful. In both non-elite departments, however, the path to multiculturalism (or lack thereof) lay in the structure of bureaucratic authority. Policy defines multiculturalism at MC State, and the lack of policy at Cathletic University inhibits the emergence of an institutionalized meaning for the word.

In all four cases, organizational routines and decisions preceded local definitions of multiculturalism. In short, *these four departments only came to understand multiculturalism through the process of coming to accept it and incorporate it into the details of their daily lives.* In that sense, there are important features of multiculturalism's meaning that the four departments have in common.

Although value, pedagogy, and meaninglessness vary a great deal across the four departments, diversity and canons were popular themes in all four research sites. This makes good intuitive sense, given the findings from Chapter 2. Diversity was the most popular arena of meaning in the overall analysis, and it is the simplest referent for multiculturalism. Canons came in a close second, reflecting the structural position of English professors as the conveyors of literary canons. This comparative analysis confirms that those trends work in all four of the departments I studied.

Thus, a non-controversial definition of multiculturalism might be identified at the intersection of canons and diversity. Note, however, that by non-controversial, I do not mean that most English professors would agree that "diversifying canons" is a good idea. I only mean that English professors in a wide variety of contexts could recognize diversifying canons as a legitimate *definition* of (literary) multiculturalism. In Chapter 2, I identified a "core" definition of multiculturalism that drew on all four arenas of meaning. Here, it might make sense to identify the "diversified canon" definition as a *universal* one for English professors—one that is less specific (and thus more vague) but easily recognized. This isn't a particularly profound discovery, but it does matter for our understanding of the way multiculturalism has been defined in the college classroom as a claim about the social relevance of literary canons.

The consistent portions of the definition (canons and diversity) indicate that national-level institutional patterns had strong influences on the outcome of the canon war. The battles fought by literature professors took place on their institutionally defined turf in what sociologist Andrew Abbott calls professional jurisdiction (1988). This effect is important for guessing whether an idea is likely to initiate widespread social change. In short, this piece of evidence indicates that English professors were unlikely to dismantle political or economic structures in the name of multiculturalism. Instead, it appears they defined multiculturalism *through* existing institutional structures, and the meaning of multiculturalism was confined to the boundaries of professional jurisdiction for most English professors. This habit of everyday life had a powerful taming effect on the potential force of multiculturalism in English literature and on national culture.

In short, organizational habits changed literary multiculturalism, and they did so through a process of boundary negotiation that allowed the routines of social organization to merge with the process of meaning-making.

The power of this particular mechanism was most evident in the experiences of a Cathletic University professor who described confronting a brand of multiculturalism produced by another academic discipline. Her dramatic response to the foreign form of multiculturalism is important, especially because her experience was not unique. It has been repeated (often less consciously) on college campuses across the country, where English literature is the discipline most likely to take responsibility for multiculturalism in the overall university curriculum.[2] *This* is the really shocking thing about the rise of multiculturalism in education, not that it is multicultural, but that it has become so narrow in the process of becoming so ubiquitous. The Cathletic University professor says of the history professor who spearheaded an experimental interdisciplinary course on multiculturalism:

> He gave me a bibliography for the course, and because he was a historian, there was no multiculturalism on it! It was all history or immigration. And I said, you know, I don't think this is really multiculturalism, to talk about when the Irish came in the nineteenth century. It was very odd. So I had to basically teach myself. I mean, I had an inkling that wasn't it. So I revised the entire bibliography for the course.

Ultimately, there is a strong relationship between definitions of multiculturalism and the work environments in which those definitions are produced. The livelier and more active institutional environments—those that were "stronger" in the sense that professors had more control of their own internal activities—produced more specific and more coherent definitions of the word. As a result, *the potential threat of multiculturalism works in reverse*: the most organizationally vulnerable department, Cathletic University, was the most "successful" at resisting multiculturalism because the word could not take

hold and earn a meaningful definition there. Ivory Towers' hands-off departmental culture produced a similar effect (despite its reputation for progressive
scholarship), in that there was no encouragement to systematically incorporate multiculturalism into departmental practices. Ivory Towers professors
generated less-grounded definitions of multiculturalism but no resistance
(claims of meaninglessness) to it.

In contrast to theories that emphasize the power of culture over more tangible institutional structures, I found that multiculturalism made real inroads
in active institutional environments, not weak ones and not merely progressive ones. In sum, multiculturalism, and perhaps cultural change in general,
does not *threaten* social cohesion, it *requires* social cohesion in order to emerge.

Chapter 4

TAKING SIDES IN QUICKSAND:
MEANING, ABSTRACTION, AND AMBIGUITY

It has been 14 years since the outbreak of civil war in Columbia
University's English department, a war that sent some professors
scurrying for more congenial settings, turned feminists and multiculturalists against traditionalists and left a fifth of the permanent positions in the department unoccupied. By some combatants' standards, an empty office was better than one filled by the
unqualified candidates supported by the enemy. . . . Now, in the
academic version of a third-party peace proposal, the department
has ceded key decisions about its future to a posse of outsiders
from five competing universities.

—*Melodramatic report by Karen W. Arneson,* New York Times,
March 17, 2002

If I'm in a joking mood, I'll say I wash brains for a living, just to
try to get a conversation going.

—*Cathletic University professor who works among real-world
disagreements*

In some ways, the popular depictions of battles over English literature were
so overblown they were just funny to insiders. It isn't only definitions of
multiculturalism that are drastically different "on the ground" inside English
departments; disagreement works differently, too. The press was selling a sen-
sationalized story about epic battles over the fate of a culture, while English
professors insisted on the value of scholarly debate. Their insistence might
have been convincing, in that it should have confirmed every college student's
suspicion that professors don't really "do" drama even if they write about it.
Yet, that was part of the allure of this alleged battle.

It was intriguing to think that some of our nation's most austere and serious educators would go behind closed doors and duke out their differences.

Moreover, professors couldn't claim that there were no disagreements. There were. English professors clearly had differing opinions about the direction of scholarship in their discipline, and there was evidence of that everywhere. Many said so in class, others published their opinions in scholarly journals, a few even spoke with the press or participated in public debates. There may not have been a war, but there was something, and even English professors expected conflict.

Professors at Cathletic University disagreed, and they knew it. They just tried to avoid talking about it. Professors at State Star and Ivory Towers also disagreed, but they overestimated the depth of their differences, so they were continually surprised to find that they agreed on important issues. A new assistant professor at State Star, for example, recounted this story, which summarizes the response of her colleagues:

> I was on a [departmental] committee on the place of writing in the curriculum last year and there were people from all different branches of the faculty, and we ran a lot of surveys. It was less surprising to me, being new, but what I noted was the committee's surprise at how much consensus there was in the department.

At Ivory Towers, several professors told me that their hiring, promotion, and tenure decisions tended to be unanimous. In fact, they said, nearly *all* such decisions were unanimous, and yet they did not accept that fact into their realm of expectations. They continued to be surprised, each time.

> It's amazing how many tenure decisions in this department have been unanimous. Virtually every one I've been involved with. And how many *hiring* decisions are unanimous, or virtually unanimous. It's quite stunning. In fact, I would say since I came here . . . I guess there have been only two or three decisions of either hiring or promotion that haven't been unanimous. It's pretty incredible, especially considering our blood-in-the-halls reputation. Typically, on hiring committees, we'll have old Ivory Towers and new Ivory Towers people on them—often people that have not spoken to one another in some time. And often the result will be a unanimous endorsement by the hiring committee. I don't know how that happens. It's really magical.

Despite trying to argue that English professors are not nearly as divided as the press would have us think, all these professors had an analysis and a critique of the real philosophical differences in their discipline, and they situated

themselves within its confines. But when they did that, they would forget
about their real lives together in the department. They would often imagine
the "abstract" version of their opposition, while thinking of themselves as
more grounded—more reasonable.[1]

In short, opinions are shaped by the environments that produce them, in
much the same way that different definitions emerge in different contexts.
For example, some of the *national* debate was shaped by conventional political concerns that resembled political party differences. That's because the
noisiest participants in the "battle" were not English professors (or artists or
cultural producers); they were politicians, such as former Senator Jesse Helms
and William Bennett, who served first as chair of the National Endowment
for the Humanities and then as secretary of education. Political figures made
direct connections between literary disagreements and conventional party
politics, especially when they talked about public funding for education and
the humanities. But such concerns had less effect on academic disagreements.
Here's how a State Star professor explained it:

> I would venture to say I have probably only two or three colleagues who
> vote Republican. Yet, what they do in the voting booth is one thing, and
> what they think about literary value is quite another. So, they would be
> horrified to think that they were in the same league with Newt Gin-
> grich. They don't necessarily see votes on tenure cases as being in any
> way connected with the same kind of conservative view.

Roger Kimball made exactly this mistake in his book *Tenured Radicals,* in
which he blamed the left-wing politics of the sixties generation for changes
in the English literature canon, saying, "It has often been observed that yes-
terday's student radical is today's tenured professor or academic dean" (xiv).
Kimball's book was an instant success, but its claim was unfounded. The most
left-leaning factions of English professors in the United States during the period were the younger generations of faculty, most of whom were *untenured.*
And no generation stood out as a radical blip in the family tree of English literature.[2] Although there were certainly even more conservative generations
ahead of them, the "sixties generation" could better be described as the *traditionalist* faction in the discipline (to the limited extent that such factions could
be said to exist at all).

Moreover, as each generation ages, its members tend to become even more
conservative. That effect is so strong, in fact, that the overall liberalism of col-

lege faculty across the United States had been *decreasing* for ten years when Kimball first complained about increasing radicalism in 1990. By the time Kimball's "tenured radicals" earned tenure, they were considerably *less* radical than their untenured colleagues. These facts not only stand Kimball's argument on its head, they put English professors themselves off balance.

Here, for example, is a "tenured radical" of sorts, talking about academic politics in his field. He earned his Ph.D. and joined the State Star English department at the end of the 1960s. But by the time the 1990s rolled around, he was genuinely dismayed by the lay of the political land around him. In what follows, note the informal language he uses to launch his attack on the Modern Language Association (MLA). This guy was no uptight prude from the 1950s, but he found himself cast very close to the right wing of literary politics. He began by commenting on the uselessness of the MLA:

> The MLA sucks. I'm not presently a member. . . . For one thing, it's too big, and, um, I would regard myself as being an extremely left-wing liberal. The MLA would define me as a Neanderthal conservative, so, uh, I think they're loony. The organization is just *Looney Tunes*. . . . I think I'm actually a member of the NAS, too. . . . An elderly friend, who is retired, joined me to that, um. I don't know whether I'm still getting their periodicals or not. Bunch of nuts! You know? All of these people with burning issues, if they had any real scholarship, they wouldn't have time for any of that stuff.

To be "recruited" into the ranks of the National Association of Scholars was a fairly serious political claim. But neither of these groups really fit his politics. He was a child of the sixties, neither a postmodern nihilist nor a Neanderthal conservative. Labeling him a "tenured radical" only added to the confusion.

In fact, many of the anti-multicultural classics of the era came to be famous because they were written by well-known scholars and left-wing public intellectuals, most notably Arthur Schlesinger, Daniel P. Moynihan, and Todd Gitlin. These "tenured radicals" made long, successful careers leading the American public down the path of progressive change, but they finally decided to put on the brakes and say, "Okay, now we've gone too far!"

Differences in opinion on academic politics were not, therefore, structured by the same factors that structure national politics. Most pertinent to the question of meaning is the possibility that the way one understands multiculturalism, the way one defines it, might have something to do with one's opinion of it. In fact, my respondents often made just that sort of claim. They would say, for example, that there were several kinds of multiculturalism in play and that they favored one while opposing the other. So, there is a need for a more sophisticated, or at least a more accurate, explanation of opinions on multiculturalism and how they are formed—one that can make sense of the tendency for individual English professors to have multiple opinions.

What follows is my analysis of how meanings shape opinion. By looking at the definitions used by supporters compared to opponents, I was able to identify which definitions were controversial and which were more benign. Abstraction also contributed to the formation of support and opposition. Remember, however, that departmental conditions played an important role in shaping the definitions that emerged there. And remember that the important departmental factors were mostly unrelated to multiculturalism. So, if departments shape definitions and definitions shape opinions, it is possible that some departments came to accept or reject multicultural changes because of unrelated conditions, like decision-making structures and departmental prestige.

In short, the implication of such a connection between organizational structures, meanings, and opinions is not only that definitions mattered for the way political battles turned out, but that political processes mattered as well.

The Role of Meaning and Ambiguity in Stance-taking

Many of the professors I interviewed suggested that their opinion on multiculturalism would depend on its definition, but that's no reason to believe them. They were often wrong about the way their own battles operated. (Although, if I had to choose between a journalist's rendering and that of an English professor, I'd choose the professor, every time.) To examine whether advocates and opponents of multiculturalism really used different definitions of the word, I compared opinions on multiculturalism (stance-taking) with the sixteen possible definitions and present the results in Figure 4.1.

In this analysis, I assumed that the causal relationship between definitions and opinions went, to some extent, in both directions. The first direction is obvious and often mentioned by respondents, one of whom said, "You tell me what it is, and I'll tell you what I think about it." But the action may also have worked the other way. For example, staunch opponents of multiculturalism may have been more resistant to learning about multiculturalism than other professors. Having less knowledge about multiculturalism would, then, limit their ability to define the word. In addition, people strongly committed to a *position* may have preferred definitions that would strengthen the logic of taking that position. This (along with the general tendency for traditionalists to overestimate the extremism of their opponents) explains why the most radical descriptions of multiculturalism often came from its opponents. It also explains the mad scramble for acceptable definitions of multiculturalism coming from supporters who decided to support it before they figured out what it meant.

Between supporters and opponents of multiculturalism, the two most obvious differences lay in diversity and meaninglessness. In all, 95 percent of the professors who supported multiculturalism drew on diversity in their use of the word, and the connection between talking about diversity and supporting multiculturalism seemed almost automatic at times. Said one professor: "My definition is the pursuit of knowledge about people other than yourself."

Diversity is a fairly obvious element of multiculturalism that one might expect to be involved in all opinions on the matter. But, compared to the 95 percent of supporters who included diversity in their definitions of multiculturalism, only 22 percent of opponents drew on the idea of diversity. Here, the definition of multiculturalism as the anti-canon reappeared as an important element in constructing opposition to the idea. If the undeniable problem of diversity in American culture was excluded from debate, then multiculturalism could be defined as a mere threat to American literary culture, and it made more sense to oppose that apparently destructive force.

Resisting definitions altogether worked the same way, possibly because the key element, diversity, was still missing. Among the few professors who opposed multiculturalism, the greatest portion (44 percent) specifically described it as meaningless and never made use of the word or offered any other definition. This contrasts with supporters of multiculturalism, none of whom maintained that the word was meaningless. On the surface, the tendency for opponents of multiculturalism to deny its meaning seems counterintuitive. How can one oppose an undefined idea? But, for opponents of

FIGURE 4.1

Percentage of Professors Using Each Definition, by Stance
(Opinion Toward Multiculturalism)

STANCE: POSITIVE (N=20)

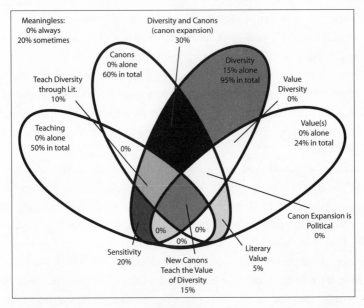

STANCE: NEGATIVE (N=9)

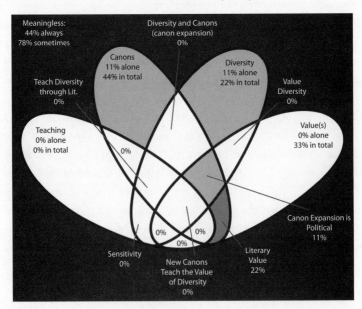

FIGURE 4.1 *(cont.)*
Percentage of Professors Using Each Definition, by Stance
(Opinion Toward Multiculturalism)

STANCE: MIXED / COMPLEX (N=31)

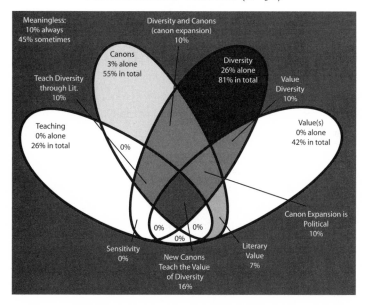

multiculturalism, the strategic value of denying meaning lay in the flip side of that question: How can one be *in favor* of making curriculum changes based on an unspecified idea? The high incidence of meaninglessness among opponents of multiculturalism indicates that defining multiculturalism, perhaps especially in the context of work routines, was an important step in the path toward partial consensus.

Even while I was interviewing professors, however, I wondered whether this evident tendency for opponents of multiculturalism to claim that the word has no meaning was an intentional display of resistance to the idea of multiculturalism and the possibility of institutionalizing it. This group had other important traits in common, however. They specialized in fields far removed from the most obvious influences of multicultural expansion. They had a tendency to make a point of saying they hadn't read most of the multicultural works in question, and (among elite professors) they tended to dis-

parage the theoretical works commonly invoked in discussions of multicultural canon expansion. In short, although some of these professors may have
feigned ignorance about the word's meaning, most had less institutional pressure to be knowledgeable about the specifics of multicultural literature than
did their colleagues in other specialties. *Professors who had no need to learn
about multiculturalism were less likely to assign meaning to the word and, therefore,
did not often support it.*

Two-thirds of the professors who used the popular, single-arena definition
of multiculturalism as "diversity" reported having a mixed or complex opinion about it—one that could not be reduced to mere support or opposition.
In addition, that definition accounted for more than a quarter (26 percent) of
all the "mixed" opinions, a little more than in the grand total. The overwhelming complexity of opinions associated with this single-arena definition
confirms that definitions that drew on a single arena of meaning were not
necessarily more simplistic or clearer than those that drew on several realms
of meaning. Rather, this effect supports my earlier portrayals of single-arena
definitions as "abstract" and less constrained in the range of implications the
word might have. Abstract definitions do not provide enough specificity to
invoke clear positive or negative assessments.

The canon-expansion definition, at the intersection of diversity and
canons, also stood out as influential, but this time in a different direction.
That definition accounted for 30 percent of the favorable opinions toward
multiculturalism and none of the negative stances. "Canon expansion" was
also one of the more popular definitions of multiculturalism overall, suggesting a possible route to widespread acceptance among English professors.
Viewed from the perspective of definitions causing opinions, two-thirds of
the professors who used that definition favored multiculturalism, compared to
only one-third of the entire group. And (again) none of the multicultural opponents used the canon-expansion definition of multiculturalism.

Among the four arenas, however, the issue of teaching had the clearest
positive influence on opinion. It is the only arena that was *never* invoked by
opponents of multiculturalism, and those who used it were more likely to
take a strong stance in favor of multiculturalism than they were to say they
had mixed or complex opinions. In particular, all of the professors who defined multiculturalism as a matter of "sensitivity" (teaching methods that accommodate student diversity) reported being supporters, and none suggested

that the topic was too complex for stance-taking. The most reluctant of the four offered a possible explanation for the power of this perspective when he said, "I guess I feel like whether we like it or not, we're living in it. And the institution has a responsibility to serve the needs of its students." Adding canons to the sensitivity definition, however, introduced more complexity in opinions. Although there were still no opponents among this group, some did report having mixed feelings about it. The same is true for that "central" definition as well.

The definition of multiculturalism at the center of the diagrams also made a strong showing among multicultural advocates. And, in light of those teaching concerns, none of the professors who opposed multiculturalism used that definition. Unlike the simple, two-arena definition of multiculturalism as sensitivity, however, the four-fold "core" definition was used by a sizeable portion (26 percent) of the professors who said that multiculturalism was too complicated to inform a clear positive or negative opinion. This might suggest that drawing on more arenas of meaning can add complexity to one's understanding of multiculturalism as it gets ever more closely tied to ideas about grounded reality. I'll explore that effect in the next section, but I want to close this analysis with a longer treatment of the definitions at the intersection of canons and values.

The literary-value definition proved to be especially volatile, in terms of the opinions associated with it. This was the second most popular definition among opponents of multiculturalism (the most popular, if we exclude meaninglessness as a definition). Yet an equal number of professors who used this definition saw multiculturalism as too complex for stance-taking, and one of them is an advocate.

The advocate presented an interesting case. She was a female senior professor at Cathletic University who began, like so many others, saying, "Tell me what it means and I'll tell you what I think about it." After I told her that I didn't really know, but that I wondered about her gut-level reaction to the word, she provided a definition to serve as the basis for her reaction, which was positive. What's interesting about her definition is that it is one I might interpret as a relatively sophisticated theoretical claim that canons have been shaped by ethnocentric understandings of literary value. But I would need to employ a great deal of interpretive license to get there, because the words she chose mimicked those of her senior colleagues in avoiding specific references to cultural difference. Unlike those colleagues, however, she managed to sustain a definition of multiculturalism that understood it as a challenge to the unfair or unfounded history of literary exclusion. She even said she acknowledged that challenge in the classroom, but she did not adjust her text-selection choices or teaching methods in light of that view. Hers was an unusual case that points to the volatility of meanings in this particular category. Here's the way she did it:

> Well, I guess what it means, then, is that we should be aware that for decades, maybe even centuries, we've only been talking about a very limited group of writers as the so-called great writers.

One of the professors who chose to describe the issue of literary value as too complex for general stance-taking was the State Star professor who mentioned race and gender differences in order to say that they were illegitimate concerns for English professors. Now it becomes more evident that there existed a boundary dispute at the intersection of diversity and value—a boundary dispute that posed a challenge for my coding decisions. In fact, that professor might have taken issue with my claim that such an intersection even existed. I think of that ambiguity as a discovery, rather than as a source of error in my analysis, however, because those arenas and their boundaries belong to English professors, not to me. The boundaries describe the way that English professors make sense of multiculturalism, and I had no reason to expect that the process would work in an especially "clean," unambiguous, or non-controversial way.

Opponents of multiculturalism who claimed that it was an assault on literary value (aka beauty) argued that any interest in the "value" of differences relative to the canon was, *by definition*, illegitimate, on the grounds that canons are defined by aesthetic value. That's what professors who *did* mention diversity meant when they said that multiculturalism was "politicizing" English literature. They meant that "diversity" was encroaching on the field of "value," which *some* wanted to define exclusively as aesthetic value. In short, opponents of multiculturalism wanted to shrink the definition of value so that an overlap with diversity would be impossible, and to accomplish that goal, they labeled all those categories that involved the overlap between canons and values as "*aesthetics*," and all those categories that involved the overlap between canons and diversity as *illegitimate politics*.

Outside the field of literary canons, however, these opponents considered the overlap between diversity and value a fine topic for national and even campus politics. After all, the English professors who opposed multiculturalism had been part of the educated liberal class during the civil rights movement and during the decade of the 1960s. They wouldn't dream of saying that political action was illegitimate, only that it shouldn't change the canon they had come to love. In fact, they would be the first on the scene to fight for unbiased access to that beloved canon and the educational model based on it. When it came to defining canons, however, they wanted a stronger boundary, a moat, a boundary that could fend off the advances of diversity. They wanted one of Zerubavel's "islands of meaning."

To keep the battle going, however, there was also an opposing camp there at the intersection of diversity and value, who said that canon expansion was political and who saw some value in such political changes. Although these professors used the same "politics" and "literary value" definitions that multiculturalism's staunchest opponents employed, they were the professors who most closely resembled D'Souza's caricatured multicultural villains—elite literary critics who were keenly aware of the boundary dispute between canonical politics and canonical aesthetics. But these professors were far too sophisticated (and too steeped in the portions of their field that were cleanly separated from teaching) to take a clear stance on multiculturalism. That's what generated D'Souza's constant and futile search for a real opponent. On paper, he had clear enemies, but none of them stood up to defend the position he attributed to them because they didn't really hold that position. At last, D'Souza managed to schedule a series of debates with Stanley Fish, a white male literary critic and chair of the Duke University English department. The following passage is the introduction to an essay Fish prepared for the first in a series of debates with Dinesh D'Souza during the 1991–92 academic year. It appears in his 1994 book, *There's No Such Thing as Free Speech*.

> I appear before you today by virtue of a mistake made by central casting that has tapped me for the role of ardent academic leftist, proponent of multiculturalism, and standard-bearer of the politically correct. Unfortunately, my qualifications for this assignment are so slight as to be non-existent. (53)

Fish offered two reasons why his true self could not occupy the role he was playing on stage. The second, which is most relevant here, was that his "true" opinions were too complex to be suitable for debate. His first reason, however, probably overshadowed the issue of opinion for most readers: he argued that his true self could not occupy the position he described because he had the demographic characteristics of the dominant groups in American society. He said, in essence, that the true Stanley Fish was not a proponent of multiculturalism, but that he would pretend to be such a person for the purposes of debate. He would play the part into which the theater had cast him, but he would not claim the position he took on stage to be his own. It's a perfect example of the gap between abstract national politics and grounded political action.

So, the most promising site of conflict over multiculturalism in English literature departments was the tension between diversity and aesthetics, but that dispute was not carried out between supporters and opponents of multiculturalism. Rather, the "sides" (such as they were) were defined by those who did and did not see literary value as inherently political. That is, supporters of canonical change did not argue in favor of inserting a politics of diversity into the selection of literary canons; they argued that the selection process is, was, and always will be political.

Moreover, the "literary value" and "political" categories did not stand out as particularly popular definitions of multiculturalism. At 8 percent each, they lagged far behind plain diversity and could only manage to tie with canon expansion and the core definition if they were combined. The theme *did* emerge in some scholarly treatments of the problem, most notably that of Harold Bloom. Most English professors would probably acknowledge it as a concern for some of their colleagues. But it wasn't the kind of concern that proved to be pragmatically useful to English professors because the idea of a pure aesthetic dissolves in the real-life problem of putting together a college reading list, and few of them had any use for irrelevant controversy in their departmental lives. (Of course, controversy is the lifeblood of cultural criticism, popular debate, and publications outside departments, and, in those venues, irrelevance doesn't matter.)

These findings demonstrate that the definition of multiculturalism played an important role in forming opinion in the local arena. The symbolic-boundaries method even identified the *source* of disagreements over that contested region where diversity overlaps with value. And this approach allows me to explain why that particular boundary dispute was also apparent in the national arena: it draws on a relatively abstract definition of multiculturalism that doesn't concern itself with teaching and seeks to exclude concerns about diversity. But for conflict-averse English professors who faced pressures from students and administrators to become more multicultural, the path of least resistance was to define multiculturalism in a less controversial way.

Abstraction, Responsibility, and Opinion

The question of abstraction and groundedness emerged as an important theme in the previous chapter, and it looked like the effects were pretty clear. English professors, most of them, anyway, used different definitions from the pundits because they faced the reality of the classroom and that reduced their tendency to talk about multiculturalism abstractly. Now it seems that abstraction and groundedness may also be related to the way opinions form on multiculturalism. But looking at the relationship between groundedness and opinions introduced another complication.

Meanings that drew on only one concept were flexible and expansive in that they were not constrained by the limits of other ideas. That's why the English literature canon can seem so powerful in its abstract form—one need not consider how difficult it is to convey those ideas to eighteen–year-old college students. So, adding more issues to the mix made abstract ideas seem more real, and at first it seemed that grounded definitions were also clearer. That was certainly true for the two-arena definitions. But as definitions moved toward three and four arenas, things seemed to get more complicated. English professors more often pointed to the complexity of the issue and reported having mixed feelings about it.

Table 4.1 provides a more careful examination of those issues and confirms that the number of arenas employed in a definition is an important factor in stance-taking, but the effect does not work in a straight line. Mixed opinions predominated where definitions were either complex (involving three or four domains) or abstract (involving only one domain). Advocacy, on the other hand, was most prevalent among professors who drew on exactly two arenas of meaning. Those definitions also tended to be clearer, in the sense that they made concrete connections between a limited set of ideas and simultaneously

TABLE 4.1

Stance-taking by Number of Arenas Employed

Opinion	0 Arenas	1 Arena	2 Arenas	3 Arenas	4 Arenas	Overall
Favor multiculturalism	0%	21%	53%	30%	38%	36%
Oppose multiculturalism	57%	14%	10%	10%	0%	13%
Mixed/complex	43%	64%	38%	60%	63%	51%
Totals	100%	100%	100%	100%	100%	100%
Overall proportion	12%	23%	35%	17%	13%	100%

excluded many other possible meanings and associations that could complicate matters. Clear meanings led to clear support. Finally, opposition to multiculturalism was most closely associated with an absolute lack of meaning.
No meaning, no support.

Moving a definition from a single, abstract principle to a "grounded" definition that connects two ideas offered the most attractive meanings—those
that were most easily accepted. Adding more connections, however, added
complexity. That is, the implications of multiculturalism became so varied
and complex that it didn't make sense to take a single position on all those
possibilities. But single-arena definitions lent themselves to complexity, too,
by virtue of their abstraction. The potential connections to an abstract idea
seemed limitless, and remained unspecified.

In order to understand the way opinions toward multiculturalism varied
across the four departments, therefore, I needed to start by examining abstraction in the four departments. Table 4.2 thus compares the four departments according to the proportion of professors in each who used zero, one,
two, three, or four arenas of meaning to define multiculturalism. The results
confirm my suspicions from Chapter 3 that Ivory Towers' definition was primarily abstract (with 41 percent using only one arena). The definitions then
funneled into applied areas, tapering from 35 percent in two arenas to 24 percent in three. State Star's large department evidenced a more evenly distributed approach centered on clear, two-dimensional definitions (mostly canon

TABLE 4.2
Number of Arenas Employed, by Department

Number of Arenas	Ivory Towers	State Star	MC State	Cathletic
0	0%	12%	7%	33%
1	41%	18%	0%	33%
2	35%	35%	40%	25%
3	24%	18%	19%	8%
4	0%	18%	33%	0%

expansion) and tapering in both directions. As expected, definitions of multiculturalism at MC State and Cathletic University weighed in at opposite ends of the complexity spectrum. The cohesive Multicultural State faculty displayed the most-grounded definitions, while the Cathletic University faculty displayed not only a reluctance to make connections among the various arenas of meaning, but (unlike the abstract definitions in play at Ivory Towers) a reluctance to make any attempts at definition at all.

In addition to the groundedness in definitions of multiculturalism, Chapter 3 also revealed differences in the way professors in each department applied the problem of diversity to other arenas of their work lives. For example, MC State faculty were more likely to see the relevance of cultural diversity to teaching philosophies, while State Star faculty tended to see the connection to canons more clearly. While I assumed that those tendencies sprang from differences in professorial expectations in the four departments (varied emphasis on teaching, for example), I wanted to be sure.

Although the question wasn't on my interview guide, I searched the interview transcripts for any evidence of this that might have emerged in the course of the conversations. In particular, I searched for accounts of the motivation to *do something* about multiculturalism, evidence that a professor was inclined to change his or her own actions, or evidence of changes in the functioning of individual departments. Table 4.3 presents the percentage of professors in each department who oriented their sense of multicultural responsibility to each of six inductively coded reference points.

English professors at State Star had two ways of grounding their multicu-

TABLE 4.3

Unsolicited Accounts of Responsibility for Multiculturalism, by Department

Multiculturalism...	Ivory Towers	State Star	MC State	Cathletic	Total
in the discipline	5%	4%	0%	0%	3%
of students	5%	13%	0%	0%	5%
for students (in world)	5%	33%	10%	0%	14%
in the U.S.	37%	0%	5%	17%	13%
globally	11%	13%	0%	0%	7%
in Western history	5%	13%	0%	8%	7%
no account	32%	24%	85%	75%	51%
Total	100%	100%	100%	100%	100%

tural responsibilities in students. The first and less popular method treated the student body as a cultural unit. That is, faculty who grounded their multicultural responsibility to the diversity of their students did so because they thought their syllabi ought to reflect the cultures represented in the classroom as a matter of equity among the students in the room. The second, and more popular, method of grounding multicultural responsibility in students treated them as individuals swimming in a larger multiculture. These professors hoped to infuse their students with a wide array of cultural knowledge and a set of skills necessary to navigate a multicultural world. It is multiculturalism *for* students.

Multicultural responsibility at Ivory Towers was less grounded in the needs of students. Rather, students were just one type of vehicle through which professors could shape and preserve national culture. Professors at Ivory Towers taught multiculturalism to students in order to make the *world* better, rather than to make students better. They felt a responsibility to the cultural diversity already present in the United States and hoped to prepare their students to act responsibly toward it. It was not what the culture would do to their students, it was what their students would do to the culture.

Table 4.3 also indicates a key organizationally produced difference between elite and non-elite faculty. Although some professors in non-elite departments did offer a specific philosophical account of their responsibility to multiculturalism, most did not (75 versus 85 percent). In non-elite departments, multiculturalism seemed to come from the walls and the sky. And dealing with it was less a matter of rationalizing one's autonomous actions than it was a question of managing the interests and constraints posed by a larger bureaucracy.

While professors in the two elite departments appeared to conceptualize canon construction in the broad terms of shaping their discipline or specialty, canons in non-elite departments had a more concrete existence. There, the cannon came prepackaged, sandwiched between the covers of textbooks and anthologies. Many professors in this context agonized about their inability to cover all the material in an anthology during a single semester. This bothered them, in part, because leaving out a work literally meant skipping pages. Anthologies made teaching a "whole" canon appear almost possible. Anthologies also increased the sense that text-selection was a zero-sum game, where adding multicultural material more clearly meant skipping traditional works—old friends from previous years.

> I got this textbook here that has over two thousand pages of American literature. There's a lot of Hispanic writing there, Native American, just an awful lot of stuff, which is quite different than when I first taught this course. And, so, I can't get it covered in fifteen weeks, and the anthology is actually getting bigger. I wrestle with it and every once in a while I say, you know, I'm just, you know, it's just wrong for me to be thinking that I'm going to be able to cover everything. I just have to go and approach this whole thing differently. . . . I still do that regularly with my class. Can we conceive of other standards by which this would be a superior work to the work that's been canonized?

The example above is useful because it chronicles a single professor's struggle with the *structuring* effects of an anthology. Although that struggle demonstrates that the effect can change (from "teach all this" to "find a new way to choose readings from this monstrous book"), professors in non-elite departments that made heavy use of textbooks and anthologies were more likely to think of canons and reading lists as someone else's responsibility. In many departments, the instructors for introductory courses did not even select textbooks. All these factors shape the way professors think of their responsibility for multiculturalism, and that, in turn, can affect their opinion of it. Notice, however, that none of these factors I've discussed referenced a department's reputation for progressivism.

Prestigious Complexity and Public Support

At the outset of this project, I fully expected the sites selected for having a more "traditional" curriculum to have the highest levels of opposition to multiculturalism, and the sites having reputations for progressivism to show more support. Of course, there would be individual variation, but a department's political reputation would, I thought, almost certainly come from the political opinions of its faculty. I was wrong.

Although the proportion of faculty opposing multiculturalism *was* substantial at Cathletic University (42 percent), that department also had the second highest rate of advocacy. And State Star evidenced extremely low levels of opposition to multiculturalism, despite the fact that I selected that department for its reputation as one of the more conservative and traditionalist elite departments in the nation. Even Ivory Towers' ultra-progressive department on the cutting edge of literary scholarship broke with expectations by demonstrating the second highest rate of opposition to multiculturalism. In fact, only one department in my study, Multicultural State, seemed to match its overall reputation and curriculum design with a strong rate of advocacy (70 percent) and low opposition (5 percent) among professors there. The sense of public responsibility to multiculturalism in elite departments and the more complex definitions of the word appeared to be stronger factors than a department's reputation for conservatism.

Table 4.4 shows that, overall, the effect of prestige (elite versus non-elite departments) is a more powerful determinant of opinions than is progressivism. The difference between elite and non-elite departments, however, occurred not in a department's left–right orientation, but in its willingness to take a stand at all. In non-elite departments, 75 to 84 percent of the professors I interviewed had clear opinions about multiculturalism, but in elite departments the vast majority (68 to 75 percent) chose to outline the complexities of multiculturalism rather than take a firm position on the matter.

For example, one of the multicultural standouts at Ivory Towers—a professor specifically hired to increase the department's reputation as the leader

TABLE 4.4
Stance-taking, by Department

Opinion	Ivory Towers (N=19)	State Star (N=24)	MC State (N=20)	Cathletic (N=12)	Overall (N=61)
Favor multiculturalism	16%	21%	70%	42%	36%
Oppose multiculturalism	16%	4%	5%	42%	13%
Mixed/complex	68%	75%	25%	17%	51%
Totals	100%	100%	100%	100%	100%

in cutting-edge literary criticism—reacted to the word "multiculturalism" by adding an extra layer of complexity that made the premise of stance-taking irrelevant. She said, "I just find it a silly word because—to think of America as anything but . . . to think of America as . . . whatever the opposite of multiculturalism is—*unicultural*—is a historical lie, an act of the most silly kind of racial or ethnic nostalgia." As a result of her views on the meaning of multiculturalism, she positions herself outside the "battle" that, in her view, both distorts and oversimplifies the issues of cultural difference and power. Of course, in stepping outside the battle, she has actually moved to the political left of it. Dinesh D'Souza and William Bennett would have called her a multicultural radical who has inadequate respect for "American" or "Western" cultural traditions, yet she says she is not a clear proponent of multiculturalism.

This notable difference between elite and non-elite professors was also apparent in the interviews. Elite faculty often treated the debate as a literary text, full of complexities and insights to be analyzed, rather than as activity in which they might have participated. Non-elite professors, on the other hand, were less ambivalent. Stance-taking seemed like an obvious and important part of their jobs. Although professors in elite departments were more reluctant to take stands on multiculturalism, they did demonstrate great familiarity with the issues by producing longer, more detailed, responses to my question. Rather than state a position, they indicated both that they were familiar with the complexities of multiculturalism (a high-status cultural cue) and that they had given the question a great deal of genuine consideration.

The next most obvious pattern evident in Table 4.4 is the low level of opposition to multiculturalism at both of the public universities in my study (State Star and Multicultural State). This pattern resonates with Victoria Alexander's (1996) study of art museums, in which she found that publicly funded institutions show more concern than private ones for issues such as multiculturalism that are related to outreach—efforts to attract audiences that do not normally frequent museums.[3] That effect is also evident in Table 4.3, where professors in both public universities more often located their responsibility to multiculturalism in students than in national culture, while professors in the private universities were more likely to cite national concerns.

But finding evidence of that effect among English professors in publicly funded universities is particularly interesting because professors are much further removed from the funding mechanisms that directly produce the concern Alexander observed among museum professionals. In universities, the concern for public constituencies filtered down in the form of moral, that is to say, cultural, repertoires about motives and decisions, rather than in the form of an understanding of explicit institutional interests. In fact, many of the direct rewards for public stewardship disappeared before they reached individual professors, to the extent that a few complained to me that the university did not acknowledge their efforts on that front.

This public–private effect on stance-taking appeared despite the strong effect of prestige. Faculty in elite public universities complicated multiculturalism in order to avoid opposing it, but non-elite faculty were more likely to form clear opinions on the matter. Therefore, if those non-elite professors worked in publicly funded universities, the stances they took were more likely to be favorable. Regardless of prestige, the mission of service to a diverse citizenry increased the chances that professors who did choose sides in the debate would support multiculturalism.

In both private universities (Ivory Towers and Cathletic), the proportion of professors who favored multiculturalism was exactly equal to the proportion of those who opposed it. Although I am certain that the exactness of the relationship was mere coincidence, there was clearly no organizational incentive for the faculty of private universities to favor one side over the other. In sum, the propensity to accept multiculturalism is already apparent in popular culture and among administrators. That effect is reinforced in public universities, but the whole package is fed through a more substantial propensity for elite professors to complicate the matter and then report having mixed feelings about it.

Refinement: Multiple Meanings Lead to Mixed Opinions

One common way for professors, especially elite professors, to avoid stance-taking was to offer two definitions, one they favored and one they opposed. Here is a fascinating example from a State Star professor who said he was a fan of multiculturalism but only if it was the right brand, not "advocacy multiculturalism," which he vehemently opposed. In his final statement, however, he turned the tables to label advocacy multiculturalism "conventional" and the administrators who were swayed by it as "reprehensible."

> Comparative literature is a multiculturalist program, though it's, in many universities, a multicultural program without the cachet of multiculturalism. . . . I'm a great believer in multiculturalism, and I think that there are lots of urgent reasons to push multiculturalism and also to question the rhetoric behind most attempts to enforce a single core curriculum. . . . On the other hand, there is the strident rhetoric of multiculturalists who are the same people that are, you know, promoting death sentences against Salman Rushdie. It has to be said that, uh, the culture of advocacy multiculturalism is not so different from the culture of hype, which again seems to me to be, uh, a kind of heresy. . . . I know that multiculturalism has the ear of the same reprehensible and interfering administrators that a substantial program like comparative literature does not have. So if comparative literature does not have access to the same stodgy hearers—stodgy and venal and, you know, basically bureaucratic hearers—that multiculturalism does have access to, that seems to me an index of how advocacy multiculturalism is simply good at playing a conventionalist game.

Here is a more subtle example from another Ivory Towers professor, who pointed to the limits of his own definition by referring to a position he does not hold. We are left to imagine that other people might have opposing views. (Also notice that his view of the proper way to proceed assumes that departments get to hire new members on a somewhat regular basis—it makes some assumptions that might not apply to non-elite departments or financially strapped universities. These issues will get more attention in the next two chapters.)

> I tend to think it's a good thing for us to be able to offer courses on a wide variety of topics, and that's one way to describe the mission [of multiculturalism]. . . . *But I don't necessarily think that every course in the English department has to be written by the Rainbow Coalition.* I think that what's important is for a department to allow people who are interested in teaching fairly traditional stuff to continue to do that, but it's also important for a department to hire some people to do some new things so the students can make choices. But for students to expect that every class is going to be the model of, you know, political correctness and multiculturalism is unrealistic and unhealthy.

The most common distinction made by elite professors, however, could generally be described as the distinction between shallow and deep. My favorite came from an Ivory Towers professor who said:

> If they're all going to Princeton or Harvard or Stanford, by the time we're through with them, they're gonna look a lot like one another and their habits and dress or cuisine are going to be pretty minor stuff. In other words, there's a kind of vulgarized version of multiculturalism that I don't have much sympathy for. . . . [But] there's a kind of deeper goal of introducing people into the universe of world cultures which has immense value and importance. And I think it is not only consistent with the mission of the university, but it always has been a mission.

The tendency for individual professors to have multiple definition-opinion pairs offered three insights. First, it was one of the most popular mechanisms through which elite professors added complexity to the issue and justified their refusal to take stands on multiculturalism. Second, it offered further support for my claims that definitions *mattered* for the outcome of those debates and that ambiguity over definitions forestalled both a resolution to the debates and strategic action relative to multiculturalism. Finally, it should be noted that these elite professors showed a strong preference for the more challenging forms of multiculturalism that involved, for example, requiring students to learn a non-Western language, or that challenged some fundamental assumption about elite education. But it was the less-difficult versions of multiculturalism that were more likely to take hold.

The reluctance of elite professors to choose sides in the battle on multi-culturalism was surprisingly incongruous with the media reports of a culture war being waged in the hallways of academe. But sociologist Steven Brint noted a similar and more generalized inconsistency between the public image of intellectuals as combative dissenters and their real tendencies to avoid obvious stance-taking in his 1994 book, *In an Age of Experts*. In fact, Brint points out that this is a long-standing tension that exists apart from any particular controversy—multicultural or otherwise. He further connects the reluctance of public intellectuals to take stands on important social controversies to their structural positions relative to their audience and market. That is, public intellectuals rely on income from royalties and benefactors, so their writings must maintain a certain level of public appreciation to survive.

Brint's study even found an increased reluctance to choose sides among the more elite authors compared to other popular critics. His analysis of articles in influential journals revealed that the authors of papers in more prestigious journals did not often produce strong arguments for the value of one position over another (what Brint calls the *stance-taking frame*). Rather, the articles were more likely to contribute to the reader's understanding of a given topic by providing a more complex rendering of the issues involved, using what Brint calls the *refinement frame*. Brint uses these findings, however, to suggest that public intellectuals (many of whom are also elite college professors in the humanities) have stopped providing strong leadership for public opinion because they must appeal to the market of public opinion.

My research lends further support to Brint's underlying claim that structural positioning can influence ideological production. In my study, many organizational factors (systems of incentives that shape individual interests and success) worked at the local department level just as they did in Brint's national study. But the evidence presented here also reveals that the connection between the cultural products of intellectual elites and their organizational circumstances is not limited to the effect of "interests." Although there is plenty of clearly self-interested behavior in English departments and elsewhere, much of the political terrain surrounding multiculturalism has formed on the different definitions of multiculturalism generated by the four departments.

That is, structural differences among the four departments encouraged different systems of meaning which, in turn, lent themselves to different patterns of stance-taking. Advocating multiculturalism just made more sense at MC State than it did at Cathletic University. But Cathletic rejected multiculturalism to its own detriment—not for a lack of knowledge about its own interests, but for a lack of a cultural apparatus that could produce a productive, non-threatening definition of multiculturalism.

Chapter 5

B O U N D A R Y   D I S P U T E S :
T H E   C U L T U R A L   T E R R I T O R I E S   O F   A C A D E M E

> If I, as dean, wanted to have one great department, it wouldn't
> be the English department. . . . Because it is a moving target,
> there's no longer a kind of body of knowledge or a kind of de-
> mand you can make, as you can in history. You can have all
> kinds of theories about how history works, but you had damned
> well better know Poland and Sweden are different countries.
> There's no sense of the discipline as a discipline. . . . It becomes
> that much harder to be sure you're hiring right or you're getting
> the right things in. . . . A lot of people in English have rejected
> that idea, so there's . . . there's, nothing! Everything is arbitrary.
>
> —*English professor turned dean*

The connection between multiculturalism and disciplinary boundaries was
central to both popular and local understandings of the crisis in English literature. What is and is not canonical? What is and is not worthy of scholarly
attention? What should students read in college English classes? How far can
English professors reach in their attempts to change or preserve national culture? All these questions challenged the boundaries of English literature, and
the answers threatened to change (or dissolve) the intellectual responsibilities of English professors. Thus, despite some confusion over the exact
meaning of multiculturalism, it was clear that the word implied an expansion of conventional disciplinary perimeters. It was also clear that the experience of shifting boundaries could be disconcerting to people who depended on them.

To make matters even more confusing, the battles among English professors came to represent boundary conflicts in the national polity, so that multiculturalism implied expanding the boundaries of citizenship as much as it
implied expanding the boundaries of literature. As is the case for other forms

of cultural representation, however, the medium (the means of expression, the book, the painting, or the symbolic struggle over culture) had its own set of technological potentials and limitations that accidentally influenced the range of expression that was possible. In other words, once the disputes over English literature came to represent larger social tensions, some idiosyncrasies of academic politics got tangled up with our larger understanding of multiculturalism outside of universities.

But the national-level battles were also fueled by a more familiar kind of turf war. This was the battle over old-fashioned resources, in the form of students.

The "Crisis" in English Literature

In the last decade of the twentieth century, the popular press made no fewer than 954 references to a "crisis" in the humanities that referred to debates over multiculturalism and its effects on core areas of knowledge within a given discipline. In a small but significant portion of those articles, however, the "crisis" also referred to declining *enrollments* in the humanities and possible connections between enrollment drops and the highly publicized battles over multiculturalism in course content.[1] In fact, declining enrollments and evolving curricula in English literature were more closely connected than most observers recognized. Students were migrating across disciplinary boundaries in droves, leaving the liberal arts and heading for more vocationally specific college majors such as Business and Accounting. All the humanities suffered from this migration, but English took the most dramatic hit. The resulting "crisis," at the axis of the trend toward multiculturalism and the decline of enrollments, set the stage for an explosive battle over multiculturalism that had two apparent causes. One cause was a concrete and observable decline in students and resources for English departments. The second cause was an intangible and alleged decline of Western culture. Why focus on the ephemeral issue? Because English professors had some control over that one.

Of course, any story of crisis is likely to overstate the degree of stability that preceded it, and the crisis in English literature was no exception. Several scholars documented—sometimes with amusement—the frequency with which commentators claimed that the once stable discipline of English literature had been propelled into a state of crisis.[2] But English literature's experience of decline did stem, in part, from it's previous successes. English was one of the most popular majors during the post–World War II boom in college enrollments (fueled by the G.I. Bill). And the discipline maintained its claim that its courses distributed elements of high culture, and thus "the" national literature. As such, familiarity with English literature was a defining feature of the college experience, and the discipline held a secure place in the core of most curricula.

But in the decades that followed, the discipline grew so rapidly that national meetings became nearly impossible. While English was losing its sense of identity, college students were undergoing changes of their own. They had become a much larger, less elite group, and they had high hopes that a college degree would propel them into the tiny social class that once had a monopoly on college degrees. When that plan began to seem less secure than first imagined, college students sought a more direct route: majoring in fields that would train them for high-paying jobs—degrees in business, engineering and computer science. That effect was far more pronounced in non–elite colleges like Cathletic and MC State than it was at State Star and Ivory Towers, where the career trajectories of elite students were more secure. But that didn't stop William Bennett from blaming English professors, and it didn't stop other cultural critics from directing their attacks at elite colleges.

By the early 1980s, English professors knew they were in trouble. Enrollments were down, anxieties were up, the job market was dismal, and English was fast losing its stronghold on the core of college education. It was also a reverberating crisis; elite departments felt the pinch, too, when the market for their Ph.D. students dried up. Inside departments, in professional meetings, and in journals, English professors talked frequently about the possible causes of and solutions to their predicament. Ironically, it was William Bennett who recognized that the discipline desperately needed to make a stronger claim for its own importance—to "reclaim a legacy," in his words—or, as it turned out, to revamp an identity.

Even more ironically, Bennett's exaggerated attack on the humanities appears to have worked. He cut through those complex realities and named a single foe: multicultural English professors. Through his framing, the enrollment crisis came to be understood as the result of a "culture war," not changes in institutional structures, student demographics, or the economic interests of parents. But Bennett also sparked that infamous controversy—the one that made English professors seem interesting. And he drew national attention to the possibility that English departments might be the most exciting places to study culture, cultural difference, even race, gender, sexuality, and migration (to the dismay of many sociologists).

The disciplines that had traditionally held domain over those topics watched in horror as the canon war dramatically redefined English literature. No longer a stale and irrelevant field devoted to glorifying books, English was the place where hip students could study all the burning questions of the day (assuming their university had experienced said transformation). Forget the social sciences with their math requirements and fieldwork!

The annual convention of the Modern Language Association, likewise, gained a risqué sense of allure. It became the place where journalists could be sure to find the craziest panel titles. For thrills of that sort, see Anne Matthews's February 10, 1991, report on the convention in the *New York Times* (43). It includes interviews with Andrew Ross and Roger Kimball, as well as the required list of flashy paper titles. Who would want to read a story about a convention for gray-haired, tweed-clad fans of T. S. Eliot?

When I attended an MLA convention for my research, I did see some tweed (and not nearly as much light-blue and brown polyester as I see at sociology conventions), but mostly it was a sea of black fabric. In the women's restroom, I found several attendees complaining about the "automatic" sink faucets that didn't seem to work. One of them noted that the electronic eye needed to be able to reflect an infrared beam off of something—most effectively, white or light-colored clothing. Those sinks would not get much use while the MLA was in town! But the "hip" feel of the MLA is exaggerated by the fact that the association has grown so large. It can't really serve its entire constituency, so it revolves around the academic job market, which is dominated by youngsters and superstars. Settled scholars in less elite positions are served almost exclusively by societies devoted to specific fields of study and sometimes regional associations. So the effect is dramatic and shocking to people both inside and outside of academe. (This theme was repeated to me often, but the most colorful rejection of the MLA came from a senior Ivory Towers professor, who said, "I'm as likely to go to the national meeting of the Bonsai Association.")

Matthews introduced her *New York Times* readers to Andrew Ross by describing his outfit, which she contrasted not to musty tweed but to "assistant professors in black leather pegged pants." Here is her description of Ross, followed, in the next paragraph, by her description of the MLA:

> He straightens his hand-painted Japanese tie, smoothes his pale mango wool-and-silk Comme des Garcons blazer. . . . Politely sidestepping a clutch of Dante experts, Ross disappears into an elevator, off to present a paper on censorship, Mapplethorpe, and 2 Live Crew.
> The Modern Language Association of America is about scholarly research and hiring, money, power and fashion—not always in that order. At the most recent convocation, members could choose among a dizzying 2,400 scholarly presentations, including the sedate ("Encyclopedias as a Literary Genre"), the arcane ("Aspects of Iconicity in Some Indiana Hydronyms") and the standing-room-only ("The Sodomitical Tourist"; "Victorian Underwear and Representations of the Female Body").

If Bennett was trying to send the humanities back to where they came from, he failed. But he did succeed in revitalizing the discipline by attracting attention to the dramatic changes underway within it. Like it or not, "English Lit" was hot!

Inside English departments, however, change happened more slowly. The MLA could offer a slightly distorted view of the changes underway in the discipline (with some overemphasis on intellectual fad), but it could not reflect the state of education in English literature because it had almost no grounding in the more permanent institutional conditions of life in academe. It's not that English departments didn't experience those trends. They did. But the grounded experience of cultural change was somewhat less exciting, and much more difficult. New fields of study clashed with disciplinary boundaries, professional expectations, and, as the next chapter will explain, curricular requirements. Taken alone, no amount of student excitement about a new course on lesbian cinema could make it count toward the major. That would require department-wide negotiation. Nor could a best-selling novel win tenure for its author in a department that only considers literary criticism when making tenure decisions. For departments that drew their disciplinary boundaries that way, writing a terrific novel would be about as useful for tenure as winning an Olympic gold medal—impressive, but irrelevant.

In an organizational sense, the way each of my four departments managed their own disciplinary boundary constituted the job description of its members and defined the legitimacy of their work, in terms of hiring, promotion, and tenure decisions, as well as teaching assignments, curriculum structure, and access to resources such as travel funds. Disciplinary boundaries also defined the limits of multiculturalism (in English literature), and that's crucial to understanding how multiculturalism worked inside English departments.

Boundaries of all kinds are often the sites of conflict, and multiculturalism challenged the boundaries of English literature by attempting to bring attention to works that had previously been excluded. Every time someone referred to a work or an author as non-traditional, they located it near that boundary. The only question was whether the boundary lay in its "traditional" location for that particular context. In short, the way a department defined its own boundary determined whether multicultural literature would be a controversial topic for departmental activity.

State Star

Not every English department of the era was especially aware of the role boundaries played in their experiences with conflict over multiculturalism. They didn't always think consciously about the way they imagined and invoked their local version of disciplinary boundaries or how theirs compared to other versions of that boundary. State Star, however, was exceptionally aware of the need to reestablish the boundaries of its jurisdiction and, therefore, made some of those boundaries more explicit than most departments. In the 1995 undergraduate catalog, the State Star Department of English began its section with the following introduction:

> From Geoffrey Chaucer's bawdy *Wife of Bath* to James Joyce's stately, plump *Buck Mulligan*, from Elizabeth Bishop's "manmoth" to Toni Morrison's *Milkman*, the study of imaginative literature is justified not only by the greatness of individual works but by the insights such works give into the origins of cultures, individuals, and modes of perception. Students will study literary achievement both in its own terms and in the context of the many cultural traditions that co-exist under the word English (African-American, feminist, Irish, and Anglo-Saxon, for example).

This statement made clear the department's attempt to demonstrate inclusiveness with specific references to a variety of authors and sources of "greatness." The English department chose to include both a canonical poet who wrote in Middle English and a popular African American woman, novelist, and scholar who is still writing successfully in the United States for both academic and popular audiences. Though broad, the range might have been even wider. For example, it could have been described as including works "from Homer to Spike Lee," or it could have named little-known authors who had earned "literary achievement" without having earned fame. Thus, the State Star English department communicated literary breadth while maintaining relatively conventional disciplinary boundaries around "literature."

Although the trend toward adopting a business logic in higher education affected non-elite universities more profoundly than the elite (as we'll see more clearly below), places like State Star were not immune. They faced hard questions from the prominent business leaders on their boards of visitors and from state legislatures, and hiring business consultants even became a routine activity for State Star's administration.[3] Those sorts of pressures eventually filtered down to departments, professors, and classrooms, and the English department was facing one of those challenges when I arrived.

State Star's departmental self-examination, prompted by budget-cutting initiatives in the state legislature, had generated a great deal of musing about the scope of its jurisdiction, and the occupational hazards of asking English professors for analytical reports were obvious. In the chair's office, under a worktable, there were two boxes of evaluative material written by individual members of the faculty. Through a long process of examining the department's mission, goals, and effectiveness, the faculty identified large areas of consensus, and most important, they clarified and formalized their own disciplinary boundary.[4]

Interviews further revealed that the department had specifically discussed the range of material that should be considered its domain and had settled on *limiting* themselves to the broadest possible definition they could generate— "works written in English." Two professors there used those exact words, and another produced a close approximation. All emphasized, however, that the department interpreted that boundary broadly, so that poems, songs, and plays would qualify because they are passed on to us in written form. Note, however, that this description of the department's intellectual boundary addressed only the object of study and not the methods literary scholars used to study them. Even the meaning of the word "works" could be a problem. Did it mean to imply, for example, words written only for the sake of writing? Would a literary analysis of a television talk show transcript be legitimate? How about newspapers, appointment planners, grocery lists, or e-mail? Any demarcation of intellectual boundaries will face clarification as it is applied in practice.

Although the new boundary was significantly broader than the de facto boundary that applied in earlier years, it did not manage to encompass all the scholarly work of every department member. One exception managed to escalate into a highly politicized tenure battle, in which the deciding factor was reported to have been whether an article in a leading feminist journal would be counted toward tenure in the English department. That crisis exemplifies the sort of problem Ivory Towers managed to avoid in its many unanimous tenure and promotion decisions.

One of the more senior State Star professors provided an interesting description of his department's evolving self-description that illuminated the way such boundaries operated over time. His description was particularly interesting because he had never considered himself to be an insider. Like most of his contemporaries, he disliked the new emphasis on literary theory, yet he was not in favor of excluding it. (The theoretical movements he references are the ones normally allied with—or, more accurately, confused with—multiculturalism.) Notice, also, that he described the department's first entrée onto the disciplinary scene as being the result of a concentration on cutting-edge literary work that challenged an earlier generation's understanding of the discipline. It sounds funny in its contemporary context.

> This was a hotbed of bibliographers for a long time, which didn't interest me at all, but it didn't make any difference because they left me alone to do what I wanted to do. Since that time, I think it's fair to say that there's kind of a schism in the department between those of us who have little interest in theory and those of us who have a great interest in theory. . . . We don't belong to the Modern Language Association anymore. We belong to that other one whose name I can't remember right now, and we do pretty much hang out together. And most of those people are very senior—been around for thirty or thirty-five years. . . . I think it's fine, that it [theory] should be here in English or in the languages, in any case. I would like to see a little less emphasis on it. I'd like to see it as ancillary to a program of study of literature. I would not like to see it take

over as it seems to have done, or nearly to have done, here. But this is the logical place to have theory.

The deliberate democracy that characterized governance structures at State Star thus allowed most professors there to act as autonomous scholars. In addition, wherever *external* forces threatened that freedom (such as when administrators went searching for good places to cut budgets), the department's collective front protected it from such threats while avoiding publicly visible battles. There were still conflicts, but subjecting field-level debates to careful scrutiny reduced the chances of *accidental* antagonisms over multiculturalism by alerting professors who remained securely in the center that some of their valued colleagues risked exclusion.

I characterize the political processes at State Star as "deliberate" because they stood out in my research as the most reflective, and that trait applied to the department's boundary management as well. They did not deny the importance of disciplinary boundaries, nor did they pretend that such boundaries were externally generated. Rather, the English department at State Star carefully defined its own boundary and it acknowledged some of the ways in which it excluded the work of some professors there. There is no doubt that such exclusionary practices could be a source of conflict and discontent in the department. (Shortly, we will meet an Ivory Towers professor who had left her previous appointment because of similar practices.) But State Star made the source of such disgruntlement obvious. It was a line in the sand.

The conscious nature of State Star's approach to defining the boundaries of its own turf also called attention to what sociologist Thomas Gieryn (1983) called *boundary work*—all the activities that create, enforce, or draw attention to the significance of a boundary—the subtle and the obvious, the symbolic and the physical, walls, laws, rituals, statuses, and linguistic distinctions (such as "us" and "them"). All these things make boundaries exist, and all the activities described, from building walls to unconsciously using the word "they," can be understood as boundary work. Although the English professors at State Star were acutely aware of their turf-marking activities, boundary work can also be simultaneously intense and unconscious. Harvard sociologist Michèle Lamont studies that kind of boundary work in relation to class, race, and nationality. In *The Dignity of Working Men* and *Money, Morals, and Manners*, she highlights the fact that people can guard the symbolic boundaries of status and identity fiercely without ever noticing the exclusionary and boundary-marking significance of their actions.

Less deliberate forms of boundary work can result in the sort of explosions often associated with battles over multiculturalism. For example, to advocate "including multicultural literature" in a college English course implies, among other things, adding works by and about people of color. By extension, rejecting multiculturalism implies excluding such works and thereby excluding the authors. Here, boundary work related to the maintenance of disciplinary boundaries aligns with the boundaries of meaning we saw in definitions of multiculturalism. When traditionalist English professors got accused of racism, it was usually because they had failed to recognize (or acknowledge) their scholarly decisions as *social* boundary work. This often happened to the complete bewilderment of "innocent" traditionalists, who failed to notice that their claims about universal literary value had worked to defend a *racial* boundary and to justify racial exclusion.[5]

In definitions of multiculturalism, professors who wanted to exclude attention to diversity generally described the issue as a matter of aesthetic judgments (values) that were, they argued, correct, *but that had been made in the distant past and that, now, applied only to literature, not to people.* Drawing disciplinary boundaries would generally activate the same kinds of concerns for deciding what does or does not belong in the discipline based on some sort of judgment. But when referring to a department's disciplinary boundaries, the judgments were applied to people—people who might have an office down the hall. At that point, any apparent biases stopped being about books and started being about people. Hence, the explosive tenure case at State Star. If the question of disciplinary boundaries had not partially coincided with a question about the legitimacy of feminist scholarship, the question would have been less explosive and more technical. It would also have attracted less attention. The story would have been less heinous and less interesting, less likely to have escaped the confidential boundaries of tenure deliberations, and then less often and less widely repeated.

No amount of literary purism can change the fact that these two boundaries collided, but State Star's strategy suggested that it was possible to acknowledge that source of conflict by making both the location and consequences of intellectual boundaries less ambiguous. In other words, State Star professors did not often trip over hidden boundaries while I was there. When they invoked their boundaries, whether for the purposes of exclusion or self-defense, they did so with full knowledge of the extent to which their actions would be controversial. Thus, the existence of that clear boundary only made conflict more conscious. It did not, by itself, make conflict less likely. In practice, English professors usually avoid a real fight if they can. It's not an easy line to walk, though. Professors often enjoy the intellectual exercise of hashing out such questions (as evidenced by the boxes of written analyses in the chair's office). That's why it's so helpful to have clear signposts at dangerous intersections.

Ivory Towers

In contrast to State Star's explicit boundary work, a key feature of Ivory Towers' reorganization in the late 1980s was an emphasis on the *destruction* of disciplinary boundaries. The chair specifically identified such boundaries as hindrances to cutting-edge work in literary criticism. Therefore, the new recruits were promised something special that they couldn't find elsewhere — an environment where their boundary-challenging work would be valued. Notice that the reference to pseudonyms in the quote below implies that writing outside the disciplinary boundary could *hurt* this professor's chances for promotion at some universities.

> I came to [Ivory Towers] explicitly because [the chair] said, "Of course you can do all those things." Whereas at several major famous institutions [references deleted], it was clear that if I stayed there or went to the other universities I would either have to keep writing some of my work pseudonymously . . . or that just sort of wouldn't count. . . . I really have incredible latitude to do what I want to do, and to get enormous support from university. In any institution you can do crazy work in different fields, but to be considered a respected member of the faculty, and even a prized member of the faculty, versus a pariah, is really rare. I feel very grateful to have that kind of opportunity. Also I think it affects the kind of work students do. Students here tend to be doing really exciting, interesting, innovative work and come up with connections that might not be the expected ones.

Having read each department's catalog entry long before case selection, I remembered that Ivory Towers' curricular requirements were nearly unspecified. I returned to the catalog for this portion of the analysis, expecting the English department's entry to say something similar to what respondents had told me—that majors would not be constrained by disciplinary boundaries. I expected an introductory statement that said something like, "We encourage our majors to take classes outside the department," or to "sample broadly," or to "construct an individualized program of study." What I found provided a poignant example of how much we take boundaries for granted.

In stark contrast to State Star's carefully defined mission, the English department at Ivory Towers *had no introductory statement at all* in the 1996 undergraduate catalog. Although that omission was consistent with the department's insistence on denying disciplinary boundaries, the lack of an introductory statement was unprecedented, in my experience. Not only did all the other departments in my study begin their sections of their respective catalogs with an introduction or mission statement, all the other departments at Ivory Towers did so as well. English was the only exception.

But here is the important point about the way the English department at Ivory Towers chose to represent its expansive breadth. To encourage interdisciplinary work would be to discourage traditional programs—to specifically map the turf of English literature at Ivory Towers as outside the center of the discipline—to draw a boundary in a different location rather than to go without. Instead, the department simply removed boundaries whenever possible. The elimination of disciplinary boundaries even extended to the graduate curriculum, where students were not required to take *any* particular course. It was possible to earn a doctoral degree in English by taking courses entirely *outside* the department, although I did not find any cases of that in practice.

Here's how a somewhat less radical member of the department described the criteria for those miraculously unanimous hires. We will see, shortly, that the department did manage to make good hiring decisions, which would be terribly important in the future. But notice, also, that there was a tension in the conscious decision not to hire people who resembled the current members of the department.

> I think what the department looks for is a great deal of intelligence and professional alertness. Uh, the department here certainly does not look for individuals who are happy to slumber in some dignified corner of this university and simply write a certain kind of criticism. I think it

looks for people who are likely to surprise at some point or other. . . . I'd rather see us occasionally make a bad choice but have taken the risk than never take the risk and always hire someone who does a certain kind of inquiry that we all recognize because it's really just *us* again. Then one makes bad hires, and there are universities [examples deleted] that have made *terrible* decisions for decades now.

The Ivory Towers English department built a strong reputation on the idea of finding cutting-edge scholars that were not just wacky but also smart. They also tried to hire good teachers, an unusual move that helped boost their sanity quotient, given the high concentration of genius there. And they tenured many of their junior faculty, another unusual move for prestigious departments. All these choices helped build a more solid social foundation for the department underneath its boundaryless reputation and the absence of obvious structure. History can record the story of Ivory Towers' sudden and glorious rise to fame as a success story. It probably won't be recorded that way, though, because sensational news stories do that kind of recordkeeping for us, and some of it is shockingly inaccurate. I have read of key figures having "left the department" only to discover that they "left" to go into administration or to take advantage of some other opportunity in the university.

Although the Ivory Towers English department has maintained a very high status in the discipline for twenty years now, it also suffered some setbacks after my visit. Today, the department is not quite as hot as it once was, but it is also less vulnerable. The department has an introductory statement that defines its boundaries far beyond those of State Star's English department. Like State Star's introduction, the Ivory Towers' introduction includes a list of authors intended to highlight the expansiveness of the discipline, but unlike State Star's statement, it also lists objects of study in the same manner and extends its territory beyond the written word.

The most serious setbacks at Ivory Towers could be described as threats from external forces (including bad publicity)—the press and the university administration. At every juncture, the key factor involved was that the department hadn't managed to do something for itself—something like figure out what its mission was or how it would make key decisions and allocate resources. Eventually, other forces would step in to take over apparently neglected duties. Even the media attention can be understood in this way. The Ivory Towers English department did not have a description of itself that could defend it from any portrayal a journalist or pundit wanted to impose on it, so, to the outside world, the media depiction was the only one in play.

In short, I would argue that when the Ivory Towers English department obliterated its disciplinary boundary, it not only gained an extraordinary degree of artistic freedom, it also lost the protective functions that such a boundary could have provided. When the department was really operating without a boundary (which, as I've said, requires a difficult cognitive leap that wasn't always possible to maintain), it was, literally, working without an institutional safety net. Progress can certainly go much faster without the inconvenience of making safety preparations, and the sky's the limit for creative genius, but the slightest mistake can mean disaster. Working without a disciplinary boundary meant that Ivory Towers was less able to describe itself or its strengths. When things went well, it was "magical," but when they went poorly, the department was entirely unable to defend its turf because it couldn't *define* its turf.

In short, the most radical structural condition at Ivory Towers—the only thing I encountered in my tour of the discipline that even *remotely* resembled the radical promise of multiculturalism to shake the foundations of the academy and possibly Western culture—was unsustainable in its institutional context. And that problem didn't come down to money and "hard structures"; it came down to identity—meaning, boundaries, and rhetoric.

Multicultural State

The definition of English literature in non-elite universities responded to a drastically different set of contextual problems having less to do with new trends in literary criticism and more to do with the expectations of a new middle class that needed some assurance that their investment in college tuition would pay off in cold cash, not just intellectual development. One effect of this shift was that, for the purpose of attracting students, the "value" of an education came to be measured primarily by the financial success of an institution's graduates.

As colleges began selling improved job prospects to potential customers, students also shifted their focus from the "gentlemanly" pursuits of enculturation to pre-professional job preparation. Multicultural State's English department turned out to provide an exceptionally clear example of these forces at work because it highlighted those changes and found ways to benefit from them.

In stark contrast to Ivory Towers' boundarylessness, the Multicultural State English department made strategic use of its ever-expanding boundary in an almost imperialist fashion, relative to the larger university community. In fact, this department stood out in my analysis for its centrality to the larger university's function. It actively extended its reach into new territories, and it moved to formalize those inroads with great speed. For example, the English department spearheaded several important trends in the university, including its policy solution to the problem of multiculturalism (described earlier), a translation of liberal arts training to career skills, and a "writing across the curriculum" program that allowed the department to *expand* its influence across the university rather than surrendering its jurisdiction over writing. One professor even initiated a faculty development writing program that put the English department at the center of a university-wide effort to nurture more scholarly publication among the faculty. That kind of expansion would not have been possible if the department had rejected the writing and composition areas of the discipline, the way every other department in my study did.

It is not surprising, therefore, that the specifically multicultural expansion of disciplinary boundaries was more firmly institutionalized at MC State than it was at any of the other sites. English professors at MC State did not report an awareness of their own boundaries as consciously as the elite departments did. Nevertheless, the introduction to the English section of the undergraduate catalog performed this important boundary work. It said: "A major in English prepares students for *careers* in which good communication, a knowledge of people, an awareness of ideas, and clear thinking are important" (emphasis added).

In terms of constraining specialties, this statement may have provided as much practical breadth as Ivory Towers' non-statement. There was no mention of literature or even English language, in particular. Instead, the statement focused on the general: people, ideas, communication. On the other hand, the unilateral emphasis on careers did specify the purpose of learning these skills—a vocational purpose that responded to the growing need for regional colleges to advertise job skills to prospective students. That definition eliminated the possibility that students should be learning to discern literary value and beauty or learning to become "cultured" (two popular ideas I plucked from the air for the purposes of contrast). Instead, the English department at MC State defined its discipline in terms supportive of local trends toward vocationalization. Although that particular framing of the discipline was broad enough to avoid affecting everyday routines, professors at Multicultural State did, in fact, take vocational concerns seriously, making frequent references to the real-world applications of the skills they taught.

Multicultural State's English department tapped another important source of power and status within the university by bringing composition courses within the boundary of its professional activity. Not only did many full-time professors (in addition to adjuncts and part-timers) volunteer to teach composition, they did so with care. The chair reported the department's history of treating composition courses like literature courses, in terms of the authority instructors had over their own syllabi.

> This department has a history and a reputation among book reps. . . . It never had any textbook selected for any course, and so every teacher could do what he or she damn well pleased. The whole idea was freedom, and the book reps were pulling their hair out because it meant that they had to sell to every individual teacher, and they couldn't go in and sell the program. . . . And they [the professors] were proud of it![6]

Many of the professors there also specialized in fields related to composition (rhetoric, linguistics, etc.), and the department's self-assured decision to remove the study of literature from its year-long sequence in freshman English further reflected its dedication to the art of writing.

Thus, boundary work at Multicultural State expanded the jurisdiction of its specialty from the study of literature to vocational writing. Furthermore, the multiculturalism policy in place there helped resolve the problem that faculty in other departments faced when I asked how they felt about multiculturalism: it defined the word for them and brought the idea safely inside the boundaries of their roles as English professors. The faculty at MC State rarely asked me what I meant by the word, and they had no stories of battles over it or the curriculum. For this department, the matter was settled long ago.

It is significant that MC State's "Multiculturalism Policy" was passed just as William Bennett began his attack on English professors, but before the specific word "multiculturalism" became synonymous with conflict. Because they settled the matter of multiculturalism before it became an issue, English professors at MC State took pity on the rest of the profession for its travails over the issue. Their policy tamed multiculturalism. It prevented critics of English departments from having control of the word's meaning, and it prevented multiculturalism from becoming an attempt to abolish canons or the discipline. It also specified faculty members' individual responsibilities relative to cultural diversity, which might have been considered a burden to some. But to those most devoted to multiculturalism, it set limits on what could otherwise have been an expansive arena of guilt.

The multiculturalism policy essentially solved the problem of predicting the "right" sort of behavior with respect to the sacred word. (Remember the Ivory Towers professor who said the word reminded him of an episode of the *Twilight Zone*, "where the children can send their parents to the cornfield where they will vanish if the parents say the wrong thing, but the parents never know what the wrong thing will be"? Problem solved.) In addition, the university administration saw the department's policy as a major accomplishment in the struggle to address multiculturalism peaceably and encouraged other departments in the university to produce similar statements (without success).

In terms of faculty autonomy, however, the policy served as a statement of intentions rather than as an enforced regulation. That was an important factor in the policy's success. With respect to boundaries, the multiculturalism policy appeared to *compel* breadth, rather than merely allow it. That was an unusual and perhaps unacceptable feature of the policy, from the perspective of other departments. But members of the Multicultural State English department did not read it as a prescription. They read it as boundary work—a powerful claim about the centrality of literary works that were once excluded from the realm of legitimate scholarly attention. As such, they defended the policy vigorously and interpreted any attack on it as an attack on non-traditional literature.

Cathletic University

Among the four departments, I found the most dramatic example of a boundary problem at Cathletic University, where disciplinary boundaries were narrowly drawn and rigidly, though unconsciously, enforced. And as the contrast with Multicultural State's success story suggests, Cathletic's English department was in some trouble with their administration and they had far less control over their own conditions than the other departments in my study.

One of the most striking features of boundary activity at Cathletic University revealed a process that probably affected all four departments to some extent: the boundaries and definitions that ruled academic activities at Cathletic built on the divisions of more familiar social categories such as age, gender, and race.[7] For example, when I asked one professor whether the definition of a "good professor" was generally agreed upon in the department, she referred to the generation gap there in a fashion typical of the local culture at Cathletic University. Rather than reporting conflict, she said that there was no point in discussing such matters. She cryptically avoided constructing sides as right and wrong, but she did point to the dividing line—something no one in other departments did.

> Ummmm, uh, I don't know that it [agreement] matters much. Everyone, except for a small handful of us, has tenure so . . . I think when you've got a lot of people who have been doing the same thing for a long time, those kinds of issues don't necessarily come up. It's only four of us in the last thirty years.

Another junior professor echoed the sentiment that (largely unspoken) disagreements in the department stemmed from a generation gap caused by the hiring freeze and a more general decline in majors. This claim was especially important because the professor who made it actually had a mixed opinion on multiculturalism—not one that was firmly structured by graduate training or age. In addition, the quote reveals some discomfort with the subject, in that it begins fairly understated and then becomes disjoined as it approaches a clearer claim at the end (which, I'll argue below, is probably misleading).

> I'd say there's some disagreement about that. There's probably some grounds for there being, disagreement, for example, as regards the canon—what should be taught, what shouldn't be taught. Uhhh . . .

some departments don't [pause] there's really armed camps in many departments. This department—people—I think, um, I—it's interesting because this department—A great many people were hired in one fell swoop somewhere in the late fifties or early sixties, and only just now those people are retiring, and so there's a big sort of [pause] gap between junior and senior faculty.

The division between tenured and untenured members of the department, however, was not merely a matter of rank. There was also a significant age gap. The primary exacerbating factor at Cathletic University, however, was the *size* of the hiring gap. Whereas Multicultural State's English department created five new full-time, tenure-track positions in addition to their normal turnover during the 1970s (when most of higher education was facing financial decline), the Cathletic English department hired no one. In fact, Cathletic University *reduced* the size of its English department during that period, through attrition. As a result of the hiring gap at Cathletic, age differences were more salient, fundamental differences in Ph.D. training were more striking, and anxiety about multiculturalism was far more common at Cathletic than at any other department in my study.

The generation gap at Cathletic did not, however, work *alone* to separate (usually younger) supporters of multiculturalism from (usually older) opponents. The dividing line between supporters and opponents was also reinforced by race, gender, age, Ph.D. generation (invoking "schools of thought" and other ideological differences), and, as mentioned above, tenure. The alignment of these five status boundaries suggests a powerful crystallization of everyday social patterns, so that reaching out to peers in one status category reinforced other boundaries. For example, friendships among junior faculty also implied friendships among women, among people under thirty-five, among people who had similar forms of training in literature, and among people who supported canonical revision. Through the same structures, friendships among faculty with tenure were friendships among white people who, for example, did not encounter post-structuralism in graduate school.

The coexisting boundaries at Cathletic constituted an impressive consolidation of six social and political categories: gender, age, tenure, Ph.D. generation, orientation toward multiculturalism, and race (in that the tenured professors were all white and the untenured ones were not all white). In the consolidation of six statuses across twelve people, there were only three people in the department who had an incongruent status on any one of those categories, and, in each case, gender was the out-of-place category. Those incongruent statuses allowed them to move across a battle line that was otherwise rigidly structured.

This boundary alignment can pose a fairly serious problem when some of the boundaries in question are destructive or unwanted while others are considered benign or legitimate. This is not only because one boundary can reinforce another, but because coincidental boundaries can cause us to misattribute the causes of the problem at hand, preferring to choose other (sometimes exotic and improbable) explanations over more familiar and painful culprits such as race or gender problems. The Cathletic professor above who cited a generation gap as the culprit made just that mistake. Faculty attributed their division over multiculturalism to the "obvious" problem of the generation gap, so the fact that the more powerful and tenured members of the department also opposed multiculturalism was just a byproduct of history. But they were wrong.

Opposition to multiculturalism was not primarily structured by generation or tenure in Cathletic's English department. Rather, the three professors in the department with incongruent statuses revealed that the primary factor was gender. Only two professors at Cathletic reported having mixed or agnostic feelings about multiculturalism, and both of them had incongruent statuses relative to their gender. The third, whom I'll refer to with both gender pronouns to preserve anonymity, was avid about his or her opinion on multiculturalism, and it did not match that of his or her status peers.

Despite the perfectly plausible claim that changes in graduate training were to blame, opinion on multiculturalism followed gender lines. The effect of the generation gap (and the tenure gap), did play a significant role, however. Ph.D. training provided the rationale for the staunchly traditional curriculum, and tenure was the reason no one bothered to pursue the issue of multiculturalism.

Given the generational rift and the boundary coincidences that supported it (most importantly, the tenure distinction), it should not be surprising that the boundaries defining the turf of English literature at Cathletic University were closely guarded. The department's brief catalog introduction, for example, drew its boundaries narrowly: "The English major aims to provide the student with a basic knowledge of the English and American literary traditions while offering a variety of more specialized courses in literary periods, authors, genres, and writing."

But Cathletic University did not merely choose to avoid accommodating multiculturalism by leaving a traditional boundary in place and failing to encourage majors to take non-traditional courses. Their curriculum requirements actively *excluded* multiculturalism from the program by *prohibiting* majors from counting more than two such courses toward a major in English. But beyond that, there just weren't many non-traditional courses offered. The department had recently begun teaching one course on women writers. On occasion, it also offered one or two of five cross-listed courses in African and African American literature (all taught by the same person), as well as two courses on Asian literature in translation. In contrast, the other three departments in my study offered so many such courses that it doesn't make sense to list them here. There were dozens to choose from at each university, and they ranged over topics that defy categorization (e.g., Henry VIII in Film and Literature).

Given limited course offerings, it might be possible for a student interested in multicultural literature to take, at maximum, the women's literature course and two cross-listed courses (African, African American, or Asian literature courses). But that would require special permission from the chair of the department, not just a faculty advisor.

It isn't likely that the two-course restriction was merely intended to prevent overspecialization, for two reasons. First, even though they were taught by professors with Ph.D.'s in English Literature who had appointments in the English department, *not even one course in Asian, African, or African American literature could be counted toward the major without special permission.*

Second, there was no rule against specializing in Renaissance Literature or Contemporary American Literature by filling all six electives with relevant courses (though, in practice, limited offerings would prevent *any* sort of specialization). Thus, the disciplinary boundaries imposed by the curriculum indicated that non-traditional courses detracted from the core of important literary studies. In addition, these curriculum requirements also served to keep enrollment numbers higher in traditional courses and, thus, to preserve coveted specialty teaching for more senior members of the department (whose courses might have emptied if students were permitted more choice).[8] I'll discuss curricula in more detail in the next chapter.

The department also enforced its narrowly drawn boundary by separating non-traditional courses from their other offerings. On the department's list of course offerings and descriptions, the courses in African, African American, and Asian literatures were listed *without descriptions* at the end of the document, under the heading "Cross-listed Courses." African American and Asian literature were not merely excluded from the major, however; specialists in these fields were also excluded from the department. Both instructors had appointments in English, but neither had an office there, and both participated little, if at all, in departmental affairs. One even referred to her exclusion from departmental governance with reference to the problem of joint appointments by saying, "Because I'm half-and-half [in two departments] and treated half-and-half, I guess I have half a vote."

Compare that professor's position to that of her counterpart at Multicultural State, an untenured African American woman who specialized in African American literature but earned her Ph.D. in a different discipline. She said of her position, "I'm comfortable in an English department and I contribute to the American Studies program and the African American Studies department." This MC State professor showed no signs of being either excluded or singled out for her "special" status as an African American woman. Her colleagues talked to her about teaching, but did not, for example, expect her to provide them with ideas for the requisite multicultural offerings on their syllabi (as discussed earlier). She was not entirely uncritical of her colleagues, but her main concern provided another fascinating contrast between the two departments.

Both professors commented on the way some of their colleagues evaluated African American students. The alienated Cathletic professor recounted this story:

> One of the students who is a major in the English department is black, and I asked him to help me to do something because I was out that day. I mentioned to other parties that I had had this person help me and the response was, "He's the worst student in the English department!" Now, that made me, first of all, wonder, "Why does this person say this to me?" And then, second, "If he is so bad, what are you doing about it? How are you helping him? Or are you just labeling him as a failure?"

The MC State professor, however, had a contrasting concern about the same issue. Although she also worried about how much her colleagues helped

African American students improve their skills, her concern was that some of her colleagues were too sympathetic.

> I believe in working with the student, showing the student how to write, pushing the student. I think a lot of my colleagues kind of acquiesce to the student that says, "I can't," or acquiesce to bilingualism or multicultural ideas like, "There's a Black English thing," and "There's a this or a that," and I try not to buy into that too much. I acknowledge that those things may exist, but that does not mean that the student cannot learn to do better. I tell my students that language is political and the world will judge you by how well you write. . . . Your writing has got to reflect your intelligence, so they cannot use that against you.

When I asked her my standard question about how she would describe a bad professor (which usually produced uninteresting responses), she continued on what became a rant about the importance of challenging all students.

> Bad professors are passive; bad professors don't make students toe the mark; bad professors accept crap from students and give them A's and B's for it. There's this whole debate about process versus product. I believe you have to go through some process, yes. You should revise and whatnot, but the end result is the product, and that's what I will look at when I assign a grade. So if the product is crappy, you know, I'm going to be very blunt. If the product is not acceptable, if the product is written with sentence fragments, if the product is written with all kinds of grammatical errors, if the product has no kind of coherence, no kind of cohesive development, that is an F product. I'm sorry. I'm not going to give somebody a C and tell them, "Well, baby, you tried." I'm not gonna do that, because I think it sends false messages to the students.

No one, not even this professor, would have dared to argue that the situation for African American students was worse at MC State than it was at Cathletic, but her complaint did point to the possibility that the way MC State chose to practice multicultural tolerance may have had some of the same effects as Cathletic's old-fashioned rejection of cultural difference. Neither approach pointed to an obvious strategy for training students from diverse backgrounds to be fluent in the dominant traditions of English literature. One approach ran the risk of labeling them unprepared or even unable; the other ran the risk of exempting them from the challenge because of their advanced abilities in other language skills. Boundary management remained a challenge, even at MC State, where multiculturalism appeared to be thoroughly absorbed into every corner of daily life.

There were two other interesting features of boundary work at Cathletic University. First, Cathletic employed a conventional distinction between literature and the social sciences to maintain its claim that English professors should not attend to issues of social class, gender, or race. The logic works like the boundary dispute around the question of aesthetic value (and the "politicization" of that arena). One of the Cathletic professors who had a mixed opinion on multiculturalism argued that such issues were primarily *sociological* in nature and not the legitimate concern of English classes. That puts questions of diversity beyond the scope of the English professor's academic responsibility.

Even more fascinating was the fact that multiculturalism had come to be viewed as a field of its own at Cathletic—a field external to English literature. One professor told me she had taught a course on multiculturalism *outside* the department. Note that the idea of teaching only multiculturalism wouldn't make sense to most of the MC State faculty, who use the word almost exclusively to describe literature, and it would be plainly absurd for elite English professors because multiculturalism does not constitute a distinct academic field (essentially the same reason, reworded). In contrast, this Cathletic University professor said:

> We had a grant here to initiate an introductory freshman multiculturalism course. I was one of the first people who taught in it, and I just sort of went in cold. Knew nothing about the field, and you know, got a textbook. Just dove in and contributed a lot to that. Of course, the minute the grant ran out. . . . They're still teaching it, but they didn't get it in the core. They didn't even try to put it in the core.

In an interesting turn of events, however, this professor immediately changed the course to fit her own understanding of multiculturalism as a literary phenomenon (as described at the end of Chapter 3).

Cathletic University's firmly bounded definition of English literary scholarship excluded more than just multicultural literature. In fact, the boundary that separated the study of literature from composition (grammar and writing) saw more action than the one that excluded multiculturalism. I will explain shortly that the exclusion of composition was relevant to the emerging definition of multiculturalism. But volatility around the literature–composition boundary might also indicate that some of the boundary work against multiculturalism could have been motivated by more general forms of territoriality that are not necessarily relevant to the merits of multicultural literature.

The Cathletic English department faced the same enrollment declines that threatened humanities departments across the nation as students gravitated toward programs with clearer vocational connections such as business management and computer science. But those trends were particularly pronounced at Cathletic University. Despite a growing student body and huge increases in the overall size of higher education in the United States, the size of the English department had been declining steadily since World War II because of a decline in the number of English majors and a shift to part-time labor.[9] When I arrived there, the department had only twelve full-time positions.

The decline in English majors meant that the department could offer very few advanced literature courses, and, thus, a greater portion of its teaching efforts went toward those English 101 classes that stressed writing skills and now constitute the "bread-and-butter" work of most English departments. But unlike MC State, Cathletic University had *not* chosen to embrace its potential domain over writing by teaching advanced writing courses, expanding its influence in the wider university, or emphasizing the importance of writing in faculty career advancement.

In that respect, the department's strategy was closer to the behavior of the two elite departments than to Multicultural State's. However, there were important differences between the elite model and the Cathletic model of rejecting composition. First, Cathletic's decision to devalue composition courses was apparently doing it harm at the time of my visit, because of shrinking opportunities to teach more advanced courses.

A marked decline in preparedness among entering classes demanded remedial preparation for the composition-based English 101 courses. In fact, at the time of my visit, remedial English courses constituted 32 percent of the department's offerings. Together with the non-remedial course in College English, the department spent 73 percent of its instructional hours on non-literary "service courses." Moreover, in light of the new expenses associated with remedial instruction and the immense "burden" (contra "opportunity") it posed for the tiny English department, the administration was considering redefining the English requirement for the bachelor's degree to incorporate an *interdisciplinary* focus on writing. That move could have devastated what was left of the department's position in the university by removing at least 75 percent of its total teaching responsibility and jeopardizing the master's degree program.

The increased emphasis on service and remediation, together with an expanding number of non–tenure-track positions and declining interest in the English major meant that only a handful of English professors at Cathletic University had enough departmental power to secure coveted teaching assignments in scarce English *literature* courses. Junior faculty and adjuncts (in addition to part-time instructors) taught composition courses almost exclusively. (That's why so many of them talked about teaching special interdisciplinary and cross-listed courses. They were funded by other parts of the university.)

Thus, the scope of departmental activity was expanding dramatically in regions outside the boundary that marked its definition of legitimate work— "the English and American literary traditions," according to the catalog. Yet that boundary remained rigidly in place, even while the proportion of work available in its domain shrunk.

A second difference between the elite model of excluding composition courses and the Cathletic model, then, was that the boundary between literature and composition *divided* full-time faculty in the Cathletic department. Full-time faculty in elite departments *never* taught the first-year English/composition courses. Some of the elite professors who were successful novelists, however, did occasionally teach small advanced-writing seminars because it was their field of expertise. But in every example I saw, the courses were not merely small seminars, they were also not available for open enrollment, not even to advanced English majors. Rather, the students awarded entry in those classes were hand-picked by the professors, who sometimes held formal competitions for that purpose. One such competition was even administered by the elite professor-author's research assistant! It was a different world.

Cathletic, conversely, did not have enough demand for advanced literature courses to fill the teaching schedules of all full-time faculty. And the department did not embrace the study of composition, as Multicultural State did, encouraging all professors to teach some composition. Three or four full professors at Cathletic even taught a full load of literature courses (sometimes as many as three different course titles at a time), while associate professors would normally teach one literature course in addition to three or more composition courses each semester. Thus, teaching assignments also divided the department along the same generation/gender/age/race/tenure fault line that operated to structure the exclusion of multiculturalism.

Again, boundary conflicts and status orders reinforced each other. Young, low-status professors taught composition and supported multiculturalism, while most of the senior faculty taught literature and objected to multicultural expansion. And because of those boundary alignments, the status order also prevented multiculturalism from making inroads into English literature at Cathletic, because the untenured faculty were not generally allowed to teach literature courses. The only exceptions were the women's literature course and the courses that were taught outside the department (Asian, African, and African American literature, plus the co-opted course on multiculturalism).

Cathletic University's response to declining resources bore a striking resemblance to what sociologist Andrew Abbott (1988) called "profession regression," a pattern he found among members of declining professions. When facing a reduction in the need for prestigious work in the abstract parts of a profession, the more powerful members of a professional group often choose to guard that territory for themselves. Regressors shun the practical application of their abstract work, even though it is their main contact point with the rest of the institutional structure and their ultimate source of legitimacy, which needs more rather than less attention when a profession is facing decline. At Cathletic, that less-prestigious, legitimacy-producing work was relegated to lower-status faculty—part-timers and temporary workers who were less able to draw strong connections between the abstract and applied sectors of their field.

The junior professors, however, constituted an exception to the general principle that the composition instructors were less qualified. They *were* different from their tenured colleagues, however. The lower-ranking members of the Cathletic University faculty were all female, schooled in newer theoretical approaches, and more familiar with multicultural literature. Excluding them from teaching the literature courses was, therefore, one of the most effective means by which the senior faculty prevented multiculturalism from infiltrating their traditional curriculum in English literature. But this effect was not a carefully devised strategic move on the part of traditionalists. It was merely a byproduct of their desire to avoid low-status work.

Conclusion

In short, the department showing the highest levels of antagonism (Cathletic University) was also the department showing the least awareness of its own boundary work. It was, therefore, sheer habit that led the tenured among them to protect their disciplinary boundary from multicultural expansion by invoking more familiar distinctions—age and Ph.D. training—to obscure more insidious tensions, especially race, gender, and ethnicity. Faculty members allowed professional regression to back them into a corner where colliding boundaries forced them to fight impossibly illogical battles in which taking sides in favor of Shakespeare was also taking sides against women, for example. Meanwhile, the university threatened to confiscate those English composition courses because the boundaries that preserved the status of the department's more powerful professors (tenure, age, gender, race, and ideological bent) could not protect them from even more powerful figures in the university administration. To do that, they would need to claim professional expertise over the very courses that they rejected.

Ivory Towers, State Star, and Multicultural State, conversely, reduced potential conflict and disgruntlement through boundary management. At MC State, embracing both literature and composition further contributed to departmental success (as measured by administrative favor and undergraduate enrollments). In contrast, elite departments did not need to accommodate composition courses to maintain their status in the university. Thus, boundary management can be an important part of defending departmental health, even when status and resources are scarce. Jurisdictional boundaries define a department's relationship to other parts of the university, and they create or reduce conflicts among department members. Nevertheless, boundary management did not promise an end to the debate over multiculturalism.

Obliterating disciplinary boundaries may reduce conflict, but that strategy only works when other conditions—such as a prestigious position in the discipline—guard the authority of individual professors over course content and curriculum. A minor reduction in prestige, or even internal conflict in a department like Ivory Towers, can leave professors vulnerable to external threats. Even State Star's far more rigid disciplinary boundary required re-enforcement in the face of encroachments from the state. Thus, strong and defensible disciplinary boundaries were essential to the survival of weak or vulnerable departments. These were the organizational conditions in which English professors made decisions about multiculturalism, and they were conditions that influenced the emergence of conflicts apparently so scandalous that they were worthy of coverage in the *New York Times*.

In the end, however, multiculturalism obliterated neither canons nor the boundaries of English literature. At most, it expanded those boundaries—sometimes onto the turf of other disciplines. It's also possible that the discipline abandoned or neglected some portions of its previous jurisdiction (biography?), but it would be difficult to demonstrate that multiculturalism or any other form of expansion was responsible for those changes. Moreover, the essential pieces of the discipline remain in place, including the study of canonical literature and the fundamental practice of selecting an evolving but remarkably similar set of literary works to assign in college courses. As one MC State professor put it:

> If instead of James Baldwin and Richard Wright being the one or two, we've changed it to Tony Morrison and Alice Walker being the one or two, then all we've done is changed the joke and slipped the yoke.

Chapter 6

MANAGING MULTICULTURALISM: CURRICULUM
STRATEGIES FOR REDUCING CONFLICT

> This is advice I sometimes give to students when they go on the
> job market and get their first job. I say, "Go forth, and enjoy
> yourself a lot, but do not join a curriculum committee because it
> is the worst and the least productive, purely transactional form
> of academic enterprise." It produces almost invariably a lot of in-
> tradepartmental conflict.
>
> —*English professor at Ivory Towers*

Curricular Battlegrounds

Anyone who read the *New York Times* during the height of the canon wars
"knew" that Western culture died at Stanford University in 1988 when, after
months of heated controversy, their course in Western Culture was stricken
from the catalog forever. Western Culture had been a long-standing part of
the Stanford tradition, a common course required of all Stanford undergraduates, but it was replaced by something more nebulous called Culture, Ideas,
and Values (known as "CIV"). Here is a journalistic account of those events,
from the June 5, 1988, edition of the *New York Times* (24):

> All over the country, editorials appeared decrying the sorry develop-
> ments at Stanford, where last year students on a march with Jesse Jackson
> had chanted, "Hey hey, ho ho, Western Culture's got to go." Days after
> the new course was unveiled, William J. Bennett, the Secretary of Edu-
> cation, showed up in Palo Alto, Calif., to deplore the university's deci-
> sion. Speaking before an overflow crowd, Bennett expressed contempt
> for the faculty senate that had voted for the change [saying] . . . "a great
> university was brought low by the very forces which modern universities
> came into being to oppose: ignorance, irrationality and intimidation."

Some form of the story recounted above appears in most of the popularly read books on the "culture wars." The metaphorical death of Western Culture is irresistibly powerful. Unfortunately, it isn't a particularly honest story, and it was absorbed into common knowledge and popular literature in an even less precise version. Authors often implied an inaccurate order of events in the story to improve its dramatic narrative. For example, Bennett's talk had been planned far in advance of the curriculum change, so he "showed up" for reasons having nothing to do with the battle. And Jesse Jackson did not visit Stanford *during* the controversy. He even counseled the students against that slogan: "Hey, hey, ho ho, Western Culture's got to go!" (It is catchy, though. Seems a shame to leave it out.)

In fact, Stanford's "traditional" Western Culture course was only established in 1980.[1] Local mythology said it was the reincarnation of a defunct history course called History of Western Civilization that had been a requirement from 1935 to 1969. But, note the substantial gap of eleven years, along with the new name and the disappearance of the history department. The historical connection between the two courses was tenuous, but it helped to justify the new requirement imposed on incoming cohorts. In short, the hype used to sell the course to disgruntled students was ultimately used against them by politicians and pundits.

Moreover, *Stanford Today* (May/June 1997) reported that "the CIV saga dates from the post-World War I decades, as America sought to secure a link across the Atlantic with European history and culture." So, if we are to believe this report, Western Culture was one of those courses that Lawrence Levine described—a late but obliging response to World War I political pressures that sought to reshape American national identity in the image of its Western European allies.[2] The effect was to abandon an earlier attempt to establish an American identity *in contrast* to Europe. Frontier culture, slavery, and nineteenth-century immigration disappeared in the transition, taking with them the influence of Native American, African, and Eastern European presences. (This is not to claim that those influences were valued or direct, of course, only that they were once an integral and definitive feature of American identity.)

Today, even the CIV course is ancient history. By 1996, the political environment had cooled off so much that Stanford was able to start publicizing reports from its reexamination of the CIV course. The university launched the new version, called Introduction to the Humanities, in 1997, with a radically restructured form. And as was the case for the previous iterations, changes to the reading list were secondary to the more fundamental changes in disciplinary authority over the course. Each time the course was reorganized, the most difficult question for the curriculum committee was not what would be taught but who would do the teaching. More on this in Chapter 7.

Many of the most interesting news stories on the canon wars were reports of localized battles in academic departments, art museums, and school boards. Those stories were more gripping because they involved conflicts over concrete decisions rather than the abstract merits of one position over another, as tended to be the case for debates within the discipline. Collective decision making provided opportunities for conflict, but curriculum reviews were *special* occasions of collective decision making. Unlike all the other contexts for the debate, curriculum review was the only opportunity for English professors to exercise direct, collective authority over large-scale cultural diffusion. They were, in effect, determining the outlines of what the next generation of college graduates would recognize as the literary heritage of the United States. As such, professors often took curriculum decisions very seriously.

But curriculum reviews were also dangerous moments when those tame, grounded, civilized definitions of the discipline and of multiculturalism would come into contact with their abstract counterparts from the national arena. If participants weren't careful to keep their discussion grounded, the results could be explosive. During the conflict over multiculturalism, the danger was even more severe because there were so many hyperbolic versions of abstract thinking about English literature in the air, and the two versions of reality couldn't mix. Comparing a program curriculum to national expectations was like time travel: it was a thrilling adventure, so long as travelers never directly encountered the other version of themselves. Juxtapositions of that sort, however, could cause a meltdown in reality.

In addition, curriculum review was the organizational context in which departments connected the daily work of English professors to field-level definitions of literary value, the qualities one would use to describe one literary work as better than another. English professors at a curriculum committee meeting would not merely be fighting with each other (if they were fighting at all); they would be making claims about their importance in the discipline and in American society. Periodic review of the curriculum, in fact, is intended to provide professors with the opportunity to assess changes in their discipline and to adjust curricular requirements to match those changes. A curriculum review committee will, therefore, spend at least as much time describing the discipline as they spend talking about their specific departmental situation, such as university regulations, faculty specialties, student interests, and resource allocation.

Here, it is important to recognize an obvious fact: the discipline does not produce a clear description of itself. The reasons for this are no secret, but they may be taken for granted. Many elite English professors make their reputations by *changing* the shape of the discipline. Although some individual scholars might like to etch their contributions in stone, others who wish to make their mark by introducing even more changes will object to the prospect. To even consider a discipline-wide statement that would help departments weigh the importance of one literary period or theoretical approach against another would produce irreconcilable conflict (and bad publicity). Therefore, national-level discussions of scholarly value are left free to *debate* central issues in the discipline but are rarely if ever required to produce decisions.

Curriculum design, on the other hand, *does* require real decisions. Curricula are sometimes authored collectively, if not unanimously, by entire departments. Representatives from across a university may investigate more general curricular questions, as was the case with Stanford's decision to revise its common course in Western culture, and such decisions may ultimately be subject to approval from an entire college faculty. Agreement on such matters is hard to come by, and opportunities for conflict abound. This is one reason the professors at Ivory Towers tried to avoid it.

Ivory Towers

Several members of the Ivory Towers faculty mentioned a distaste for curriculum review and extolled the virtues of avoiding the process, as evidence by the quote which introduced this chapter. One of the newcomers to the Ivory Towers English department expressed the sentiment, saying, "Our department has been quite smart about it and has never had a curriculum committee [during my time here] . . . and God willing, it will stay that way." But the following quote goes closer to the heart of the matter in explaining why curriculum review is contentious.

> Because it's a curriculum committee, you have to have principles. You can talk in the hall any day of the week about all kinds of things, but suddenly you're in the curriculum committee and they're proposing, "All undergraduates must have A,B,C, and D," [and they're seeing] hidden agendas. I hate them. . . . In your classroom, you do your own thing anyway, but it forces people to articulate themselves in the most extreme and often silly ways imaginable.

But it wasn't just curriculum review that the faculty disliked. Ivory Towers professors avoided administrative work of all kinds. When I asked my first respondent there about service to the department, she said, "Oh just the various—whatever I can't get out of." There were obvious benefits to this kind of work reduction, not just because of the extra time it offered for scholarly production, but also because it reduced occasions for conflict. In general, though, Ivory Towers professors just wanted the administration to take care of things and leave them alone.

They assumed a great deal of autonomy in their work and encountered very little governance. Hierarchical control inside the department was conspicuously absent, even when there *were* committees. And the chair described his role as that of a *liaison* between individual professors in the department and the dean, not as that of an advisor, administrator, coordinator, or moderator for the department as a whole. In short, the department imposed minimal constraints on its members, treating them as superstars rather than employees. The side effect of this benefit, however, was a reduction in collegial engagement.

According to the logic of their superstar governance model, the best thing an administrator could do for such a department was to remove barriers from the path of its stars. Teaching assignments, disciplinary boundaries, committee work, and generalized bureaucracy all dissolve in the path of a well-maintained star, and in many ways, this department treated *all* members of the faculty like stars. There were differences. Some faculty taught more courses than others, some advised more graduate students, some worked in university administration, and others devoted all their energies to their scholarship or to more generalized fame. But all reaped the benefits of individual and departmental autonomy. All took for granted that the content of their courses was a matter of individual discretion. All could train their own graduate students as they pleased. And their curriculum model (described below) eliminated most constraints on teaching assignments. Without the need to cover a litany of required courses, professors had the freedom to teach whatever they liked.

The logic of the superstar model did not, however, imply rampant individualism and anarchy so much as it assumed that professors there were leaders in their specialties. Individual autonomy at Ivory Towers derived from two assumptions: (1) that each professor was more knowledgeable about standards in his or her own specialty than any other member of the department, and (2) that divergent (aka "cutting edge") work from them was likely to become institutionalized in the discipline. Furthermore, I do not mean that all members of the department were superstars. Even graduate students at Ivory Towers had unusual amounts of autonomy. Most were funded by a system that employed them through the writing program in fall semesters, and allowed them to teach spring semester undergraduate seminars individually *on the topic of their choice*. Each year, the graduate instructors would submit three topic proposals along with their own ranking of preference among the three. According to the graduate students, they almost always got their first choice.

When I asked graduate instructors what reason the committee might give for not accepting an instructor's first choice (thinking I would learn the secrets of making baseball sound literary), they cited only overlaps with other seminars and the importance of being able to attract students. Thus, one instructor suggested that medieval literature might be a risky topic—unless the course title incorporated something sexy like death, betrayal, or, well—sex. Instructors could choose to seek guidance in constructing a syllabus (just as some faculty did), but no one administratively approved or disapproved the syllabus.

The superstar model of curriculum structure was even more interesting. The addition of new faculty was not the only major change that took place in Ivory Towers' English department during the 1980s. There were also concurrent changes inside the department, among them the obliteration of disciplinary boundaries and the (related) decision to eliminate most of the specific requirements from the department's nine-course undergraduate major curriculum. What remained was one required course in critical reading (available in three flavors), three courses selected from menus (a major author course, a British literature course, and a seminar course). Those three courses and the remaining five were "to be organized into a coherent plan of study approved by the student's advisor."

By allowing students to select the requisite number of credits from the department's course offerings under the guidance of a faculty advisor, Ivory Towers' department brought curriculum management in line with the rest of scholarly production there. Although it was highly institutionalized and dependent on available resources, curriculum management at Ivory Towers appeared to be the individualized product of independent scholars. The end result was a model that suggests there was more than one *good* way to design a curriculum and that all members of the department were qualified to define their own good ways of doing that. Following the "academic star" model of department control, the underlying logic of the curriculum at Ivory Towers seemed to be based on the belief that stars perform better with less direction rather than more.

Even in this elite multicultural department—a darling of the academic tabloids, where the curriculum was pared down to a skeleton and English classes were offered on the topics of sex and baseball—I saw no evidence of conflict over multiculturalism during my visit. In fact, most professors I interviewed shared a belief in the dual importance of both traditional canonical works and more recently recognized works that might be considered multicultural. Several members of the department did oppose multiculturalism, both among friends and in national debates, but opposing multiculturalism did not translate into hallway ambushes or a general sense of disorder, as the press would have had us believe.

If conflict *were* to emerge at Ivory Towers, multiculturalism would have been among the least likely candidates for its cause. Unlike other possible topics for local-level debate, such as teaching assignments or the allocation of resources, professors at Ivory Towers had successfully deferred the job of hashing out multiculturalism to the public debates where several of their members were active combatants. Together with the absence of disciplinary boundaries to fight over, an infinitely flexible curriculum structure (that would never become outdated), and maximum individual autonomy, Ivory Towers had disabled nearly all the mechanisms that lead to most local battles over multiculturalism. (The missing piece was hiring, promotion, and tenure—something the Ivory Towers institutional review board wouldn't allow me to investigate—but the professors who mentioned those decisions unprompted said they had it all under control.)

Because the superstar model of departmental organization increased individual autonomy and reduced interaction in general (both formal and informal), there were few opportunities for open conflict. I am not suggesting that anyone there would have asked for more committee assignments in order to combat isolation, but the overall effect was evident. For the canon wars to produce blood in the halls at Ivory Towers, there would need to be *faculty* in the halls!

State Star

From the perspective of a journalist hoping to uncover a story about the death of Western Culture or of refined public intellectuals coming to blows over the choice of a book, it might have seemed that nothing interesting was happening at State Star. There was no army of "tenured radicals" (or untenured radicals, for that matter), and there was no battle. But change was, nevertheless, on the horizon. State Star had managed to stay out of the limelight by taking a slow, deliberate approach to changes in the curriculum and a laissez-faire approach to changes in the classroom.

As with almost every other aspect of departmental function, I found the State Star English department in the middle of assessing and revising its curriculum. The requirements for English majors that were in place when I visited, though, demonstrated the strongest sense of responsibility to current disciplinary standards evident across the four departments. The core of the program was a two-semester sequence titled History of English Literature, and the department was in the midst of considering a change (adopted the following semester) to increase that history to a three-semester sequence.

In addition to the two required courses, four more electives could be chosen freely from the department's offerings, and another four could be selected in menu fashion. Two of those came from a list of historical period courses (e.g., Nineteenth-Century American Writing, or Renaissance Literature), another was to be selected from a list of author-driven "major figure" courses, and a fourth was to be selected from a menu of non-traditional offerings. In this way, the department required of its majors both tradition and breadth, while allowing enough room for specialization. Program requirements totaled 32 hours. (Students earned four credits each semester in the history of literature sequence; the other eight courses were calculated at three credits each).

In contrast to Ivory Towers' flexible and individualized curriculum, State Star's undergraduate program in English had a more specified structure. But the shape and existence of that curriculum was also highlighted by the department's attempt to revise it. Thus, more than their counterparts at the other three universities, professors at State Star were likely to mention the curriculum in their conversations about multiculturalism, literary value, and departmental conflict.

Although there were core courses required of all English majors at State Star, professors there made no attempt to control the content of those courses beyond their description in the catalog. Members of the department spoke of changing their syllabi in response to student reception, their current research interests, or changes in a book's availability, without any apparent concern for the way other professors might interpret the change.

The autonomy of English professors who taught required courses was so profound, in fact, that two respondents mentioned a culture of privacy surrounding course content at State Star. Although the university required that syllabi be on file and available, they need not include detailed reading lists or course schedules, and professors in that department did not make a habit of reading others' syllabi without their permission.[3]

Although this sort of secrecy about reading lists was unusual, faculty in most elite colleges can expect to have near total autonomy in selecting reading assignments. This is in stark contrast to non-elite colleges, where consistency across instructors can take on the seriousness of, for example, the statewide learning objectives that preoccupy high school teaching. Even graduate instructors in my elite research sites had wide discretion in such matters. One professor at moderately conservative State Star who was a recent graduate of Ivory Towers' untraditional Ph.D. program conveyed to me his surprise at discovering the full extent of his autonomy relative to the hotly contested subject of reading lists:

> When I was a graduate student, I got the impression that we were being trained to go out into a battle of some kind and that there would be all these, you know, nasty reactionaries trying to keep us from doing this work, but the reality is: Nobody ever checks my syllabus.

So much for the "war."

The large size of the faculty in State Star's English department probably made the activities of one assistant professor seem even less significant, but having a large department also reduced some of the difficulties that their highly specified curriculum might otherwise have imposed on teaching responsibilities. Between the large, well-funded graduate program, an ample supply of majors, the popularity of English courses among non-majors, and the relegation of service courses to graduate instructors, opportunities for teaching specialized subjects abounded at State Star. Respondents in the department generally acknowledged the importance of the department's size only in terms of their being able to avoid antagonists and find a niche. But having a large faculty and a team of graduate instructors also helped preserve some choice in teaching assignments so that professors could spend more time teaching in specialized fields where they were highly qualified—areas where no one else could claim enough expertise to question the syllabus.

Although State Star's democratic collectivity potentially imposed some constraints on individual autonomy, faculty at State Star gave me the quizzical look I had come to expect from my question about authority over new courses. "What do you mean, course approval?" They spoke of specialized courses as something of a citizenship right. Professors produced a course description in order to have a new course listed, but did not consider the possibility that someone might object to the course itself.[4] They also took for granted their ability to teach small, specialized seminars—usually graduate seminars—that focused on their own research interests. They did not merely say that they had a right to teach topics that interested them; they described those courses as their contribution to the department—their reason for being there. Some even seemed to take pity on my naiveté for asking such questions, as though no English professor in the world has ever been made to teach a service course or check with higher authorities before inventing a new class. Faculty at State Star were hired for their specialties as much as their general competence. If they spent all their time teaching generalized survey courses, their special knowledge would be wasted.

When I asked faculty members at State Star how they might construct a syllabus on a given author, period, or genre, some mentioned how the course should fit with others in the department. Student interests also entered the decision. Professors often reported changing their courses after discovering that most of their students were headed for professional school rather than a lifelong dedication to literature. But responses did not begin with a need to accommodate anyone else's syllabus.

Professors at State Star did not construct their syllabi in a vacuum, however. They chose among works available to them through institutionalized channels of evaluation and distribution—those that seemed obvious, important, standard, canonical, or merely available and convenient.[5] But they were not constrained by departmental decisions about the content of particular courses. Department-level concerns such as the way courses relate to each other had even less influence on specialized courses. Graduate students in the English program at State Star taught introductory literature courses, and they constructed a common syllabus each semester under the guidance of a member of the faculty. The graduate instructors, then, had a fairly high level of autonomy from the faculty, but they were constrained by a need to work together and under some degree of supervision.

Because of their chronic engagement with issues of curriculum revision and self-definition, professors at State Star seemed to take multiculturalism very seriously. By this, I mean that State Star professors universally responded to the word as an important unresolved problem. None ever said, in effect, "Oh, *that* again!" Most produced critiques of their own response to the problem at both the level of the department and the discipline, and none implied that they stood on higher ground than other participants, as many Ivory Towers professors did.

State Star professors were also least likely to laugh or smile when I asked them about multiculturalism. I suspect this was because such conversations were a routine part of their working lives. Therefore, they did not experience the awkwardness that some professors in other departments did when I introduced the topic. I did not interpret their seriousness as anger, though I often felt I was listening to the middle of a conversation begun earlier. That is, some professors began their response as a sort of self-defense. But even those respondents never took the position that they had the only correct view on the issue.

Their eventual agreement on a new curriculum might have permitted faculty to regard the challenge of multiculturalism as resolved, but I found them quite literally in the middle of a complex *conversation* about it—not a conflict. Even if individual faculty members hid bitter resentments and unspoken grievances over the issue of multiculturalism, there was no evidence that they engaged in open conflict, though they were aware of such conflicts in the discipline and possibly in the department. Rather, they held a common belief that their department had been reasonably successfully in avoiding such conflicts in recent years with a carefully democratic strategy designed to avoid oversimplified and polarized rhetoric.

Despite this general feeling of having been spared the bloodshed reported in the press, however, I did see hints of the typical problems caused by curriculum review—namely, that it was one of the few moments when a State Star professor might dare suggest anything about what ought to be going on in the department's courses, beyond his or her own classroom. One such hint came from a female professor who answered my "bad professor" question by saying, "A poison colleague is somebody who has a sort of expansionist notion of competence without a particularly expansive grasp of the subject matter." In the end, though, such tensions didn't amount to much (at least not for tenured faculty, who didn't need to worry that their tenure case might get caught up in such a controversy). Another spoke of the same kind of event, concluding, "It's not virulent or savagely harmful to the department because nobody is going to tell me how to conduct a course."

Comparing State Star's English curriculum with Ivory Towers' in terms of the constraints placed on faculty autonomy reveals some more specific mechanisms through which State Star alleviated the conflict-producing features of its more rigid curriculum. First, the wide variety of course offerings for both majors and non-majors tended to reduce the ratio of standard core courses to specialized (autonomy maximizing) courses. Second, State Star professors maintained the connection between literature and writing and carefully managed the quality of those courses taught by graduate instructors, thus fending off any attempts to confiscate the writing program from the English departments.

Third, State Star's resource-rich English department employed ample graduate assistants to lead discussion sections so that one professor could serve hundreds of majors with one or two lectures a week. This eliminated the temptation for multiple instructors to attempt coordinating efforts across several sections of a course—coordinating efforts that might have been threatening to some professors. Finally, the department was able to offer an array of topical seminars because its strong reputation in the university attracted non-majors and because of a college-wide requirement that students must take a writing-intensive course (in addition to the standard "College English" course) in some department before graduation.

Note that each of these autonomy-preserving mechanisms required extensive resources. A department with a small faculty, a limited graduate program, a shortage of funding for instructors, or an inability to claim specialized expertise among the faculty could not have protected individual authority the way State Star did.

Multicultural State

The experiences of professors in the two non-elite departments, on the other hand, provide stark contrast to those at Ivory Towers and State Star. Non-elite professors spent very little time worrying about autonomy. In fact, professors in non-elite departments faced de-skilling from several sources. They could rarely claim to be leaders in a specialty at the disciplinary level, and they made greater use of textbooks in all their courses. Although textbooks often make it possible to manage heavier course loads than elite professors face, they also serve to define non-elite professors as generalists who can cover a course in an unfamiliar field with the aid of a good textbook and instructional materials from the publisher. Thus, one serious threat to the autonomy of English professors in non-elite departments came not from other English professors, but from administrators (and politicians, in the case of public universities) who hoped to gain some control over course content or the curriculum.

The non-elite Multicultural State English department, however, managed to avoid the external threats to autonomy that most non-elite departments faced. The department employed a quintessential "menu" curriculum—a style that allowed students to select from a variety of courses in each required category. The effect was a high level of flexibility and a wide variety of specialized topical teaching opportunities, which were generally more rewarding to instructors than survey courses that are usually deemed "service" assignments in elite departments. The heavier teaching load that MC State professors handled furthered that effect. They taught six courses per year, compared to four or fewer at Ivory Towers and State Star. Therefore, Multicultural State professors also had more chances each semester to teach a specialized course, merely because they taught more classes overall.

The particular features of MC State's menu system, furthermore, allowed each professor a great deal of mobility across menus. Because menus were organized by approaches, genres, and topics rather than time periods, the training of any particular professor probably allowed her or him to teach in at least four or five of the menu categories. For the faculty, this flexibility meant that a demanding curriculum (the major required 33 percent more credit hours than Ivory Towers' degree) did not restrict their teaching to a few required courses.

The curriculum model in effect at MC State can only be described as *enforced breadth*. English majors took one common course, Approaches to Literature, five electives, and six courses selected from as many menus: history, major figure, genre, non-traditional, writing, and linguistics. The enforced breadth encouraged students to explore topics in areas they might otherwise have ignored, but it did not enforce historical diversity. A student could satisfy the program requirements by focusing almost entirely on Renaissance literature or twentieth-century African American literature, to the exclusion of other specialties. Thus, the program at MC State was similar to the program at Ivory Towers, in that the curriculum did not require historical coverage, but different from it, in the sense that MC State did attempt to encourage non-traditional approaches. Ivory Towers left *all* these issues up to the individual student and his or her faculty advisor.

Conflict over literary multiculturalism was essentially non-existent at MC State. Several members of the faculty corroborated the story that their multiculturalism policy was adopted unanimously, and their continued support for the policy was unwavering. Many expressed the desire to continue pushing the bounds of multiculturalism, and none seemed complacent in the security of knowing that the "problem" was solved there. Rather, the entire faculty seemed committed to continued action in the area.

Faculty often had to reach decades into the past to produce a suitable grievance, and even accusers tended to sketch out high levels of understanding for their antagonists. Furthermore, the tendency for professors to express specific grievances *to me* was characteristic of non-elite departments (and of graduate students in elite departments). This difference, however, was rooted less in the relative contentment of people in elite versus non-elite departments than in the unconscious hope among lower-status academics that I might be able to improve their situation. Elite professors took a more mentoring approach to our sixty–minute relationship, carefully explaining the complexities of literary and academic politics rather then lamenting their effects.

Despite a happy consensus on the issue that might have been expected to divide the average English department, therefore, English professors at MC State did report disagreements. One member of the department referred to her section of faculty offices as "multicultural row" because nearly all the women and non-white professors in the department were located in a short corridor that branched off the main hallway. None of her neighbors were white men. Another spoke of the difficulties he had faced revising his sexist language to suit his feminist colleagues. A third complained that some women and non-white faculty failed to understand that their lower rank was the result of past (rather than present) discrimination. He argued that he and his senior colleagues wanted a more diverse department and that the lack of tenured minorities was not indicative of discrimination but of the department's attempt to change the situation, by hiring female and non-white faculty at the level of assistant professors. At the time of my visit, those professors had earned tenure, though most of the full professors were still white men. The more important observation on this point, however, is that MC State was the only English department where these ubiquitous issues managed to make their way into public discussion.

Cathletic University

The English curriculum at Cathletic University, conversely, was not only more demanding of its majors, in terms of credit hours required, it was also the most highly specified, with eight prescribed core courses out of the thirteen required. Thus, it was also the most demanding of the faculty. The Cathletic department, however, was the least equipped to handle such extensive and highly specified requirements. Whereas the sixty-five–member English department at State Star only needed to offer two specific required courses for English majors (with an army of graduate assistants), the twelve full-time professors in the Cathletic University English department taught eight core courses each year. Furthermore, those eight titles were largely survey courses that covered, for example, all of American literature in two semesters. Thus, they were not the sort of highly specialized courses that could preserve the authority of the instructor through claims to expertise. And no graduate students assisted the professors who taught those classes.

The place of specialized teaching in each department reveals a stark contrast between State Star and Cathletic University, the two programs that stressed common courses. Whereas specialty courses were a rewarding component of *every* professor's teaching schedule at State Star, the faculty at Cathletic University had almost no opportunity to teach them. The State Star course-offering directory listed the writing courses required of all undergraduates under a unique course mnemonic (not ENGL 101), and the offerings in literature ran for pages. At Cathletic University, a long list of 101–level writing courses (all with the same title but different meeting times) dominated the English department offerings. A few lines of literary survey courses in the English curriculum appeared at the end of the long list, almost as an afterthought.

The meager resources available to the English department at Cathletic University precluded any resistance to their rigidly structured curriculum of survey courses. Most faculty spent their time teaching courses that were constructed by committee (freshman English) or informally structured by a need to produce consistency across semesters in survey course content. At every turn, someone attempted to influence the content of someone else's course, and there was very little opportunity to teach topics in which one might be able to claim ultimate authority, relative to one's colleagues, by way of scholarly specialization. The result of that mix was a regularly scheduled reminder from senior professors about the appropriate content of almost all courses offered by the department, and a great deal of quiet antagonism among the faculty as a whole.

Most of the thirteen-course curriculum for English majors at Cathletic University consisted of prescribed courses. Majors took three two-semester sequences in American Literature, English Literature, and Great Books of the Western World, as well as an introductory course and a majors' seminar—for a total of eight required courses, plus five electives. There were a few courses on record that featured a special interest of some kind (e.g., The Psychological Novel, Poetry and Science, and Introduction to Literary Criticism), but for any individual professor the opportunity to teach such courses was rare. And that rigidly enforced disciplinary boundary prevented students from counting courses in African, African American, or Asian literature toward the English major without the chair's permission.

Some of the emphasis on survey courses with predictable titles could be attributed to the bureaucratic process of new course approval. The abundance of survey courses could also be explained by limitations in resources and an extensive and highly specified curriculum. Providing enough courses for a student to complete the major requirements in two or three years, plus college English courses for the entire university, strained the resources of this twelve-professor department. Moreover, the curriculum in place had not been seriously revised for more than a decade. The department had made small changes, such as adding a Majors Seminar and moving it in and out of "required" status, as well as specifying the credit-worthiness of cross-listed courses, but the faculty expressed no interest in giving the program a major overhaul. Based on the hints of conflict provided by faculty in the department (discussed in more detail below), I suspect a major curriculum revision would have been contentious at least, and maybe impossible.

In contrast to the other departments in my study, professors at Cathletic University appeared to have the least control over their own work. Individual faculty members had a more limited ability to make independent choices about teaching assignments and course content. Professors there treated departmental and university decisions as authoritative constraints. Even the linguistic style of faculty at Cathletic University stood out for the tendency of faculty members to define their own positions in opposition to those of the overall department using a "me-versus-them" frame. It was particularly unusual that so many of the professors in the department appeared to imagine themselves as solitary outsiders to a unified group of colleagues, most of whom also saw themselves as solitary outsiders.

For example, the procedure for approving new courses stood out at Cathletic University as the most difficult. In fact, the Cathletic University department was the only one in which course approval was considered something of a serious venture concerning questions of disciplinary boundaries as well as hierarchical structures of authority. Like most other universities, new courses at Cathletic required approval from a university-level committee of faculty peers. Unlike the other three sites in my study, the committee at Cathletic sometimes rejected new courses and often demanded changes in course design. To the extent that new courses had to demonstrate importance and legitimacy, surveys of well-established topics were more likely to pass than narrowly defined courses—no matter how legitimate the topic. A course called Love and Honor in Shakespearean Tragedy would be legitimate and potentially interesting to students, but it would not likely be offered at Cathletic University because it is not clear that this is an important question worthy of so many resources. Instead, a course titled Shakespeare provides legitimacy with the authorities while offering a (potentially) broader return on resource expenditures.

Textbooks and the process of text selection also played starring roles in the conflict over multiculturalism at Cathletic University. Unlike other departments, Cathletic chose only one book for the freshman English course. They did this every year, and the process of choosing brought multiculturalism to the center of departmental contention each time. One professor said of the experience:

> In freshman English, one of the problems is, in the first semester, what are the students going to write about? Are we going to get one of these readers, which has essentially sociological essays in it, and not be teaching literature, but simply be teaching rhetoric? And do we like these essays? Are they too lightweight? Are they too . . . do they involve us in political discussions that we don't need to get in—involved in? That's one issue. On the other hand, if you go to a more rigorous [traditional] reader, it takes so long for the students just to understand what's going on in the reading that the emphasis on writing gets [lost] and that's the quandary that we're always in.

Notice, however, that the conflict this professor described was not really between committee members. No one in her story stood up for multiculturalism. Rather, it appeared to be a quarrel between professors and *textbooks*. Opponents of canon expansion could not win that particular battle over textbook selection because of their belief that strictly canonical material was too difficult for their students. They could, however, make their hostility abundantly clear to their silent and terrified junior colleagues.

The role of textbook offerings in the problem of multiculturalism is particularly intriguing and largely ignored by the cultural critics who dominated national conversation on multiculturalism and literary canons. When the rare critic referred to multiculturalism as a "dumbing down" of literary studies, his adversaries would react with angry disbelief because the study of non-traditional texts in research institutions is associated with some of the most difficult literary theory one could expect to encounter in an undergraduate course.

The Cathletic University English department had an annual confrontation with multiculturalism in the form of a textbook selection process that shaped decisions, interactions, and (most of all) avoidances throughout the year. Open conflict is rarely visible in any professional setting, however, and Cathletic University was no exception. The professors there were not eager to describe the department as conflict-ridden, but they did provide evidence that they took conflict for granted and harbored various kinds of resentment and bitterness. Many of those disagreements, however, were deflected from issues of race and gender onto questions of textbook offerings, student abilities, disciplinary boundaries, and that infamous generation gap.

Conflict and the Curriculum

Even though multiculturalism was a problem framed at the national level, some departments experienced conflict over the matter while others did not. The difference between such departments was not necessarily that the professors in one department were more belligerent or zealous (though personal characteristics of the faculty could certainly make a difference). The more systematic difference between departments that disagreed over multiculturalism and those that did not lay in how they organized their decision-making activities. Multiculturalism just happened to complicate routine decisions.

In all four departments, the *structure* of the curriculum, not its progressivism, profoundly affected the level of autonomy that professors enjoyed. And it was that freedom that mitigated conflict over multiculturalism, not the political leanings of the department. A nearly non-existent curriculum at Ivory Towers allowed professors to avoid conflict by avoiding each other altogether. The State Star case indicates that abundant resources can mediate the effects of a more rigid curriculum so that faculty autonomy is largely preserved.[6] Multicultural State managed to use a highly flexible menu curriculum to achieve levels of autonomy similar to those in elite departments. Again, plenty of undergraduates, a steady flow of public school teachers seeking master's degrees, and generous budget allocations for the English department at MC State helped support the curriculum model in marking out areas of autonomy for individual members of the faculty. Cathletic University, however, had neither the resources nor the curriculum to protect professors from each other or from outsiders.

It is already known that flat structures of authority generally allow people to practice avoidance in the face of potential disagreements.[7] And university departments are the prime example of flat structures, in that college professors, even deans and department chairs, have few formal mechanisms to control each other. In this case, however, flat structures were constant across the four research sites, while evidence of conflict and antagonism varied. As a result, I was able to address the mitigating effect of other organizational practices in preserving or weakening the individual autonomy that might otherwise result from a flat authority structure.

First, any collection of autonomous professionals is likely to be subject to various constraints in the form of rules or procedures. To the extent that rules define the boundaries of individual autonomy, however, adding a rule can both reduce autonomy and protect it from an encroachment. For example, people who disagree about philosophical, political, or aesthetic principles, will fight over a rule, a boundary, the thing that offends their principle, rather than fight over the correctness of the principle itself.

It makes sense, then, that the professors in Cathletic's highly structured department were the most divided. When the committee finally agreed on a textbook, all the instructors were compelled to use it. By contrast, when MC State professors chose composition textbooks, their discussions yielded a menu of possibilities that prevented the group from having to make a final selection. Professors in elite departments, on the other hand, did not make collective decisions about course content. And they relegated the whole matter of designing the composition courses to graduate instructors, so they avoided the most likely source of contention over multicultural expansion in literary canons. Rules that took the form of curriculum requirements affected conflict the same way that rules governing text selection did: the more rigid the constraints, the greater the possibility of conflict.

The quotes above also indicate that, although rules reduce structural flexibility and faculty autonomy, they do not create conflict universally. In fact, the multiculturalism policy at MC State (a rule that constrained individual autonomy) *reduced* conflict, by providing a symbolic response to internal and external pressures while decoupling the symbolic rule from classroom activities.[8] Rules and other official written statements can, therefore, act not only as constraints but also as cultural resources that may tame and reframe potential conflicts.[9] In the case of MC State, the multiculturalism policy tamed controversial elements of multiculturalism, and pre-framed the problem. That is, the faculty agreed on a "treaty" for representativeness before anyone called it multiculturalism, and before anyone declared a war on culture.

One key to the survival of MC State's policy, therefore, was that no one appeared terribly concerned about enforcing it. As such, the policy was an important symbolic resource when the administration (or a nosy sociologist) came around asking what they had done about multiculturalism. They pointed to it. It meant something. But it did not act like a policy in the sense that it directly determined their behavior (or the consequences of their behavior). The policy was entirely benign relative to departmental conflict because it remained valued but unenforced. Therefore, it did not threaten the *autonomy* of English professors, and as a result, multiculturalism had itself become benign for the faculty at Multicultural State. In fact, the policy helped *preserve* the department's autonomy by defining its mission and demonstrating that it had this volatile issue under control.

State Star also used structural mechanisms to buffer the faculty from repeatedly teaching lower-status core courses in the English major, which could raise the autonomy-threatening problem of consistency across instructors. Offering the core courses as large lectures and allowing graduate assistants to hold discussion sections buffered the effects of structural rigidity in State Star's curriculum, but that strategy required ample departmental resources (teaching assistantships enough to cover both the composition courses and discussion sections for literature courses).

When disciplinary boundaries were conceptualized as rules (as when they were applied as tenure criteria), they could clearly constrain the legitimate activities of English professors by making some courses and publications more important than others. Disciplinary boundaries could also protect individual autonomy, however, by marking the lines within which the authority of outsiders (such as administrators and politicians) should not apply.

In broader terms, two forces threatened English literature during the troubled years of the canon wars. The first was declining enrollments of English majors associated with vocationalization. The second threat came in the form of political heat—some of which was cast broadly, as when William Bennett attacked the humanities in general, and some of which had direct effects on the budgets of state universities. But whether the general public saw a "canon war" unfold among English professors in a given department, or across the discipline, had as much to do with funding structures and curriculum design as it did with Homer and Homi Bhabha.

The question of external encroachments highlights another important problem for departments that were trying to preserve their autonomy. The task was much easier for powerful departments—those that had a strong standing in the discipline or strong standing relative to other departments in their home university. Furthermore, departments often instituted rigid structures in order to appease some external force. An elite department that is slipping in the national rankings or that has received a negative program review may be pressured to increase the rigor of its graduate program, in the hopes that better training will make its graduates more successful on the job market. A department that is doing well, on the other hand, is unlikely to face such pressures.

Thus, successful departments are characterized by organizational structures that offer autonomy and freedom for academic stars to challenge current assumptions (otherwise known as tradition). "Unsuccessful" departments (where success may be judged relative to the department's performance in previous years rather than relative to other departments) may face even more hurdles, in the form of conflict-producing organizational tasks and structural conditions that discourage the addition of more superstars (because star professors will prefer departments that offer fewer constraints and more professional autonomy). In short, resources beget autonomy and autonomy attracts resources, while failure begets constraints and constraints may produce infighting, which may lead to more failure. The rich get richer, and the poor, poorer.

In short, the difference between antagonistic departments and happy ones was not the multiculturalness of curricula or departmental culture, it was organizational structure: autonomy, flexibility, and hierarchy. This does not mean that multiculturalism was not a cultural problem, at root. It was. Organizations are not merely material structures and flows of resources; they are also cultural entities—structures consisting of symbolic boundaries, habits, rules, norms, and meanings.

Chapter 7

CONCLUSION: CULTURE TO BLAME

During the 2002–2003 academic year, the national press reported three serious incidents of racial hatred among students at State Star. They were unsettling and sometimes violent reminders of persistent racial tensions there, and they were the kind of event that multiculturalists hoped to alleviate.

Could the incidents at State Star have been prevented if the English department had defined multiculturalism as something more than canon expansion? It is certainly possible that an inspirational English professor could change a few hearts, but the preceding chapters demonstrate that such meanings are rooted in larger and more permanent cultural conditions. The more powerful effects of culture, therefore, are literally in the walls and in the kinds of culture that sociologists more often call "structure." In short, my research reveals that people who are interested in cultural change are almost always asking the wrong questions.

Attempting to understand the culture of a university as something separate from the buildings, the curriculum, and the organizational structure—attempting to understand the culture of a university as something separate from *the university*—makes culture vague, intangible, unmeasurable, and, in the policy arena, ineffective. Understanding culture as an integral part of the university, however, actually makes culture bigger and more important, even though it removes some of the mysterious allure associated with *imaginary culture*. If, for example, a university's culture lies in the way it draws disciplinary boundaries, as described in Chapter 5, then specific policy initiatives can be directed at culture without needing to aim for the clouds. Cultural policy need not attempt the impossible task of directing human thoughts, values, or imagination. It only needs to direct social organization because social organization is the most universal tool of human cognition—of idea systems—of *culture*.[1]

Cultural Policy for Cultural Problems

To most people at State Star, the racial tensions on campus during 2002 and 2003 didn't feel any different from their usual plight. Racial tensions and misunderstandings were common occurrences—not that anyone would consider them philosophically acceptable. Some national journalists, however, had noticed a pattern. They reported the recent history of such problems each time a new story broke, and they started probing for new stories. In addition, campus activists began calling for action from the administration.

The scenario added up to a serious problem both within the university community and on the public relations front, where officials began to worry that minority applications would drop even further. All this prompted the university administration to conclude that they had a *cultural problem*, one rooted in human psyches and in the campus "climate." State Star appeared to need more sensitivity and stronger values—a better culture.

Of course, State Star is not the first organization to lay blame on culture. Politicians and cultural critics blame a whole host of social problems, including crime, poverty, and divorce, on "bad values." Military commanders and athletic coaches have pointed to cultural problems when their organizations faced multiple rape allegations. NASA has even blamed culture for two separate space shuttle disasters.[2]

In short, pundits and policy makers are just as likely to blame culture for our problems as they are to rest their hopes on the idea that a perfect culture can rescue us. But theories of *imaginary* culture lead to bad policy.

State Star University was (is) an elite research university. It is consistently ranked in the top-25 universities in the nation, and it has a strong commitment to education. The university is not a bastion of intellectual traditionalism. It is a place where lots of smart, dedicated scholars who study race could help solve the apparent cultural "crisis." Under mounting pressure to take action on its cultural problem, however, State Star *hired an outside contractor to tackle its cultural problem by developing an online diversity-training course.*

The proposed training program was not to be part of the standard curriculum. Rather, it would be required of each student, in the way that tuition and vaccines are required—not as a matter of academic credit. Although the online course proposal was not the university's only response to its cultural problem, it was the first response to make a real splash.

In short, the university commissioned the construction of a Web site to improve its cultural glue so that it could bring an increasingly diverse collection of people together into a single, well-functioning community. Unfortunately, this proposal emerged in response to an implicit theory of culture as something that serves to unite its members and exists independent of other structures. The university devised a plan for changing campus culture that ignored the cultural implications of the plan's unusual structural location— outside the academic function of the university.

As a result, the corporate-style diversity-training course looked like an awkward and ineffective response to a serious problem, and it seems that much more so because education is the best remedy we have for interracial hatred. Why, then, would a respected institution of higher learning turn over its most important mission to a for-profit Internet enterprise?

The reason is exactly the same as the reason Stanford had so much trouble managing that Western Culture course (aka Introduction to the Humanities, or CIV). It is a structural misfit. Is "sensitivity training" an intellectual pursuit worthy of placement in the required undergraduate curriculum—or even of college credit? Who would be responsible for administering such a course? Does it either *manage* students or *treat* their psychological problems? If so, the program is not academic and it belongs to another part of university operations (student affairs, for example). Such organizational problems can best be described as jurisdictional, in that they amount to questions about institutional identities, responsibilities, and boundaries.

But here is the point when it helps to know that the organizational conditions of meaning-production matter, and that they matter in a fairly profound way. The online diversity-training course was to have been disconnected from academic life because it was not developed in an academic setting and would thus be carefully separated from serious college courses.

Yet it would be required. This arrangement put "diversity education" in a curious structural location. As a result, one student organization began opposing the course by arguing that the university had no right to impose it on students. Such an argument would have been nonsensical if a class on race and gender relations had been proposed as part of the core curriculum. Universities have every right to impose educational requirements on students, but the diversity course was cast outside the boundary of legitimate scholarly pursuits, and as such, it was vulnerable to all sorts of problems not normally associated with university courses.

Most significantly, the meaning of racial sensitivity was altered by State Star's extraneous structural problem. The proposal temporarily changed the terrain of racial politics at State Star by turning racial hate crimes into a "diversity" problem and by locating that issue outside the jurisdiction of legitimate academic activity. The inaccurate illusion was that the university did not consider the original problem (race relations) to be worthy of serious scholarly attention—much less the status, professorial authority, and other institutional protections afforded by the very idea that students are there to be educated. Of course, the program's originators never intended to devalue their own project, much less the importance of race. They merely wanted to treat an imaginary cultural problem with an expedient and semi-therapeutic intervention. Administrators quickly recognized the emerging political pitfalls and scuttled the program. (They'll use the Web site for training non-academic staff, which is a much better cultural and organizational fit.) But the experience highlights the fact that translating meaning across institutional contexts can turn a structural convenience into a moral or political disaster with shocking speed.

Of course, State Star was not unique in the troubles it had translating the national "value" of racial harmony into an academic environment. Although it seems like educational institutions would be good places to attempt such changes, the proper course of action for ending hate is neither easy nor obvious. One popular, though ill-fated, "remedy" was the institution of hate-speech regulations on college campuses, better known as "politically correct" (or PC) speech codes. These constituted a second aspect of the flare-ups over multiculturalism in the late twentieth century.

Opponents of the codes argued that such regulations constituted a violation of free speech. That controversy, too, appeared to come down to a battle between crazy radicals who wanted a fascist version of sensitivity and reactionary right-wingers who, for some reason, wanted to defend their right to say awful things about their students or peers. But like State Star's online diversity training, speech codes were largely administrative responses to specific incidents on college campuses where administrators have a responsibility to react but not the authority to teach—or even (in most cases) to direct the content of teaching.

In short, speech codes were a perfectly logical and deliciously inexpensive administrative response to student harassment. To an administrator, hate speech is not free expression; it's children behaving badly. It's only when we consider the academic side of universities that the political questions look more complicated. So the problem of abstraction works in both directions. Big, abstract ideas are often difficult to interpret inside specific local situations. But the other direction can be equally confusing: removing important structural details from a story and reading it only through the lens of abstract ideas like free speech and the politics of difference can make a routine (if imperfect) administrative decision look absolutely nuts.

Powerful Abstractions

At times the contrast between the overblown claims of cultural critics and the real lives of English professors have made the pundits seems silly and out of touch. It is clear that much of the canon wars did consist of hot air. But I also want to stress that abstraction is not just harmless fantasy. Abstraction is powerful!

In fact, the term "hot air" already implies that abstract ideas can fuel emotion with surprising ease. They can provoke moral outrage without requiring any of the "real-world" specificity that would limit the scope of their implications. More seriously, abstractions can make persuasive calls to action.

To this point, I have repeatedly said that abstract ideas cannot inform strategic action, but I have not mentioned the opposite effect (because English professors don't fall victim to this kind of persuasion). Abstraction may not be able to *inform* action, but it is often used to *justify* action—and there are few limits to the kinds of action that can be justified by an abstract idea.

Patriotism, for example, encourages flag-buying and war-mongering rather than political participation because the idea of patriotism (in the contemporary U.S., anyway) doesn't inform political action. Rather, it invokes a nebulous sense of allegiance and, in certain contexts, enraged defensive sentiments. So patriotism can inform loyalty and violence, but not democratic participation.

It is also possible that the more important a word becomes, the more difficult it is to hold its definition steady. That's because national conversations are prone to higher levels of abstraction. This possibility deserves further exploration.

So meanings matter, but this story suggests that they might matter even more when a word manages to become important without acquiring a clear definition. Like "family values," "multiculturalism" is here to stay because its label makes a vague reference to a sacred idea. That posed a moral dilemma for its would-be opponents. In the late-twentieth-century U.S. political climate, opposing cultural diversity was just as difficult as opposing family values. Thus, the struggle was not to determine whether multiculturalism was important, but to determine what it would become.

A second clarification I should make involves the fact that the word "multiculturalism" remained so ambiguous and contested throughout those conflicts over English literature. Whereas my research design was carefully constructed to maximize the explanatory power of my findings by preventing me from attributing one department's idiosyncratic experiences to the entire discipline, I selected the word "multiculturalism" *because* of its idiosyncratic characteristics—because it was contested, not because it was average or representative.

Multiculturalism posed a perfect opportunity to study the meaning-making process because it was ambiguous and unclearly defined. Giving it meaning was hard work, so I was able to see that process in action. But I have no reason to believe that multiculturalism is representative of *all* ideas produced at the national level when it comes to that kind of ambiguity. Remember that, by ambiguity I mean something different from abstraction, which I suspect probably *is* fairly common in national conversations. Even abstract uses of the word "multiculturalism" in the national arena were rare and unstable.

As a case in point, consider another word that emerged during the battles over English literature. The word "canon" (from the Greek, *kanon*, meaning "law") is equally new to the literary scene. The word has long been used to refer to a set of sacred religious texts, and it has more specific applications in Catholic and Anglican Church vocabulary (the canon laws govern church activity and the canonical parts of a religious ceremony are the parts that don't change). Amusingly, a canon is also a musical "round" (like *Three Blind Mice* or *Row, Row, Row Your Boat*) that repeats itself over and over.

Twenty years ago, "canon" wasn't a part of the typical English professor's daily vocabulary as it is now. And no one would have claimed that its application to literary studies could constitute a formal definition of the word. Using it for that purpose would have been a dramatic extension of its usual meaning.

The word "canon" only became synonymous with English literature during the height of these battles in the late 1980s. In fact, when William Bennett published his 1983 NEH report, the word and its implications were *both* conspicuously absent. He wrote:

> I have long suspected that there is more consensus on what the important books are than many people have been willing to admit. In order to test this proposition . . . I recently invited several hundred educational and cultural leaders to recommend ten books that any high school graduate should have read. . . . They listed hundreds of different texts and authors, yet four—Shakespeare's plays, American historical documents (the Constitution, Declaration of Independence, and Federalist Papers), *The Adventures of Huckleberry Finn*, and the Bible—were cited at least 50 percent of the time. (10)

That little claim reversed itself in short order, however. Soon, the charge was that "educational and cultural leaders" were doing everything wrong! In fact, surveys just like the one Bennett described were brought to the *defense* of English teachers to demonstrate that there was consistency—exactly the same thing Bennett found in his survey. And no one "long suspected" anything about English literary canons anymore. Suddenly, everyone was *certain* that, up until the early 1980s, all students read the same set of texts. Here's a description from journalist James Atlas that appeared in the *New York Times* (June 5, 1988, 24). This introduction was presented as factual background information for a story about "The Battle of the Books."

> Generations of Eng. lit. majors in American colleges followed his advice. You started with the Bible, moved briskly through Beowulf and Chaucer, Shakespeare and Milton, the 18th-century novel, the Roman-

tics, a few big American books like "The Scarlet Letter" and "Moby Dick"—and so on, masterpiece by masterpiece, century by century, until you'd read (or browsed through) the corpus. . . . The masterpieces of Western civilization. The Big Boys.

Done. One "canon" fully formed, written in stone, and rewritten in history. Already I can imagine Plato's students in long white togas and leather sandals, pouring over their well-worn paperback copies of *Moby Dick*. Maybe it *is* easy to change culture.

There were problems with the word "canon." The most serious among them was that "the canon" didn't exist. Anyone who wanted to teach the whole thing or read the whole thing would be disappointed to discover that it didn't have clear boundaries. Their work would never be done, and they would have the unsettling experience of discovering that English literature is not at all canonical. But most English professors were fairly comfortable concealing that little inconvenience.

Unlike the cumbersome word "multiculturalism" (with all its political pitfalls and calls for various kinds of change), the word "canon" suited English professors very well. It emphasized the importance of their jobs and the power of literature. Even if they wanted to continue updating or expanding the standard set of widely read works, or if they wanted to destroy canons and the very process of literary valorization, "canon" was a useful word. It gave a shape to the contested object, but it didn't require that they do anything differently. In short, before there was the idea of a canon, it was far more difficult to say that there was something worth fighting over, as demonstrated by Bennett's awkward attempt to articulate his claim without it.

The upshot of all this, however, is that meaning-construction is not always difficult. Literary canons took on a clear meaning in both the national arena and in academe. That meaning was relatively specific (as big meanings go) and the *meaning* of the word was not generally contested—even if the idea that we ought to have canons *was* contested. Finally, users of the word did not seem to mind its imperfections. Defining a new word in the abstract national arena does not require that the word be a perfect fit to real life.

That's part of the reason theories of omnipotent culture are so alluring. Abstract culture *is* easy to manipulate. Pundits can quickly convince their audiences that an imaginary form of culture is important and powerful. But when the English professors I studied tried to make sense of the imaginary cultural ideal called multiculturalism, they had trouble translating its abstract meaning into their local contexts. In addition, those who were successful at enacting cultural change were the ones who engaged structure in the process. Those who attempted to do their cultural work in the *isolated* world of ideas failed.

Radical Change Requires *Structure*

The theory of *omnipotent culture* warns that we should pay attention to the kind of culture that is understood as norms, values, and ideas. But the *grounded culture* of these English professors demonstrates that we should pay even more attention to other kinds of culture—the culture that structures our lives without drawing so much attention to itself.

The kind of culture that I found to be at work in the canon war was not located in the messages of literary texts. It was in the *ordering* effects of culture. In some ways, it's the kind of power described by French philosopher Michel Foucault (1982, 1990). But Foucault described structure as mysterious and intangible, and in his view, it has a power of its own making. It surrounds us, it controls us, and people have very little to do with it. In short, Foucault easily blamed culture for everything, but he didn't think we could do much to change it.

Inside English departments, I found that people *often* tinkered with the cultural order. Sometimes they did so consciously, and when they did, they were able to institutionalize change. When they didn't recognize and engage the cultural order, however, it *did* control them, and things didn't go so well. People leaned more heavily on structure when they denied its existence and when they denied their own role in its continued existence.

The problem with ignoring structure is that it can't really operate on its own for very long. That's because social structures are made of social action. Without it, they don't exist in quite the same way. In addition, no structure works in exactly the same way in all instances. Despite the fact that structures can have enormous unrecognized power, it is human tinkering that keeps them alive.

For example, the rigid structure in effect at Cathletic University served its inhabitants poorly. If they wanted to preserve a traditional approach to literature (although they didn't all want that), supporters of that position would have needed to step in and do something to protect it. When I left them, however, they were in a situation that political scientist Theda Skocpol (1979) might have described as ripe for revolution. They faced overwhelming external pressures and encroachments that badly tasked their own resources, a breakdown in internal governance, a politically entrenched upper class (those few full professors who monopolized the literature courses), and a brewing peasant insurrection from junior faculty and adjuncts who, though silenced in public, had an obvious group consciousness and ideological opposition to the weakening aristocracy in their department. In short, they were all leaning heavily on an old structure that suffered from the combined effects of erosion and neglect.

Conversely, the two public universities were intensely engaged with collective decision making. Both reported low levels of opposition to multiculturalism, and both continued to move steadily along that path—despite the fact that State Star had a reputation for conservativism.

The two departments that avoided engagement with the governance structure (elite, avant-garde Ivory Towers and rigidly traditional Cathletic University) were political opposites, but both can be described as unsuccessful in their efforts at cultural change. In both places (but for opposite reasons) multiculturalism remained unclearly defined and professors avoided democratic or even bureaucratic engagement. Both departments also experienced a fair amount of opposition to multiculturalism (for lack of a definition) and neither managed permanent structural change. In fact, the Ivory Towers department, despite its reputation for cutting-edge scholarship, would eventually experience a move back toward the center.

The Ivory Towers case is particularly interesting because it was an attempt at radical structural obliteration—a sort of experiment with postmodernism. When the Ivory Towers English department dispensed with disciplinary boundaries and curricular requirements, it was literally attempting to operate in a deconstructed environment—one that removed the constraints of organizational structures rather than substituting a new structure for the old one. Although it was a radical move, in some senses, the "experiment" took place in the context of a conventional university administration. In the long run, therefore, that part of the project failed, in the sense that new boundaries have since been erected and bureaucratic constraints restored.

Although Ivory Towers English professors attempted to support their boundary-smashing intellectual work with an analogous structural change, that change prevented them from functioning as expected within the larger institutional environment. A structural change that radical cannot be accomplished by ignoring external structures. Working without a boundary would have required *intense* engagement with governance and procedure in the external environment, specifically because the English faculty lacked the sociological auto-pilot that a well-maintained structure can provide. That's the problem at the extreme opposite of Cathletic's tendency to lean too hard on a brittle and poorly maintained structure. Reliable structures like those in effect at State Star and MC State require consistent (though not necessarily intentional) support and maintenance.

"Active structural engagement" doesn't require that structures remain constant, but that is the easiest way to do it. This strategy is more commonly known as "changing the system from within." What the Ivory Towers department tried to do was a partial version of what's known as "radical" structural change, in that they attempted to tear down as many structures as possible. But they also tried not to replace them. The result was that old, familiar structures reappeared in the empty spaces—sometimes through informal habit, sometimes through university mandate. Solid structures are more difficult to tear down than the canon warriors imagined, but they are even more difficult to replace. That's one (of many) reasons that change *through* structure is more effective than change *to* structures—just because it's easier and so it's more often successful.

Racist Structures

Remember that the reason I argue structural change might be important for cultural change is that structures *constitute* cultures. They contain meaning and they categorize thought. Extending that argument to the kinds of issues that concern multiculturalism would suggest that many of our problems with cultural difference may be located in the structure of academe. Here, I'll draw on bits of evidence I encountered in my research to sketch out some of the implications of this approach for one example, that of racist structures.

Can organizational arrangements be racist? Sure. The institution of slavery in the antebellum American South was clearly rooted in race, and marriage is premised on a system of gender biases. But I did not set out to explore such questions. I wasn't looking for instances of institutionalized racism or patriarchy, and I never dreamed that they would be so central to my findings.

What I found, however, was that unrelated organizational structures were *often* implicated in problems of cultural difference. In short, structures don't need to be directly biased in order to protect racism, gender bias, and a multitude of other arcane conditions that most English department inhabitants would adamantly reject. In fact, I found that the best way to explain resistance to multiculturalism inside these four English departments was not according to the beliefs, convictions, or actions of the people within them. Most English professors were working hard to accept multiculturalism into their worlds, their jobs, and their lives. It was the (cultural) structure that resisted.

There are *far* more powerful forces at work inside academic departments than the occasional ego clash between political positions and acerbic personalities. One of the reasons structures can do their work without facing much scrutiny is that they are so subtle and so innocent. For example, organizational structures don't need to be notably oppressive in order to protect old habits. They can do that just by virtue of being weak or brittle, as was the case at Cathletic University.

In fact, one thing that keeps these politically "irritating" structures in place may be their alleged innocence. By definition, structures cannot have intentions because they are not human. Even the word "habit" signifies human action minus intentional thought. *Our tendency to think of social structure as something separate from thoughtful human action is a practice that protects the vast majority of our actions from criticism.*

Facing up to institutionalized bias, therefore, must include taking a good hard look at structures and the way they operate. It also requires recognizing the fact that structures are created by people and that people are responsible for keeping them alive.

Some structures are beloved for one reason or another and so will be consciously protected, but many structures are easy targets for change. Just giving some conscious thought to the curriculum, to disciplinary boundaries, and to the unintentional effects of those structures could go a long way toward reducing conflict and unintentional social exclusion. With slightly more effort, a department could examine how it orders race, gender, and other differences in its current practices, or how it uses such distinctions to order other ideas.

Boundary alignment was the other key structural factor that concealed race and gender bias inside English departments. This structural effect was more direct than the ones that merely preserved old habits. It took a little more rhetorical spin and strategic forgetfulness for the professors at Cathletic to conclude that a generation gap was the source of their problem. But when a gender or race boundary becomes aligned with a more legitimate boundary (such as a disciplinary boundary or a status distinction), "innocent" boundary work *can* function as discrimination.

Thus, the symbolic-boundaries approach points to one possible way to specify the mechanisms at work in institutionalized racism (Knowles and Prewitt 1969; Feagin and Feagin 1978; Bonilla-Silva 1997). The powerful and legitimizing effects of boundary alignments for explaining race and gender bias according to some other correlated factor are emerging in the work of Michèle Lamont (2001) and Karyn Lacy (2002), both of whom demonstrate that their respondents prefer to attribute negative assessments to class bias rather than race bias when both explanations are culturally available.

Beyond Socialization: Speaking Truth to Structure

One of the most tragic and distracting misunderstandings I encountered in this cultural conflict was the idea that resistance to multiculturalism came from bad people (racist people, for example), when the more serious form of resistance (in this story at least) came from structures.

Crude theories of oppression often appear to argue that powerful people knowingly and consciously devise schemes for brainwashing their publics with ideas like the greatness of Western culture. And those theories get some support from the fact that powerful people do sometimes make decisions that they know to be undemocratic or unethical. But all the Enron scandals, Tuskegee syphilis trials, and Agent Orange in the world cannot add up to the kind of power that cultural theorists have in mind when they talk about large-scale *social* structures. (See, for example, Bonilla-Silva 1997).

Social processes imply something larger and more sinister than greedy CEOs, racist English professors, and smoke-filled rooms. The focus on social processes tells us that we can't solve social problems by treating them as individual problems—the aberrant failings of a few people to live up to the high moral standards of a good and just society. The more difficult and more sociological question is not, "Where did these people go wrong?" Rather, the question is: "Where does the structure go wrong, and where do we all go wrong in supporting that structure?" If it is a social problem, it is socially patterned; and if it is socially patterned, it is structural. If it's a structural problem, there is a structural solution for it.

Despite the fact that (imaginary) cultural change *seems* easy and inexpensive, it's not. It is only easy to resocialize a nation of citizens in the abstract theoretical world where an omnipotent culture is entirely divorced from all the other parts of human existence. In the real world, however, socialization is extremely difficult, expensive, and inaccurate. It is a messy process.

Two other studies of curriculum development support this claim. First, sociologist Julian Dierkes found, in 2001, that the postwar history curricula in the Germanys and Japan had more to do with the organizational structure of educational policy regimes than national culture. And in a 2001 report, Brint, Contreras, and Matthews found an effect almost identical to the one I describe here. They studied "socialization messages" in sixty-four primary school classrooms and found that perfectly good "values" were repeatedly altered to fit what they called "organizational priorities." Because it was an unexpected result, however, the authors did not specifically analyze the mechanisms that caused it. Nevertheless, it is clear that translation problems are a key stumbling point for the values-socialization approach to cultural change.

The most immediate problem with imaginary cultural change, however, may be its overbearing directness. Trying to change a culture in the usual way implies an individual-level intervention, even if it is applied to every individual member of a society. It means trying to change the content of individual minds, it means making endless judgments about who is in need of more socialization, and it places an awful lot of blame on individual people for the kinds of thoughts that we genuinely understand to be *gut-level* reactions—beliefs, prejudices, worldviews, affinities, and tastes. Even with a theory that says those gut-level responses are socially trained, it is not very useful to say that English classes are racist because of them.

Structural change is cleaner. It is more direct. It can be less painful and it can be less expensive than endless blame and re-re-re-socialization. The difficult thing about attempting cultural change through structural change, however, is learning to "read" structures for their cultural messages and for the ways they order and categorize meanings.

The multiculturalism policy at MC State, for example, produced profound social and cultural change, but, I would argue, not because it ensured that every student would be exposed to literature written by every category of person on the planet. It did not accomplish the latter goal. Rather, the policy affected *order*. It said that multiculturalism would be an integral part of everything the department would do—every course professors taught, every instructor they hired, and every textbook they chose. It put cultural difference at the center of all their activities, and it defined multiculturalism as something important. *That* effect constituted a profound cultural change.

Moreover, social change requires more than individual convictions and the willingness to act on them. Change requires meaning and structure. For that reason, the people who were involved in change were often unaware of it. They were just trying to "make sense" of a new idea in their local context, or they were changing a routine to suit their own preferences. The professors and administrators who *were* trying to bring about cultural change, conversely, were often changing very little because they isolated culture or otherwise ignored the important role of structural meaning.

In placing blame on structure, however, my intent is not to let individuals off the hook. Rather, my point is to explain that we have them on the wrong hook. The "norms and values" view of culture does not account for the enormous challenges real people face in translating their abstract "convictions" from one context to another and trying to balance the ones that clash. It puts too much responsibility on people to behave as autonomous beings in situations when they have less autonomy than is generally assumed. And it absolves us of our responsibility to pay attention to the powerful influences of structure and habit. *Instead of asking people to be accountable for their beliefs, I suggest that we ask them to be accountable for their structures.*

Translating Cultural Change

In sum, I argue that the central problem for cultural policy is translation. When an idea is established in the abstract national arena, it generally lacks the specificity necessary to have concrete meaning in any given context. So, for example, if one wanted to make a mathematics curriculum more multicultural, the kinds of challenges and questions involved would be very different from the ones faced by English professors. Translating an abstract idea across institutional contexts is a meaning-making process. It is complex and difficult, but it is not an unfamiliar process. It is the everyday task of trying to "make sense" of a new situation—to bring old understandings to bear on new information. We all do it many times every day.

Making meaning can be simultaneously elegant, complex, creative, and constrained. It can sometimes be a simple task, and it can sometimes be maddeningly difficult, but whenever there is a shift in the structural arrangements on which meanings rest (as when the context shifts from literature to history to mathematics), meanings must be reassessed.

How an abstract idea or moral conviction like multiculturalism will translate into specific real-life contexts is not obvious or singular. But the implication of this fact goes much further. Changing culture by changing ideas is a nearly impossible task because so much of culture has established an institutional permanence for itself. Taking an abstract idea like multiculturalism and bringing it to life inside a firmly established institution like U.S. higher education exposes the abstract idea to alterations. Even though higher education is, itself, a *cultural* institution—an idea, or set of ideas—the ideas associated with education are more permanent and more protected than new ideas about cultural change.

So when English professors attempted to make sense of multiculturalism, they did so in a way that supported English literature, not in a way that threatened it. And the idea of multiculturalism did not fundamentally alter the practice of English literature.[3] Rather, it appears the reverse is true: *the practice of English literature changed multiculturalism.*

Thus, for English professors, multiculturalism was not (often) about immigration, history, or international relations—things outside their professional jurisdiction; it was about literature, values, teaching methods, and cultural difference. Of course, both sets of ideas are logically related, but there were powerful organizational boundaries between them, both symbolic and physical. To the extent that English professors did resist multiculturalism, though, it was because it seemed to threaten the structure of their work. Reinventing multiculturalism to fit within those structures solved the problem.

For better or worse, the multiculturalism that emerged from the smoke of the canon war was the one that best fit the patterns of life and culture that already dominated our major institutions. In concrete terms, multiculturalism is a product of the way teachers, administrators, and college professors struggled to adapt in the face of cultural change. In the process, the habits of work inside educational institutions made multiculturalism into something achievable and enriching but not too far from ordinary and not terribly threatening.

This is the most powerful way that institutional structures manage to resist change. It is not merely that they can develop more permanent structures in the form of buildings and organizations. *Institutions also preserve themselves by shaping the way people think.*

In this study, I have characterized the production of meaning for multiculturalism as a locally constructed byproduct of concerned, sympathetic, and well-meaning English professors attempting to navigate a new political terrain. I have done so in order to provide an honest and ethnographically sensitive portrayal of meaning-construction at the local level.

From the perspective of larger social structures, however, this is a story about the power of existing social arrangements to impose conservative meanings on a word once offered as the rallying cry for radical cultural and social change. Until now, most national attention has been directed toward the occasional battles between opponents and defenders of multiculturalism, but my research demonstrates that many English professors chose to dilute multiculturalism rather than fight about it. They made sense of multiculturalism in a way that supported the current institutional structure and their position within it.

So this is yet another story in which well-intentioned human agency served only to reinforce structures of power rather than to transform them. But there was a moment—a moment when most of my respondents faced the fact that they had been asked to change that structure. Most concluded that the request was unreasonable, and, given the structures that define reasonable activity for them, it was.

It is unreasonable to change the world.

CHAPTER I

1. The first figure comes from El-Khawas and Knopp 1996; the rest are from A. Levine and Cureton 1992.

2. The main books are D'Souza's *Illiberal Education* ([1991] 1992) and Kimball's *Tenured Radicals* (1990).

3. See Huber 1994 on English literature syllabi, Sax et al. 2003 on student attitudes, Hamilton and Hargens 1993 on faculty attitudes, and on persistent prejudice, see Jackman 1994, DiMaggio et al. 1996, and Bobo 2001.

4. The term "culture war" is not just an empty umbrella term for cultural conflict. It refers to *all* such conflicts as part of a single phenomenon—one allegedly caused by a deeper rift between orthodox religious and progressive/secular cultures (Hunter 1991). Paul DiMaggio, John Evans, and I (1996) showed that there was not much alignment in the way the U.S. public understood those disputes and that such alignments had not increased. For that reason, I use the term "canon war" when I want to emphasize the merely hyperbolic image of warlike conflicts over literature, as opposed to the apocalyptic merger of all symbolic struggles into a single moral unit.

5. In this context, the word "canon" refers to those works generally considered to be the most important examples of literature written in a given language, era, or field, but it is a politically charged word that became popular *during* these battles, not before. I provide a little history of that in Chapter 7.

6. Literary critic Stanley Fish actually argues this point, too. His book *The Trouble with Principle* (2001) explains that the abstraction at the core of our legal system (and even the general principles of universal freedom and equality) are, in fact, logical impossibilities and that our insistence upon them only masks locally generated prejudices that we cannot really escape.

7. Classical social theorist Max Weber ([1921] 1978) proposed a theory of the fit between culture and social structure that assumed some variance in the extent to which the two would be aligned. Weber presented his view as an alternative

to Marx's insistence that culture is a mere byproduct of economic conditions. But Weber refers only to hierarchies of status culture and class, not to complex systems of meaning. And he conceptualized variation in the fit between culture and society only at the macro level—by historical periods and nations. My examination of the conflict over English literature suggests that such variation is also far smaller and more frequent.

8. See Schuman and Bobo 1988.

9. The quote is from DiMaggio 1991 (268–69).

10. Ibid., 286.

11. I interviewed one black woman at each research site. (The even balance of that race-and-gender pattern was not intentional on my part; it merely represents the structure of race and gender in academe.) In my entire project, I encountered only one black man. Unfortunately, he insisted that his specialization in film studies would preclude his ability to answer my questions about literature—a pitfall of my strategy of cloaking my real interest in multiculturalism.

12. This reference to the categorization process involved in meaning-making foreshadows my plan to study the symbolic boundaries of meaning, similar to Zerubavel's (1991) study. His useful term for the categorization process is "lumping and splitting." I add "subtracting" to this idea to account for all the stuff that just disappears into the gaps between meanings. This sort of cultural exclusion can be understood as something more serious than categorical exclusion, where ideas can be consciously defined as opposites.

13. The fact that the word "multiculturalism" doesn't inspire English professors to talk about the realities of cultural difference doesn't mean that those kinds of discussions don't happen. It only means that "multiculturalism" doesn't offer an opportunity for them and that the attempt to make sense of infinite cultural differences as a single philosophical problem imposes some serious limitations.

14. According to Nielsen Media Research (http://www.nielsenmedia.com/), the *Oprah Winfrey Show* has about eight million viewers and *Monday Night Football* gets between eight and eighteen million (depending on the game being broadcast and the competition in the prime-time lineup). Together, their sixteen to twenty-six million viewers are a larger group than the fifteen million students enrolled in U.S. colleges in 2003, but when it comes to reaching that eighteen-year-old audience, college professors win, hands down.

15. See Jacoby 1994 for a lucid argument in favor of attending to non-elite universities. I will use the term "elite" to refer to those universities and the departments within them that frequently hold national rankings in the top twenty-five institutions of their kind (nationally ranked universities, liberal arts colleges, and Ph.D. programs in literature). Colleges and universities not regularly appearing on such lists would, then, be non-elite, even if they are well known.

16. On this point, see Glaser and Strauss 1965.

17. My analytic focus on constraining and enabling structures comes from

DiMaggio 1991, 1997; Sewell 1992; and Bourdieu 1992, 1993; and before them, Durkheim [1912] 1965; and Giddens 1986. Bourdieu argues, for example, that fields of power (e.g., social structure, professional associations, universities, and departments) intersect, encompass, and constrain one another to the point where ignoring one field can seriously distort our view of another. Methodologically, he suggests that learning everything there is to know about the context of the topic at hand will provide the answers. Thus, the question demands a research design that can cast a wide net, yet offer sufficient depth to yield qualitative richness.

CHAPTER 2

1. On text selection, see Corse 1996; Franklin, Huber, and Laurence 1992; and Robinson and Keltner 1996. On ideological positioning, see Yamane 2001; Gitlin 1995; and Gless and Smith 1992.

2. For a complete overview of symbolic boundaries perspectives in sociology, see Lamont and Molnár 2002.

3. As it happened, much feminist thinking of the day followed a similar logic, one that emphasized the negative role played by cultural differences (aka socialization) between men and women. From both perspectives, it seemed prudent to reject the devalued culture and assimilate.

4. The popular understanding of cultural difference in the United States has not moved far from assimilationism in its journey through "color blind" policy in the Reagan era to "multicultural capital" (Bryson 1996) in the 1990s. The sociological literature on intercultural adaptation, however, has experienced a more sophisticated development than the one I describe here. Sociologists have moved from the concept of assimilation to those of institutional racism (Feagin and Feagin 1978), symbolic racism (Kinder and Sears 1981), and identity construction (Soysal 2000; Gamson 1995; Winant 1999, 2000).

5. See Ohmann 1976 and Graff 1987.

6. There are, of course, many other definitions of multiculturalism in play at any given moment, and there are many other strategies for achieving multiculturalism (including recruitment strategies and even structural reforms, on occasion). Although that diversity of meaning is the subject of this book, it is still useful to describe a starting point. My claim that multiculturalism is essentially understood as canon expansion is supported by the evidence to follow that the "canon expansion" definition is the most popular, and that it is the least controversial definition in play among English professors (see chapter 4).

7. See, for example, D'Souza's *Illiberal Education* ([1991] 1992), Kimball's *Tenured Radicals* (1990), Bennett's *To Reclaim a Legacy* (1984), and A. Bloom's *The Closing of the American Mind* (1987).

8. Ellen Messer-Davidow (1993), for example, offers a lucid and well-documented description of this process.

9. See Amy Binder's book *Contentious Curricula* (2002) for an incisive analysis of Afro-centrist claims on educational policy. Also note that there were plenty of multicultural literary scholars who *didn't* fit the image described by our pundits. There are dozens of them in this study alone.

10. Zerubavel didn't claim that people always divide the world into categories or islands of meaning. Rather, he argued that it is our tendency, but that we often impose clear, unambiguous meanings to our own detriment.

11. In methodological terms, my work with the snippets was an inductive search for thematic elements, but the final stage of coding was a more accurate "measurement" of the extent to which each respondent invoked each theme. In returning to the full interviews, I also confirmed the validity of my four categories.

12. On these topics, see especially Binder 2002; Brint, Contreras, and Matthews 2001; McClelland 1990; Yamane 2001; and Young 1997, among many, many others.

13. Diane Ravich's (1990) attempt to separate pluralistic multiculturalism from particularistic multiculturalism is probably the most widely known example, but there are countless others; see, especially, Raz 1994.

14. Graduate students and graduate instructors are not included in the percentages used for the figures.

15. See, especially, Corse 1997 and Smith 1988.

16. This last phrase comes from a longer response (quoted above) about the parallels between "real" multiculturalism in English departments and traditional American values, in contrast to the overblown rhetoric of the culture wars.

17. One exception to this claim is the work of Gerald Graff, who advocated that English professors "teach the conflicts" rather than preaching to one side or the other of the battle over multiculturalism. Journalists often called on Graff to represent the Cultural Left when, for example, the National Association of Scholars issued a new report. However, most English professors read Graff's contribution as an attempt at compromise.

CHAPTER 3

1. The reference is to A. Bloom's (1987) complaint, in *The Closing of the American Mind,* about changes in higher education.

2. See A. Levine and Cureton 1992.

CHAPTER 4

1. See Robinson and Keltner 1996 and Keltner and Robinson 1997 for a fascinating study of this predictable effect.

2. This discussion is based on a study by Hamilton and Hargens (1993).

3. See Alexander 1996.

CHAPTER 5

1. These figures are based on Lexis/Nexis searches in the file called "all-news."

2. See, for example, Graff 1987; Ohmann 1976; and Gates 1992.

3. Across the nation, the process of attracting and processing students has begun to resemble a sales pitch. Russell Jacoby (1994) has been particularly vocal on this point, especially as it relates to the culture wars. Joye Mercer (1997) provides more specific evidence of this in a May 23, 1997, article in the *Chronicle of Higher Education*.

4. Readers interested in disciplinary conflict more generally will be curious to know that there were also broad areas of consensus on goals for teaching literature. Most prevalent among these was developing critical-thinking skills in their students.

5. For further discussion on this point and evidence from these four case studies, see Bryson 1999.

6. Although it is tangential to my point here about embracing composition courses, I should note the astounding contrast between elite and non-elite departments on the matter of text selection. Elite English departments would not *dream* of caring what a sales representative thought about their selection of texts, nor would they be very likely to encourage consistency across professors. Therefore, the thought of imposing consistency in order to appease sales representatives would be unfathomable in elite departments.

7. Lipset and Rokkan 1967 refer to this general process in political alignments as "cross-cutting cleavages."

8. I get this insight not from my own imaginary estimate of student preferences, but from the trendier professors in the other three departments who taught in Medieval and Renaissance fields. They reported being in favor of more traditional-sounding course requirements, just to ensure that they would continue to have an audience. It was just one more piece of evidence that political cleavages inside departments didn't work as expected.

9. The size of enrollment since 1945 increased at Cathletic despite the fact that the university often failed to enroll its *targeted* number of students. The reason for this discrepancy is that the target numbers also increased every year.

CHAPTER 6

1. See Edward Fiske's *New York Times* article of March 12, 1981.

2. Levine's book was published in 1996, and the *Stanford Today* article is by Diane Manuel. I have no particular reason to doubt the trustworthiness of the information in that article, except that no source is cited to support the claim that the history department bowed to the pressures of war propaganda.

3. Although the department's administrative office guarded the secrecy of

course syllabi, students did not. Among students, there was broad public knowledge about whose courses were easy, whose were left-leaning, etc. Some professors would also learn of those general characteristics from their own students. And, of course, professors *did* sometimes share syllabi with friends and colleagues.

4. There was, in fact, a review process for any new course that a department wished to offer more than once, but because those reviews almost always turned out positive, and several mechanisms allowed departments to avoid them, the course approval process was repeatedly forgotten, imposed as a bureaucratic inconvenience, and forgotten again.

5. On this point, see Ohmann 1976.

6. For further treatment of these factors, see Patricia Gumport's 2002 study.

7. Two important works, by Morrill (1991) and Black (1990), address similar issues at a more generalized level. Morrill focused on the shape of conflict more than on the probability of its emergence, but his main point is relevant to the issue of academic conflicts. When conflict does appear in flat organizational structures, it is more visible because no authority intervenes to settle or squelch disputes.

8. There is a rich literature on this, but the classic is Meyer and Rowan 1977.

9. See Sewell 1992 for a treatment of the "enabling" features of structures we normally think of as constraints.

CHAPTER 7

1. Sociologists will recognize the influence of Levi-Strauss (1963, 1969); Durkheim ([1912] 1965); Mary Douglas (1986); Lamont (1992); and DiMaggio (1997), among many others.

2. After the *Challenger* exploded on national television, a presidential commission concluded that the infamous O-ring had been the primary cause of the disaster but that NASA's organizational culture had been a "contributing cause." In the wake of the disintegration of *Columbia,* however, the Columbia Accident Investigation Board found that NASA had repeated many of the same mistakes it had made with the *Challenger* and concluded that "NASA's organizational culture had as much to do with this accident as foam did" (CAIB 2003, 12). See Diane Vaughan's fascinating analysis of NASA's organizational culture in her 1997 book, *The Challenger Launch Decision.*

3. The modest effects of multiculturalism on the teaching of English literature have been well documented. The Modern Language Association conducted the most comprehensive assessment (see Huber 1994). But, on this point, it is more important to understand that multiculturalism never was the impetus for increased attention to cultural difference. This confusion is explained more fully in Chapter 2.

Abbott, Andrew. 1988. *The System of Professions: An Essay on the Expert Division of Labor.* Chicago: University of Chicago Press.

Alexander, Victoria D. 1996. "Pictures at an Exhibition: Conflicting Pressures in Museums and the Display of Art." *American Journal of Sociology* 101 (4): 797–839.

Atlas, James. 1990. *Battle of the Books: The Curriculum Debate in America.* New York: Norton.

Bennett, William J. 1984. *To Reclaim a Legacy: Report on the Humanities in Higher Education.* Washington, DC: National Endowment for the Humanities.

Bérubé, Michael. 1994. *Public Access: Literary Theory and American Cultural Politics.* New York: Verso.

Binder, Amy J. 2002. *Contentious Curricula: Afrocentrism and Creationism in American Public Schools.* Princeton, NJ: Princeton University Press.

Black, Donald. 1990. "The Elementary Forms of Conflict Management." In *New Directions in the Study of Justice, Law, and Social Control,* prepared by the School of Justice Studies, Arizona State University, 43–69. New York: Plenum.

Bloom, Allan David. 1987. *The Closing of the American Mind: How Higher Education Has Failed Democracy and Impoverished the Souls of Today's Students.* New York: Simon and Schuster.

Bloom, Harold. 1995. *The Western Canon: Books and the School of Ages.* New York: Riverhead Books.

Bobo, Lawrence. 2001. "Racial Attitudes and Relations at the Close of the Twentieth Century." In *America Becoming: Racial Trends and Their Consequences,* edited by N. Smelser, W. J. Wilson, and F. Mitchell, 262–99. Washington, DC: National Academy Press.

Bonilla-Silva, Eduardo. 1997. "Rethinking Racism: Toward a Structural Interpretation." *American Sociological Review* 62 (3): 465–80.

Bourdieu, Pierre. 1984. *Distinction: A Social Critique of the Judgment of Taste.* Cambridge, MA: Harvard University Press.

———. 1993. *The Field of Cultural Production: Essays on Art and Literature.* Edited and introduced by Randal Johnson. New York: Columbia University Press.

Bourdieu, Pierre, and Loïc J. D. Wacquant. 1992. *An Invitation to Reflexive Sociology.* Chicago: University of Chicago Press.

Brint, Steven. 1994. *In an Age of Experts: The Changing Role of Professionals in Politics and Public Life.* Princeton, NJ: Princeton University Press.

Brint, Steven, Mary Contreras, and Michael Matthews. 2001. "Socializing Messages in Primary Schools: An Organizational Analysis." *Sociology of Education* 47 (3): 157–80.

Bryson, Bethany. 1996. "'Anything But Heavy Metal': Symbolic Exclusion and Musical Dislikes." *American Sociological Review* 61 (5): 884–99.

———. 1997. "What about the Univores? Musical Dislikes and Group-Based Identity Construction among Americans with Low Levels of Education." *Poetics* 25 (2–3): 141–56.

———. 1999. "Multiculturalism as a Moving Moral Boundary: Literature Professors Redefine Racism." In *The Cultural Territories of Race: Black and White Boundaries,* edited by Michèle Lamont. Chicago: University of Chicago Press; New York: Russell Sage Foundation Press.

Buchanan, Patrick J. 2001. *The Death of the West: How Dying Populations and Immigrant Invasions Imperil Our Country and Civilization.* New York: Thomas Dunne Books.

Collins, Randall. 1988. "The Durkheimian Tradition in Conflict Sociology." In *Durkheimian Sociology: Cultural Studies,* edited by Jeffrey Alexander, 107–28. New York: Cambridge University Press.

Columbia Accident Investigation Board. 2003. *Report,* vol. 1. Washington, DC: National Aeronautics and Space Administration and the Government Printing Office.

Corse, Sarah M. 1996. *Nationalism and Literature: The Politics of Culture in Canada and the United States.* Cambridge: Cambridge University Press.

———. 1997. "Cultural Valorization and African American Literary History: Reconstructing the Canon." *Sociological Forum* 12 (2): 173–203.

Corse, Sarah M., and Victoria D. Alexander. 1993. "Education and Artists: Changing Patterns in the Training of Painters." *Current Research on Occupations and Professions* 8:101–17.

Dierkes, Julian. 2001. "National Identity Construction and the Teachers' Union of the Germanys and Japan, 1945–1955." In *Modern Roots: Studies on National Identities,* edited by A. Dieckhoff and N. Gutierrez, 174–95. Hampshire: Ashgate Press.

DiMaggio, Paul J. 1991. "Constructing an Organizational Field as a Professional

Project: U.S. Art Museums, 1920–1940." In *The New Institutionalism in Organizational Analysis*, edited by W. Powell and P. DiMaggio, 267–92. Chicago: University of Chicago Press.

———. 1997. "Culture and Cognition." *Annual Review of Sociology* 23:263–87.

DiMaggio, Paul J., and Bethany Bryson. 1995. "Americans' Attitudes Towards Cultural Diversity and Cultural Authority: Culture Wars, Social Closure, or Multiple Dimensions." General Social Survey Topical Report No. 27. National Opinion Research Center, Chicago.

DiMaggio, Paul J., John Evans, and Bethany Bryson. 1996. "Have Americans' Social Attitudes Become More Polarized?" *American Journal of Sociology* 102 (3): 690–755.

DiMaggio Paul J., and Walter W. Powell. 1991. Introduction to *The New Institutionalism in Organizational Analysis*, edited by W. Powell and P. DiMaggio. Chicago: University of Chicago Press.

Douglas, Mary. 1986. *How Institutions Think*. Syracuse, NY: Syracuse University Press.

D'Souza, Dinesh. [1991] 1992. *Illiberal Education: The Politics of Race and Sex on Campus*. New York: Free Press.

———. 1996. *The End of Racism: Principles for a Multiracial Society*. New York: Free Press.

———. 2003. *What's So Great About America*. New York: Penguin Books.

Durkheim, Emile. [1912] 1965. *The Elementary Forms of Religious Life*. New York: Free Press.

El-Khawas, Elaine, and Linda Knopp. 1996. *Campus Trends, 1996*. Higher Education Panel Report Number 86. Washington, DC: American Council on Education.

Feagin, Joe R., and Clairece Booher Feagin. 1978. *Discrimination American Style: Institutional Racism and Sexism*. Englewood Cliffs, NJ: Prentice-Hall.

Fish, Stanley. 1994. *There's No Such Thing as Free Speech . . . and it's a Good Thing, Too*. New York: Oxford University Press.

———. 2001. *The Trouble with Principle*. Cambridge, MA: Harvard University Press.

Foucault, Michel. 1972. *Archaeology of Knowledge*. New York: Pantheon Books.

———. 1990. *History of Sexuality: An Introduction*. New York: Vintage Books.

Franklin, Phyllis, Bettina Huber, and David Laurence. 1992. "Continuity and Change in the Study of Literature." *Change* 24 (1): 42–53.

Gamson, William A. 1996. "Safe Spaces and Social Movements." In *Perspectives on Social Problems*, edited by G. Miller and J. A. Holstein. Greenwich, CT: JAI Press.

Gates, Henry Louis. 1992. *Loose Canons: Notes on the Culture Wars*. New York: Oxford University Press.

Giddens, Anthony. 1986. *The Constitution of Society: Outline of the Theory of Structuration*. Berkeley: University of California Press.

Gieryn, Thomas F. 1983. "Boundary-work and the Demarcation of Science from Non-science: Strains and Interests in Professional Ideologies of Scientists." *American Sociological Review* 48 (6):781–95.

Gitlin, Todd. 1995. *The Twilight of Common Dreams: Why America Is Wracked by Culture Wars*. New York: Henry Holt and Company.

Glaser, Barney, and Anselm Strauss. 1965. "The Discovery of Substantive Theory: A Basic Strategy Underlying Qualitative Research." *American Behavioral Scientist* 8 (6): 5–12.

Glazer, Nathan, and Daniel Patrick Moynihan. 1963. *Beyond the Melting Pot: The Negroes, Puerto Ricans, Jews, Italians, and Irish of New York City*. Cambridge, MA: MIT Press.

Gless, Darryl J., and Barbara Herrnstein Smith, eds. 1992. *The Politics of Liberal Education*. Durham, NC: Duke University Press.

Graff, Gerald. 1987. *Professing Literature: An Institutional History*. Chicago: University of Chicago Press.

———. 1992. *Beyond the Culture Wars: How Teaching the Conflicts Can Revitalize American Education*. New York: Norton.

Griswold, Wendy. 1987. "The Fabrication of Meaning: Literary Interpretation in the United States, Great Britain, and the West Indies." *American Journal of Sociology* 92 (5): 1077–1117.

Guillory, John. 1993. *Cultural Capital: The Problem of Literary Canon Formation*. Chicago: University of Chicago Press.

Gumport, Patricia J. 2002. *Academic Pathfinders: Knowledge Creation and Feminist Scholarship*. Westport, CT: Greenwood Press.

Hamilton, Richard F., and Lowell L. Hargens. 1993. "The Politics of the Professors: Self-Identifications, 1969–1984." *Social Forces* 71 (3): 603–27.

Hays, Sharon. 1994. "Structure and Agency and the Sticky Problem of Culture." *Sociological Theory* 12 (1): 57–72.

———. 1996. *The Cultural Contradictions of Motherhood*. New Haven, CT: Yale University Press.

———. 2004. *Flat Broke with Children: Women in the Age of Welfare Reform*. New Haven, CT: Yale University Press.

Hirsch, E. D. [1987] 1988. *Cultural Literacy: What Every American Needs to Know*. New York: Vintage Books.

Huber, Bettina J. 1994. "Recent Trends in the Modern Language Job Market." *Profession* 94:87–105.

Hunter, James Davison. 1991. *Culture Wars: The Struggle to Define America*. New York: Basic Books.

Jackman, Mary R. 1994. *The Velvet Glove: Paternalism and Conflict in Gender, Class, and Race Relations*. Berkeley: University of California Press.

Jacoby, Russell. 1994. *Dogmatic Wisdom: How the Culture Wars Divert Education and Distract America.* New York: Doubleday.

Keltner, Dacher, and Robert J. Robinson. 1997. "Defending the Status Quo: Power and Bias in Social Conflict." *Personality and Social Psychology Bulletin* 23 (10): 1066–77.

Kinder, D. R., and D. O. Sears. 1981. "Prejudice and Politics: Symbolic Racism versus Racial Threats to the Good Life." *Journal of Personality and Social Psychology* 40 (3): 414–31.

Kimball, Roger. 1990. *Tenured Radicals: How Politics Has Corrupted Our Higher Education.* New York: Harper and Row.

Lacy, Karyn. 2002. "'A Part of the Neighborhood?': Negotiating Race in American Suburbs." *International Journal of Sociology and Social Policy* 22 (1–3): 39–74.

Lamont, Michèle. 1992. *Money, Morals, and Manners: The Culture of the French and American Upper-Middle Class.* Chicago: University of Chicago Press.

———. 2001. *The Dignity of Working Men.* Cambridge, MA: Harvard University Press.

Lamont, Michèle, and Virág Molnár. 2002. "The Study of Boundaries in the Social Sciences." *Annual Review of Sociology* 28:167–95.

Levine, Arthur, and Jeanette Cureton. 1992. "The Quiet Revolution: Eleven Facts About Multiculturalism and the Curriculum." *Change* 24 (1): 25–29.

Levine, Lawrence W. 1996. *The Opening of the American Mind: Canons, Culture, and History.* Boston: Beacon Press.

Levi-Strauss, Claude. 1963. *Structural Anthropology.* New York: Basic Books.

———. 1969. *Totemism.* Boston: Beacon Press.

Lipset, Seymour M., and Rokkan Stein. 1967. *Party Systems and Voter Alignments: Cross-National Perspectives.* New York: Free Press.

Knowles, Louis L., and Kenneth Prewitt, eds. 1969. *Institutional Racism in America.* Englewood Cliffs, NJ: Prentice-Hall.

McClelland, Katherine, and Carol J. Auster. 1990. "Public Platitudes and Hidden Tensions: Racial Climates at Predominantly White Liberal Arts Colleges." *Journal of Higher Education* 61 (6): 607–42.

Messer-Davidow, Ellen. 1993. "Manufacturing the Attack on Liberalized Higher Education." *Social Text* 36:40–80.

Meyer, John W., and Brian Rowan. 1977. "Institutionalized Organizations: Formal Structure as Myth and Ceremony." *American Journal of Sociology* 83 (2): 440–63.

Miller, John J. 1998. *The Unmaking of Americans: How Multiculturalism Has Undermined the Assimilation Ethic.* New York: Simon and Schuster.

Morrill, Calvin. 1995. *The Executive Way: Conflict Management in Corporations.* Chicago: University of Chicago Press.

National Association of Scholars. 1996. *The Dissolution of General Education: 1914–1993.* Princeton, NJ: National Association of Scholars.

National Center for Education Statistics. 1996. *Digest of Education Statistics.* Washington, DC: National Center for Education Statistics.

Ohmann, Richard Malin. 1976. *English in America: A Radical View of the Profession.* New York: Oxford University Press.

Powell, Walter W., and Paul J. DiMaggio. 1991. *The New Institutionalism in Organizational Analysis.* Chicago: University of Chicago Press.

Presidential Commission on the Space Shuttle Challenger Accident. 1986. *Report to the President.* Washington, DC: Government Printing Office.

Raz, Joseph. 1994. "Multiculturalism: A Liberal Perspective." *Dissent* 41 (1): 67–79.

Ravitch, Diane. 1990. "Multiculturalism: E Pluribus Plures." *The Key Reporter* 56 (1): 1–4.

Robinson, Robert J., and Dacher Keltner. 1996. "Much Ado About Nothing?: Revisionists and Traditionalists Choose an Introductory English Syllabus." *Psychological Science* 7 (1): 18–24.

Sax, L. J., A. W. Astin, J. A. Lindholm, W. S. Korn, V. B. Saenz, and K. M. Mahoney. 2003. "The American Freshman: National Norms for Fall 2003." *38th Annual Report of the Higher Education Research Institute,* UCLA Graduate School of Education and Information Studies.

Schlesinger, Arthur Meier. 1992. *The Disuniting of America: Reflections on a Multicultural Society.* New York: Norton.

Schuman, Howard, and Lawrence Bobo. 1988. "Survey-based Experiments on White Racial Attitudes toward Residential Integration." *American Journal of Sociology* 94:273–99.

Sewell, William H., Jr. 1992. "A Theory of Structure: Duality, Agency, and Transformation." *American Journal of Sociology* 98 (1): 1–29.

Skocpol, Theda. 1979. *States and Social Revolutions: A Comparative Analysis of France, Russia, and China.* Cambridge: Cambridge University Press.

Smith, Barbara Herrnstein. 1988. *Contingencies of Value: Alternative Perspectives for Critical Theory.* Cambridge, MA: Harvard University Press.

Soysal, Yasemin Nuhoglu. 2000. "Citizenship and Identity: Living in Diasporas in Post-War Europe?" *Ethnic and Racial Studies* 23(1): 1–16.

Stevens, Mitchell L. 2001. *Kingdom of Children: Culture and Controversy in the Homeschooling Movement.* Princeton, NJ: Princeton University Press.

Swidler, Ann. 2003. *Talk of Love: How Culture Matters.* Chicago: University of Chicago Press.

Swidler, Ann, and Jorge Arditi. 1994. "The New Sociology of Knowledge." *Annual Review of Sociology* 20:305–29.

Vaughan, Diane. 1997. *The Challenger Launch Decision: Risky Technology, Culture, and Deviance at NASA.* Chicago: University of Chicago Press.

Watt, Ian. 1957. *The Rise of the Novel*. Berkeley: University of California Press.

Weber, Max. [1921] 1968. *Economy and Society*. Translated by G. Roth and C. Wittich. Berkeley: University of California Press.

Winant, Howard. 1999. "Racial Democracy and Racial Identity." In *Racial Politics in Contemporary Brazil*, edited by M. Hanchard, 98–115. Durham, NC: Duke University Press.

Yamane, David. 2001. *Student Movements for Multiculturalism: Challenging the Curricular Color Line in Higher Education*. Baltimore, MD: Johns Hopkins University Press.

Young, Alford, Jr. 1997. "Political Engagement and the Rise of African American Public Intellectuals." In *The Black Intellectuals,* edited by R. Dennis, 117–46. Greenwich, CT: JAI Press.

Zerubavel, Eviatar. 1991. *The Fine Line: Making Distinctions in Everyday Life*. New York: Free Press.